Ain't Gonna Let Nobody Turn Me 'Round:

A Coming-of-Age Story and Personal Account of the Civil Rights Movement in Hattiesburg, Mississippi

By

Anthony J. Harris

ISBN-10: 148188459X
EAN-13: 9781481884594

Library of Congress Control Number: 2013900718
CreateSpace Independent Publishing Platform, North Charleston, SC

Contents

Acknowledgements

This book has been in the works for nearly 20 years, and I owe its completion to several individuals. I start with my wife, Smithenia, who has always been my chief encourager and when necessary, my chief critic. She has helped me to stay grounded and centered, thereby keeping me from becoming too complacent or overly confident.

Next, I acknowledge the presence and importance in my life of my daughter, Ashley, and my son, Michael. I am enormously proud of them; and I hope they know that I meant what I said when I told them years ago that there is absolutely *nothing* they could ever do to make me stop loving them. I might get angry or disappointed, but anger and disappointment pass. My love for them endures. I take to heart Paul's words in 1 Corinthians: "Love bears all things, believes all things, hopes all things, endures all things."

Thanks also to my brothers, James and Harold, who are among my biggest supporters and I theirs. The three of us feel exceedingly blessed to have each other as brothers and to have been loved and nurtured by great parents.

I also express thanks to four of my very special high school class-mates, whose friendship is an essential part of my life. Since the five of us collaborated on our 25th high-school reunion in 2001, we have grown enormously in our respect, admiration, and fondness for each other. Thanks to Martha, James, Sandra, and Odis Ruth for being there for me. I also acknowledge the friendship and support of my best friends, Lewis Slay and Stan McKee.

I also express my deep thanks to my late cousin, the Reverend Maury Booth, who passed away in 2012. He was an amazing example of patience, love, and courage. His life and his death touched me in indescribable ways. Despite the emotional and physical pain he endured through decades of fighting kidney disease, he consistently maintained a positive outlook on life. He possessed and was willing to share an unshakable belief in his Christian faith. He and I shared many conversations about life, our fraternity, and our respective writing projects. Without fail, I looked forward to those conversations because we invariably had something to say that would keep each of us focused and motivated.

I want to also express my appreciation to Dr. Earle D. Clowney, for his expertise as an editor. Although he is now retired, I understand why he was appointed University Editor at Clark Atlanta University.

I want to thank the staff of the Special Collections Department of the University of Southern Mississippi Library for their assistance in securing the photo for the book cover. Thanks also to the photographer, Mr. Herb Randall, for his permission to publish the photo, which was taken at the Mt. Zion Freedom School in the summer of 1964. The individuals in the photo are Pete Seeger (left), Anthon Harris (center), and the late Ratio Jones (right).

I acknowledge the wisdom bestowed upon me by my late father, James Harris, Sr. He was a man who loved his family, made whatever sacrifices needed in order to provide for our well-being, and he stood by his beliefs. I, too, possess those qualities, and I owe much of it to him.

Finally, I acknowledge the role that my mom, Daisy Harris Wade, played and continues to play in my life. Faith, family, and freedom, in that order, have continuously been her priorities in life. She not only embraced and lived her Christian faith, but she instilled it in each of her three sons. Whenever the doors at Star Light Missionary Baptist Church were open, no matter the reason – Sunday School, regular church service, choir rehearsal, eating on the ground, singing unions, revivals, pastor's anniversary, Easter programs, or Christmas programs – Daisy and her sons were always present. Unlike many parents today, she never *asked* if we wanted to go to church; and there were never any debates or negotiations about whether something else was more important to do at the time. We just had to make sure we were ready to hop into the car when she started it.

She was an unsung hero of the civil rights movement and a solid and consistent warrior for freedom and justice. She and other unsung heroes and warriors do not always receive recognition and credit for their contributions to the movement. One of the purposes of this book is to acknowledge and honor those heroes and warriors; and her name is at the top of the list.

Inspirations

The following stories are my recollections (and a few borrowed from family and friends) of the civil rights movement in a southern town in the 1960s and how that movement and other events of that time and beyond influenced my coming of age. While the recollections are personal, and in some instances quite subjective, they are not unique. The thoughts and emotions contained in these written words transcend time and geography and are inspired by heartfelt reverence, faith, and hope that manifest themselves in both people and events. The thoughts and emotions blend to tell a story that is inspired by the memory of the deaths of millions of Africans who died during the Trans-Atlantic slave trade (Middle Passage); by the courage and zeal for freedom of such warriors as Sengbe Peih (Cinque), Denmark Vesey, Gabriel Prosser, and Nat Turner; by the bravery of such civil rights pioneers as Rosa Parks, W.E.B. DuBois, A. Phillip Randolph, and Fannie Lou Hamer; by the heroism of such trailblazers as Crispus Attucks, Harriet Tubman, Ida B. Wells and Jesse Brown; by the boldness of such risk-takers as Marcus Garvey, Paul Robeson, Angela Davis, John Carlos, and Tommie Smith; and by the martyrdom of the countless named and unnamed brave souls whose ultimate sacrifices will never be forgotten. Most important, these words are inspired by a deep reverence of the past and by eternal hope and faith in future generations whose vigilance will guarantee that the horrible events that occurred before and during the civil rights movement do not occur again.

Introduction

As I reflect on the tumultuous days of the civil rights movement in Hattiesburg, Mississippi, it is easy to recall that my feelings ran the gamut from fear to elation. Indeed, throughout the nearly five-plus years I was involved in the movement, my emotions were all over the board. I have felt the bone-chilling fear that accompanies a pointed, face-to-face threat from an unprovoked, police officer who wanted to beat me with a blackjack. There was also the unforgettable and breathtaking fear that comes from the gut-wrenching sights and sounds of snarling, barking police dogs leashed by hate-filled police officers. There were also feelings of unbridled exhilaration that come from the classic triumph of good over evil as embodied by the simple but courageous act of a brave elderly black man taking that long trek up the steps of the Forrest County Courthouse and demanding his constitutional right to register to vote. There, too, was overwhelming joy and excitement while sitting in hot, tiny, overcrowded Mt. Zion Baptist Church in the wee hours of the morning listening to the inspiring words of Dr. Martin Luther King, Jr. And there was also the indescribable sadness while watching helplessly as my mother wept uncontrollably on the front porch of our home after learning that Mississippi State NAACP Field Secretary Medgar Evers had been murdered.

Emotion, both pleasant and unpleasant, played a critical role in the civil rights movement and was a constant source of individual and collective motivation to persevere when the purveyors of hatred wanted to destroy those who believed in and worked for equal rights. Fear was always our companion, but so was courage. Anger was a familiar partner as well, but was always accompanied by forgiveness. Despair was often close by, but so was hope. Sadness was ever present, but so was the unshakable belief that joy comes in the morning. Excitement and happiness were by our side, but so were humility and gratitude.

As unusual and ironic as it may seem, I am eternally grateful to God that He allowed me to experience, and therefore, appreciate the civil rights movement as it played itself out, daily, in all its glory and its ugliness before my very eyes. I regard it a special blessing and a privilege to have been present during so many mass meetings, marches, and protests and to have been in the presence of so many courageous men and women whose indomitable spirits might have been bent but could never be broken and whose love for freedom, justice, and equality was more powerful than any amount of hatred directed at us by the bigots in Hattiesburg.

My involvement in the civil rights movement stems directly from my mother's involvement. Daisy Harris instilled in my two brothers and me the importance of standing up for what is right and of challenging the evils of bigotry, racism, and segregation. She embodied courage in the face of fear. When it was easy to do otherwise, she always chose commitment over vacillation and resistance over capitulation. She was small in stature, but grand in courage. Her voice was sweet, but always commanded attention, even from the mean-spirited and cold-hearted. Nothing was more important to her than her religion, family, friends, and the civil rights movement.

Although she graduated from high school with a full scholarship to Alcorn A&M College, she declined and chose instead to become a full-time wife and mother.

As mother, wife, daughter, and civil rights worker, she possessed boundless energy, uncommon inner strength, and a remarkable ability to balance disparate responsibilities among her family, church, work, and the movement. She could simultaneously cook a meal, iron clothes, help with homework, and discuss civil rights strategy on the telephone – and do justice to each of them. Her motivation for becoming involved in the civil rights movement was based on the strong religious beliefs she acquired in childhood. She took to heart her obligation, as a Christian, to resist evil, to challenge injustices, and to seek relief for the oppressed. She never doubted the correctness of the movement itself, and she never doubted the correctness of her decision to be a part of it. She felt moved by God's spirit and His call to her to be a part of His divine plan to end racial segregation in Hattiesburg. I remember her saying on several occasions, "Ant, segregation is evil and ugly. But in the end everything will be okay 'cause God don't like ugly!" Given the strengths and needs of each, the civil rights movement and Daisy Harris were made for each other. She served as secretary for the local NAACP chapter, participated in marches, transported marchers, cooked meals for marchers, put marchers up in her home, and raised bail money to get marchers out of jail. She also helped design and implement strategies for conducting economic boycotts. She did all of that while taking care of her own home and working as a maid in the home of a white family.

Although her active days of fighting for equality and justice have passed, she remains a shining example of commitment to Christian principles and to fairness. She knows the struggle has not ended and subscribes whole heartedly to the view espoused by Frederick Douglass over a century ago – *Without struggle, there is no progress*. Today she still responds with outrage and with action when she witnesses an injustice and with compassion and aid when someone is burdened with grief or with hard times. Whenever someone she knows is ill or has passed, she is there with a kind, uplifting word and a basket full of her wonderful cooking. And although she does not have a lot of money, she constantly gives to people who have less than she does. By the grace of God, she has not lost her inclination or ability to be involved.

I was relatively young (age 12-17) during the heyday of the civil rights movement in Hattiesburg; nevertheless, I understood the purposes of the movement, as well as its dangers and rewards. Many children my age and even children today, missed the opportunity to participate in an extraordinary history-making experience that was uniquely American. Most have never attended murder trials like the one we read about, as school children in Harper Lee's *To Kill a Mockingbird* or in John Gresham's *A Time to Kill*; to walk picket lines and participate in marches; to lead freedom songs at mass meetings; to desegregate public schools; and even to go to jail for refusing to obey an illegal and immoral law. I regard myself as extremely blessed to be able to speak from firsthand experience about the civil rights movement and what life was like during that time. Cherishing it as a blessing to be shared, I view as a moral imperative the obligation to pass it on to others in the hope that those days are not revisited.

I regard myself as not only a participant in the movement, but as a product and beneficiary of it as well. The civil rights movement was, in large part, responsible for the development of my personal and life-enhancing values (belief in God, patience, love of self and others, respect of self and others, unselfishness, acceptance of differences, commitment, perseverance, forgiveness). As a result of the influence of the movement as well as the loving influence of my mother, father, teachers, and other members of the village, I successfully navigated the treacherous and unpredictable waters of adolescence and teenage years, and thus far have been successful in remaining afloat in the puzzling and sometimes dangerous waters of adulthood.

Perhaps the most enduring lesson of the civil rights movement for me has been the importance of a well-grounded spiritual life, especially as an infallible defense against the forces of evil (hatred, racism, violence) that existed so pervasively during the civil rights era and to a large extent remain prevalent today. Indeed, a sound spiritual grounding is what got me through lots of toils and snares and made me appreciate just how amazing His grace really is. More than just a part of the civil rights movement, the Church and the spiritual consciousness it engendered among all who were open to it were at the movement's core. The Church, indeed, was unquestionably foundational in both its meaning and significance to the movement. An unwavering belief in the presence of God in every aspect of the civil rights movement permeated both the leadership and the rank-in-file of the movement and was singularly responsible for the resilience and perseverance that contributed to the movement's many successes.

When I think back to the days of the civil rights movement in Hattiesburg, I also lament about the needless and senseless loss of life, freedom, and dignity that so many were forced to endure so that basic, constitutionally guaranteed rights as free citizens of the world's most powerful democracy could be realized. When one thinks about the absurdity, stupidity, and expense required to maintain the vestiges of racial segregation, e.g., separate drinking fountains, restrooms, eating facilities, accommodations, and schools, etc., it becomes clear that the white power structure of Mississippi gave little or no regard to whose rights they violated or to the fact that by oppressing black people, the entire state suffered – educationally, socially, economically, and politically. It is not by accident that Mississippi has long claimed the title of the nation's poorest state. And there is little doubt that the state's tradition and legacy of racial segregation has been a major factor in laying claim to that shameful title.

What was most important to the white power structure of Hattiesburg and all of Mississippi was the maintenance of a political, social, economic, and educational system that guaranteed the perpetuation of, not a democracy, but a *pigmentocracy*, in which skin pigmentation was the principal determinant of one's status as a citizen. *Pigmentocracy* accompanied the time-honored axiom that was created, maintained, and passed on by the power structure: *If you're white, you're all right! If you're brown, stick around! If you're black, get back!*

Chapter 1

Early Recollections and Memories

When I revisit my head and heart about growing up in Hattiesburg during the civil rights movement, memories and feelings come forth like a gushing spring. One of the first memories entering my consciousness is my grandfather (Daddy, as my brothers and I called him) and the many indignities he was forced to endure because of the color of his skin. The first memory of that dear, sweet man came to me as I recalled a story told to me long ago by my mother.

Early one morning in the early 1950s Daddy rode his bicycle home from his job at Hercules Powder Company as he had done for years. Not long after he had gone to bed after working the graveyard shift (11:00 p.m. –7:00 a.m.), two police officers came to my grandparents' home and without knocking and, without a search warrant entered their home, rousting everyone from bed. With hands on their pistols, the two officers stood in the middle of my grandparents' living room; and one began to yell at my grandmother (Mama, as we called her) in a way that was intentionally threatening: *"Where's Joe B. Griffin and you bet not tell me no lie, gal."* Shaking from the bone-chilling fear of the present moment, as well as from the all-too familiar fear induced by decades of living under Jim Crowism, Mama offered a simple, albeit vain, plea to the officers, "Joe B. jest got home and he so tired. Why you come in us house like this? What you want with him?" *"I told you, gal, what to do. Now goddamit, git em out here or you know what's good for you!"* yelled the officer at this harmless, trembling, sobbing, frightened woman. The officers claimed that a black man was alleged to have stolen a bicycle and that my grandfather was a suspect because he was seen riding a bicycle. Despite the fact that one of the officers knew Daddy and also knew he rode his own bicycle, he was ordered by the officers to get dressed and was about to be taken to jail. Desperately pleading with the officers, Daddy tearfully repeated his claim of innocence. *I didn't steal nobody's cycle. I gots my own cycle.*

1

You knows that. You knows that. I didn't steal nobody's cycle. Suddenly, without uttering a sound, one of the officers abruptly bolted from the house, clearing a path to the front door by shoving Mama out of his way, causing her to lose her balance and fall to the floor. Fortunately, only her pride and spirit were hurt. The suddenness, aggressiveness, and inexplicability of the officer's exit caused everyone, except the remaining officer, to gasp in unison and immediately caused the confusion and tension in the living room to markedly increase.

It was not until the officer returned a few minutes later with a silly smirk plastered across his beet-red face that everyone discovered the cause of the preceding moments of confusion and tension. *Well, I just talked with dispatch and they fount the boy who dat stole the bicycle. Some nigger boy down in Gomo Alley. Let's git the hell outta here and let deese niggers go to bed.* They then left the house as loudly and as abruptly as they had entered. No apology was given. Under the rules of Jim Crowism, an apology was never a consideration. The mere fact that my grandfather was a black man who rode a bicycle was cause enough for him to be accused of a crime that he did not commit, and possibly did not even occur. For my mom and grandparents, what had just occurred was nothing short of terrifying. They knew that some black men had been beaten or lynched for a lot less than allegedly stealing a bicycle. What was more terrifying was that the forces of evil masquerading as peace officers had just frightened the heebie-jeebies out of them and there was absolutely nothing they could do about it.

Daddy

The memory of that gut-wrenching story of mistaken identity triggers the start button on another mental movie, which featured my grandfather and me, playing our all too familiar roles in a Jim Crow classic. In one of its most malignant forms, Jim Crowism required black people to physically show deference to whites at all times, no matter when or where. I recall, for example, on numerous occasions walking downtown with Daddy to pay bills and frequently having to demonstrate our deference to whites wherever and whenever we encountered them – on the sidewalk, in the crosswalk, or at the entryway of a business. Whenever a white person approached us, regardless of his/her age or how much room there was on the side-walk, Daddy would slow our pace until we both came to a complete stop; and with a firm and loving grip, he would grab my tiny hand with one of his huge calloused hands and pull me closer to his side. As the two of us stood hand in hand, joined together physically and emotionally across three generations of Jim Crowism, with our feet firmly anchored among the cracks in the sidewalk, he leaned down to my ear-level and whispered to me, *Here we go, Ant. Now get ready, Son.* He and I knew the drill and what we were to do next. The two of us had played this scene numerous times and had it down pat. As the white person got closer to us, in a classic *Pavlovian* response, the two of us stepped off the sidewalk, slowly lowered our heads in tandem, and allowed the white pedestrian unfettered and unobstructed access to the entire sidewalk. Daddy always wore a hat of some type, usually a small straw hat with a colorful cloth band around the top, which he cheerfully tipped in an added show of reverence. Once the white person had passed, it was safe once again to raise our heads, at least until the next one walked in our direction. By the time Daddy and I finished paying bills and walked back home, we probably bowed to white folks at least a half-dozen times. Tragically, in the process of doing so, Daddy and I were unwitting contributors to the perpetu-ation for the nth time, of the time-honored and ubiquitous display of an unholy affirmation of many white people's belief in their God-given superiority and dominion over black people. Many whites ar-rogantly took for granted that blacks would always honor them in this fashion and acknowledge their perceived natural superiority, in much the same way they took for granted that the sun would always rise in the morning and that spring would always follow winter. At the end of the day, there must have been an enormous sense of satis-faction among the white folks for whom Daddy and I had obediently bowed while walking around downtown Hattiesburg. Whether they approved or disapproved of Jim Crowism, every white person we en-countered in downtown Hattiesburg knew either implicitly or ex-plicitly that the Jim Crow System was still in place, and, once again, everyone had perfectly performed his/her role in ensuring that it remained so. Daddy and I played our well-rehearsed parts especially well. We were acutely aware that failure on our part to show deference to whites by bowing to them as they passed would have meant that we regarded ourselves as equal to a white person, which would have resulted in our being labeled "uppity niggers." We were fully aware of the consequences of a black person being labeled an "uppity nigger" – harassment, beating, or worse. No doubt Daddy remembered that such were the cases of John Hartfield, lynched in June 1926 by an angry group of white vigilantes in Ellisville, Mississippi, 20 miles north of Hattiesburg; Emmett Till, a young black teenager beaten to death by a group of white vigilantes in Money, Mississippi, in August 1955, and Corporal Roman Ducksworth, a black GI shot by white police officers in Taylorsville, Mississippi, 45 miles north of Hattiesburg in April 1962 after being mistaken for a freedom rider.

Bowing to whites and allowing them to believe in their innate racial superiority, my grandfather and I concluded, was a prerequisite for survival in Mississippi. The cumulative psychosocial effect of this ritual on me, as a young impressionable black child, was the thorough inculcation of my status in segregated Hattiesburg as a person unworthy of respect from white people. And that was the unmistakable intent of Jim Crowism. By instilling fear and a sense of inferiority in the hearts and minds of young babies, the Jim Crow system was able to perpetuate and regenerate (or more aptly, degenerate) itself for generations. The debilitating effect on Daddy, even more sadly, was the continued erosion of his God-given humanity and a diminished belief in his own worth and dignity as a man.

Unfortunately, this scene was played out with thousands of black boys and their grandfathers all across the south. Whether my grandfather's and my existence as real, alive human beings was ignored and unseen by whites as in Ralph Ellison's *Invisible Man*, or the object of cruel racist acts as in Alex Haley's *Roots*, our lives and the lives of millions of other black people forced to live under Jim Crowism were emotionally draining.

The experience of bowing before white shoppers and pedestrians and giving them exclusive access to the sidewalks must have been both familiarly comfortable and embarrassingly dehumanizing for my grandfather. A short, dark-skinned muscular man with a very gentle spirit, who epitomized the subservience of black men in the "old" south, Daddy was exceedingly deferential to whites; and he always responded to them, regardless of age, with a polite and soft, *Yes sir, No sir* or *Yes ma'am, No ma'am.* Even in interactions with whites in which he was older, he was always addressed as Joe B., never Mr. Griffin. Sometimes, his first name became nigger and his last name, boy. Even so, he always addressed whites as Mr., Miss, or Mrs., regardless of their ages. Such salutations, of course, were required under Jim Crowism. One of the saddest memories of my grandfather seemed to come as a final sequel to this Jim Crow Classic, this time starring my grandfather and mother with me playing the role of witness/observer.

Following his retirement from Hercules Powder Company, Daddy lost his home to foreclosure. He was typical of many black men of his era who, because of low wages, needed to borrow money to make ends meet. Loan-sharking operations masquerading as legitimate loan companies gladly loaned him money at exorbitantly high interest rates, with his home as collateral. When he was unable to meet the monthly repayments, the "loan" company repossessed his home and all of its contents, forcing him, my grandmother and aunt to move into my family's home. I recall their moving into our home being an intensely bittersweet time. I loved my grandparents and my Aunt Emma and was downright giddy over having them around every day, rather than visiting them periodically at their home on the other side of town. At the same time, however, they clearly felt deep pain, shame, and disappointment brought on by the loss of not only a house, but also a loving home and all the dreams that go along with it. I am sure they also pondered and appreciated the harsh irony of having to move in with my parents. A decade and a half earlier, my parents and their three children lived with them for several years after they were married, and now misfortune had caused life to come full circle, bringing everyone back together again under the same roof.

Interestingly, it was while my parents, my brothers, and I lived in our grandparents' home that titles and names were switched and were never changed. While living in the same house, my mother and Aunt

Emma called my grandparents *Mama* and *Daddy*, and my parents *Daisy* and *Woofie*. Because kids learn to talk listening to their parents, we naturally started calling our grandparents Mama and Daddy and our parents Daisy and Woofie. That has never changed. Such informal salutations are used always with supreme reverence and love.

Not long after moving in to our home on Fredna Avenue, Daddy became critically ill with kidney failure. He routinely had blood in his urine; and I think he knew he was dying. Even so, he bravely attempted to bring closure to his rapidly fleeting life. One attempt at closure was to let my mother know that he was gravely concerned about her participation in the civil rights movement. One day he called her to his bedroom as I looked on; and in a barely audible but discernible voice, he tearfully begged my mom, in his words, "To get out of that mess before you get yourself killed." The "mess" to which Daddy referred was the civil rights movement. Daddy was proud of his daughter, but was deathly afraid for her, fearing that harm would come to her if she continued her civil rights activities. He knew how dangerous it was for a black person to challenge Jim Crowism. After all, he had been a victim of Jim Crowism all his life and had seen many lives destroyed by evil men who hated people because of the color of their skin. Naturally, he had a deep-seated fear that harm would come to his eldest daughter and her three boys if we continued participating in the civil rights movement. Although Daddy never actively participated in the civil rights movement, I believe he was privately pleased with many of the changes that resulted. With tears rolling down her face, my mom capitulated and said that she would get out of that mess. She knew, however, that was a promise she could not keep, and that God would not mind if she did not keep it.

I never knew Daddy to be a particularly outwardly religious man, which belied the fact that he truly was a believer. Not many days after his plea to my mother to cease her civil rights activities, I witnessed an amazing and heart-warming gesture on his part that revealed a great deal about his religious faith. While still confined to his sickbed, and still suffering the agonizing pain brought on by the debilitating and relentless assaults on his kidneys, he began to feel the need to bring closure to his life, in his own way and on his own terms. He had certainly begun that process by pleading with my mom to quit the civil rights movement. But perhaps the ultimate and most moving act of closure was his request to my mom one Sunday morning to see his pastor, the Reverend W.M. Hudson of St. James A.M.E. Church.

Following Sunday church services, Reverend Hudson came to the house to visit Daddy. During that one and only visit by Reverend Hudson, Daddy asked Reverend Hudson to pray for him. We all bowed our heads and felt the spirit move among us as Reverend Hudson offered up a very fervent and passionate prayer of intercession. He prayed for strength for the family and relief for my grandfather. He asked that all sins be forgiven and that the love of Christ be known and felt by all those present. Following that moving and intensely powerful prayer, Daddy asked Reverend Hudson, in a soft, raspy whisper, *Rev, do you think the Lord will let me come home now?* Hearing Daddy's words triggered in me an unexpected and involuntary gasp followed closely by a feeling that can only be described as like a knife being thrust into my stomach. I felt and tasted the salty tears flowing down my cheeks. No matter how much I tried, there was no stopping them. My heart was broken, and crying was the only response my body could offer me. As I took a quick glance at others gathered at Daddy's sickbed that had now become his deathbed, I noticed that they were bawling as much as I was. That included Reverend Hudson, who, searching for the right words, said, *Sure, Mr. Griffin. The Lord is ready for you anytime. Just put it all in His hands.* Those simple but powerful words were as much for the benefit and comfort of those of us standing vigil at his bed as they were for Daddy's. A few hours later, one of God's most precious gifts went home to be with his Father.

Chapter 2

Stepping Up to the Plate

Not long after Daddy's passing, I found myself in the midst of a rather dangerous and risky situation that profoundly affected my sense of well-being as a black child living in segregated Hattiesburg, Mississippi. I was about to be placed right in the middle of the local civil rights movement. This situation further helped to bring home to me in a very personal and frightening way, the risks and dangers of being involved in the civil rights movement and the reality of feeling utterly helpless to counter those risks and dangers. Up until that moment, I could be called a participant/observer of the movement. I actively participated in the movement but was hardly a central player. However, that all changed on a cold, wet January morning when I unexpectedly became an active, *in vivo* participant in the movement. I was about to be placed on center stage in the movement in Hattiesburg, and in the process was to become both an unwitting victim and challenger of Jim Crowism. I was called upon by the leaders of the local movement to step up to the plate of courage and to challenge a morally and legally flawed local ordinance; and instead of succumbing to the enormous fears engendered by Jim Crowism, I chose to challenge this unlawful local ordinance.

That dangerous and risky situation took place on a cold, rainy day in January 1965, when, as a 12 year old, I was participating in a peaceful demonstration outside the Forrest County Courthouse. This courthouse was the location of the office of Theron Lynd, whose job as Circuit Clerk was to register people to vote. For years he steadfastly maintained that black people would not be allowed to register, or if they attempted, were subjected to the archaic and intimidating practice of taking a literacy test and paying a poll tax. Ironically, the literacy test required the registrant to read a passage from the U.S. Constitution, which contains amendments that guarantee the right to vote to all eligible registrants, and then to interpret its meaning to the Clerk. If one could not read, as many black citizens could not, or if one was unable to interpret the passage in the manner required by the Clerk, one could not register.

To make matters worse, the City of Hattiesburg had passed a local ordinance making it illegal for anyone under the age of 18 to walk a picket line or to participate in a march or demonstration. This desperate and illegal action by the City of Hattiesburg was in response to an emerging and thoroughly effective strategy throughout the South among civil rights strategists. As jails were being filled to capacity, the result of increased civil rights protests, marches, and demonstrations in cities all across the South, anti civil rights forces believed that massive and large-scale incarcerations would prove successful in weakening the civil rights movement. They apparently believed that if substantial numbers of adults were in jail, there would be no one left to march or to demonstrate. They further reasoned that this tactic of intimidation through incarceration would cause the national media to go away, thus precipitating a quick and immediate demise of the civil rights movement.

The anti civil rights forces, however, found themselves in uncharted waters. Never before in the history of race relations anywhere in the south had there been such a sustained, albeit peaceful, rebellion and uprising against Jim Crow. They were pretty much at a loss as to how to maintain their advantage over us. The previous tactics of inducing fear and control over black people through murder, beatings, and jailings were simply not having the same effects as they had in previous decades.

In a brilliant but risky countermove, civil rights strategists decided that children should take the places of adults in marches and on picket lines. They took a calculated gamble that police would not dare treat children with the type of inhumaneness visited upon adults in the ubiquitous scenes of police brutality that were broadcast daily across the nation. If they did, that would be a major public relations disaster for the police and the segregationists and a major public relations victory for the civil rights movement. The national media would be more than willing to broadcast scenes and print pictures and headlines of black children being brutalized by mean, vicious, club-wielding white police officers. The city of Hattiesburg was aware of this new tactic by the civil rights strategists and sought to neutralize its effectiveness by passing a bogus and clearly unconstitutional ordinance decreeing who could and could not demonstrate.

So, in defiance of the ordinance, my older brother, James, my friend Ratio Jones, and I, all under the age of eighteen, showed up early at the Forrest County Courthouse, prepared to walk the picket line to protest the county's harassment of black men and women who sought to exercise their constitutional rights to register to vote. Mr. Lawrence Guyot, a civil rights worker and a leader of the local SNCC (Student Non-Violent Coordinating Committee), was also there to provide supervision and to make sure we would be safe. As we three trail-blazing teenagers were marching with cardboard placards strung around our necks, peaceably and orderly along the Main Street-side of the Courthouse, a police vehicle made a U-turn in the middle of Main Street and pulled up to the curb. The officers jumped from their car, made a B-line to the three of us, ripped the signs from our necks, and literally threw the three of us into the back of the car. The sudden and unexpected noise caused by the slamming of the car door induced an unfamiliar fear and dread in me that made me shudder like I have never done before. Ratio, my brother James and I were actually in the back of a police car, not on a joy ride or a school field trip. No! These were mean vicious men who were not happy at all with these three troublemaking black boys. *God! Please help us!* kept running through my 12 year-old mind.

I sat between Ratio and James, momentarily feeling a bit safe and protected from the police officers. It was not long, however, before our faces revealed that that fleeting and fragile sense of security had turned into real spine-tingling fear. Sensing our fear, Mr. Guyot walked over to the rear window of the car, knelt down, and tried to reassure us that we would be okay. But I had an intense, visceral reaction that informed me that it was going to be up to Mr. Guyot whether we would be okay or not. In fact, the next few moments would show that the only people who could determine whether we would be okay or not were the two men in the front seat of the police car.

As the police car sped away from the Courthouse, the officer in the passenger side of the vehicle decided to induce additional fear in these three law breakers packed in the back seat of their black-and-white cruiser. With a quick glance at his partner and then to us, he picked up the two-way radio and spoke these exact words, "Headquarters, have the dogs been fed today? Oh, they haven't. Well we're bringing in fresh meat for them!" The three of us young "delinquents" seemed to gulp at the same time as we could only look at each other and notice that each of us was eerily speechless and thoroughly frightened. The butterflies were totally out of control now. My heart was pounding like an offbeat bass drum. With that ominous and purposefully threatening remark, this officer was trying his gut-level best to scare the daylights out of us, and in my case he was succeeding. I knew the type of dogs to which he was referring – attack German Shepherd dogs that were notorious for their merciless and vicious attacks on black demonstrators.

After arriving at the police station, the three of us boys, still wearing our rain-soaked car coats and shaking and shivering from both fear and cold, were led by one of the officers down a long hallway. As we marched, single file along the tiled, black-and- white checkerboard course to some unknown location, I had only one thing on my mind – where are the dogs? I was intently listening for barking, snarling, or even yelping, which might indicate how imminent the attack would be. After a long minute, a slight smile creased my face as I could not detect any canine sounds at all. We were finally led to a dimly lit interrogation room. It was not unlike the interrogation rooms that I had seen many times on my favorite television detective shows, *Peter Gunn* and *M Squad*. Inside the cold, musty, smelling interrogation room were several well-worn, rusty metal folding chairs and a long rectangular, rickety, wooden conference table; but we were not allowed to sit in the chairs. Instead, we were ordered to sit on the cold, wet cement floor with our backs pressed up against the cold, wet cement wall. There was a noticeable and bothersome bright light hanging from the ceiling that shone directly onto the table beneath it creating a mesmerizing funnel-like effect. In a flash of surreal fantasy, I thought that at any moment one of the actors in my favorite

TV detective shows, Craig Stevens or Lee Marvin, was going to stroll into the room with a lighted cigarette dangling from his lips and start shining that bright light into our faces in an attempt to force a confession out of us. I had seen both characters do that many times with hundreds of bad guys. However, unlike the bad guys in scenes from the detective shows, the bad guys in this scene were the ones who wore the blue uniforms and carried a badge. No. This scene was not from a television show. This was the real McCoy; and I was not expecting to hear a director yell, "Cut!"

Being the oldest and the most defiant of our thoroughly trauma-tized triumvirate, my brother James decided to engage one of the officers in some not-so-friendly dialogue about the law. "Why are we here?" James asked assertively. "Cause you broke the law. You know that, don't you boy," the officer responded. Not satisfied with that flimsy explanation, James followed, "But the U.S. Constitution gives us the right to march as long as it is nonviolent, don't you know that?" Placing himself between the rickety table and the three of us, the officer glared at James and said "But we have our own con-stitution in Mississippi, boy, and the law say you can't be out there making no trouble for us. And we don't care what no nigger-loving communists up north say no how." Feeling that he needed to put an end to this little diatribe and to reassert his control of this situation, the officer spun around 180 degrees and with all of the force he could muster, slammed his open hand down hard on the table making a loud noise, like an exploding firecracker, causing the table to shake and causing the three of us to shake even more. He then plopped himself down on the edge of the rickety table, made one of the scari-est faces I had ever seen, and proceeded to pull from his back pocket, a weapon which we recognized immediately – the blackjack (a piece of lead, about half the size of a baseball bat, wrapped in black leather). He asked whether we knew what he was holding. We answered ner-vously, "Yes, sir." Getting up from the table, slowly moving toward us, and tossing the blackjack from hand to hand, he replied, "This is what we use to beat niggers' asses with." I thought to myself, "Oh my God, we managed to not get eaten by the dogs, but now this man is going to beat us to death in this room!" Suddenly, the door to the interrogation room burst open, causing it to hit the wall with a loud bang. In rushed a petite black woman, scarcely 5 feet tall, obviously very angry and upset. Despite her diminutive size, she spoke forcefully. "Why are you holding these children? I demand to know right now. If you have them here because they were on the picket line, then you'd better let them go right now. The U.S. Constitution guarantees them their right to be on that picket line. So, let them go, right now. And I do mean right now!" That was my mom, Daisy Harris, coming to the rescue. I was never more relieved to see my mom as I was at that moment. Her actions were, undoubtedly, motivated by the cruel injustice of three innocent and frightened children being held in that awful interrogation room, but also because two of those children were hers. As any mother will do when her children are threatened, my mom innately did what she needed to do to protect us. Incredibly, following a few pleas for her to calm down, these two officers reacted the same way we always reacted when she raised her voice – do exactly as she says, now! So, to our relief, we were allowed to leave with her.

The picture lives vividly in my mind today of that awesome display of courage by a hands-on-hips-totally-without-trepidation, lone black woman confronting and challenging bully, white police officers, and not even bothering to knock or ask permission to enter the room. Concerns for her own safety were secondary to her concerns for the safety of three young, frightened and terrorized boys. When I became older, I found it apropos to compare her actions with those of the Good Samaritan. The Good Samaritan did not consider, as the Levite and the Priest had done, what might happen to them if they provided aid and comfort to the man who had been victimized by robbers. Instead, the Good Samaritan had a much different perspective. Instead of wondering what would happen to him if he helped the man, he became motivated by the selfless notion of what might happen to the man if he *did not* help him. My mom and the Good Samaritan shared the same perspective on selflessness. Her concern was not what might happen to her if she entered that interrogation room and demanded our immediate release. Her concern was what might happen to those three boys if she did not intervene. I also use this incident as a reminder to myself to do the right thing, even if it gets me into trouble. Admittedly, there are those moments when, initially, I cannot seem to find the courage to overcome my fears and anxieties when I am confronted with or observe an injustice. But fears and anxieties ultimately give way to courage when I remind myself that if Daisy Harris was willing to give her life to stand up for right, then there is absolutely no reason for my doing anything less. A very important footnote to this story: I want to be very clear in stating that this incident occurred during the turbulent 60s and does not, in any way, cast aspersions on the many thoughtful, respectful, and courteous police officers who protect our communities today. Unfortunately, during the era of the civil rights movement, this type of conduct was the rule and not the exception.

Chapter 3

Life under Jim Crowism

Aside from that incredible experience with two of Hattiesburg's finest, there were other distant yet fresh memories of both subtle and not-so-subtle evidence of Jim Crow's presence throughout the city of Hattiesburg. As a youngster, I regularly came face-to-face with Jim Crow, for example, on the many occasions my parents would drive us kids to one of the local ice cream parlors. Except for the ice cream that black-owned Smith Drug Store served, the white-owned Bouie Street Ice Cream Parlor served the best soft-serve ice cream I ever tasted. My favorite flavor was vanilla, served on a crunchy cake cone. The only problem with buying ice cream at the Bouie Street Ice Cream Parlor, however, was that black patrons had to go to a separate window for service, even when there was a long line at the "black window" and there were no whites at the "white window." Such was the absurdity and senselessness of racial segregation. And the undeniable and cruel irony of this form of racial segregation is that black people unwittingly participated in this racist drama. Incredibly, the owner of the ice cream parlor seemed willing to risk losing black customers who might have grown tired of waiting in a long line, just for the sake of upholding the Jim Crow tradition of requiring black and white customers to be served at separate windows. But the owner banked on his belief that black people would always play their part in the drama; thus, in his mind, there was no real threat to his economic well-being by forcing black customers to stand in long lines. He, like many other white business owners who refused to give up their practice of separate dining facilities and separate entrances, felt completely justified in his actions, without any modicum of guilt or remorse. Most white practitioners of Jim Crowism believed themselves to be bulletproof when it came to any effort to alter what they believed was the natural order that had been established by the legacy of slavery and segregation.

Oddly, youthful inquisitiveness never compelled me to ask my parents why we always went to the same little window that only blacks went to and why we could not be served at the window where no one was present. I am certain that I saw that as just as normal and as routine as putting on my shoes. I am not sure, however, how my parents would have answered me had I asked about the separate windows at the Bouie Street Ice Cream Parlor; but I suspect that they would have been unable to give me a logical answer, because there was not one. Jim Crowism and logic were profoundly oxymoronic.

Of course, one did not have to possess a craving for ice cream to encounter Jim Crow in Hattiesburg, 24/7. Just the simple routine of driving anywhere within the city of Hattiesburg or Forrest County, one was constantly confronted with the reality of Jim Crowism via the ubiquitous signs and symbols that announced the city's and county's racial apartheid system. For example, there is the vivid image indelibly imprinted in my mind of a well-known washateria on River Avenue inside a white building in a white section of town. The image of the building that housed the washateria is so unforgettable because the words **WHITES ONLY** were so prominently printed in huge black letters across the entryway of the establishment. I remember always being afraid to go anywhere near that washateria. That snow-white cinder block building with its hideous and purposely intimidating block-style black letters seemed to represent all of Hattiesburg's Jim Crow establishments and appeared to just yell out at me in the loudest and the most blood curdling scream: *Nigger, keep out! Nigger – we hate you!*

There is also the crystal-clear image of two drinking fountains in the basement at the Forrest County Courthouse that had the words **COLORED** and **WHITE** professionally printed on a metal plate conspicuously placed at eye level above one of the drinking fountains. (Think of the cost of printing multiple drinking fountain signs.) I drank from the colored water fountain often during frequent downtown and cross-town treks with my friends and always wondered if the colored water tasted any different from the white water. Evidence of the thoroughly intimidating nature of Jim Crow drinking fountain signs and the crippling social conditioning that they produced was the fact that even when white folks were not around, I would still drink from the COLORED water fountain. The fear of being caught by a white person violating one of Jim Crow's most sacred and visible laws was enough to discourage me from any thought of tasting "white" water. So, I really never found out if there was any difference in the taste of white and colored water. But taste of the water was not the real issue at all. The real issue was that the business, religious, and political leaders of Hattiesburg concocted, created, and condoned separate accommodations and services, including water fountains, ice cream parlors, public transportation, schools, clinics, birth and death announcements in the newspapers, and eating establishments as a means of perpetuating the time-honored practice of racial segregation.

Eating in or near downtown Hattiesburg was not unlike drinking from the COLORED water fountains, being served at the COLORED window at the Bouie Street Ice Cream Parlor, or riding on the back of the city-owned buses. All involved choices – choices of surrendering to the Jim Crow practices, challenging them, or ignoring them altogether. Because of the natural desire to eat, making choices about where to eat or not eat produced a more intense relationship with Jim Crow. Two eating facilities in particular, the California Sandwich Shop and the Coney Island Cafe in downtown Hattiesburg came to represent my alimental and gastronomical relationship with Jim Crow. With each encounter with hunger that guided me to one of the sandwich shops, I found myself faced with the same choices that every black person in Hattiesburg encountered every day of our lives – give in to Jim Crow, challenge it, or ignore it.

Both sandwich shops provided service to black patrons, but only at a small square-shaped sliding glass window cut out of the wall, where the customer accessed from the outside and remained there until the order was ready, even in bad weather. Two competing emotions accompanied me whenever I visited one of the white downtown cafes – hunger and humiliation. If I were sufficiently hungry, the natural desire for food usually won out over humiliation. The idea of having to accept humiliation in order to eat a chili burger went to the core of what it was like for me as a black person living in a segregated southern town because I was being presented two choices. One, accept the diminution of my dignity as a human being and swallow the chili burger along with my pride. Two, suppress the pangs of hunger, thereby elevating my pride to a more dominant status and refuse to request service. Admittedly, the honorable choice would have been to challenge the Jim Crow practice of separate dining options; however, I must also admit that most of the times, capitulation won out over contestation. As I had done many times with my grandfather when he and I played our part in the Jim Crow drama, without any deviation from our predetermined scripts, I continued to play my role when being served at one of the sandwich shops. In stark contrast, at least from my vantage point, white customers sat inside the sandwich shops in comfortable chairs, and were cooled with air conditioning or fans in the summer and with warm heaters in the winter. In addition to enduring the humiliation of having my food handed to me through a window, while standing in rain, cold, or heat, I imagined the white customers as being more menacing and hateful towards blacks and more authentically redneck than those who dined at finer establishments in town. By enjoying the comforts of dining inside, while black customers endured the discomforts of standing outside, most of the white customers were able to affirm their superiority over black citizens, although many of them were situated at the same rung on the prosperity ladder as many black citizens. Further, well-founded beliefs that one of the white patrons would have been more than pleased to serve as an enforcer of Jim Crowism also compelled me to stick with my Jim Crow script and not deviate in the least.

Another café located midway between downtown and a contiguously situated black section of town created more eating dilemmas for me. Right there in the semi-deracialized zone, just south of the ubiquitous and symbolic railroad tracks that divided white and black stood the famous Jack's Café or better known as the *Hole in the Wall*. Owned and operated by Jack Bevon and later by his son Jack, Jr., Jack's Café earned its decades-long fame and notoriety by serving mouth-watering and inexpensive chiliburgers, ham sandwiches, and hotdogs. Each sandwich was prepared only when ordered, never ahead of time and never warmed under a heat lamp. Unfortunately, Jack's Café was also famous for its racially segregated entrances and seating arrangements. White patrons entered the café through the front door and were provided ample seating at the bar or at one of a number of eating tables. The white section even had a couple of pinball machines and a jukebox for added entertainment. The black entrance was accessed through a narrow graveled alleyway adjacent to the café. Once inside, black patrons sat in worn, dirty, greasy converted wooden school desks that numbered fewer than 10, all crammed into an area that measured no more than 15 feet x 15 feet. In sharp contrast to the white section, the black section of the café had no regular tables, pinball machines or jukebox; just 10 dirty, greasy school desks that accommodated both the customer and his food. During the lunch rush, there was standing room only in both sections of Jack's Café. People from all socioeconomic groups – college professors to day laborers – flocked there at lunch time, and it was not unusual to see more than a few black and white customers in their separate dining areas ordering and eating their food standing. What was intriguing to me about Jack's Café, more so than having to enter through a side entrance and the food being so mouthwatering, was the fact that my dad's brother, Uncle Sonny Boy, worked at Jack's as cook, cashier, and waiter. He waited on black and white customers; and it was an absolute delight to watch him in action. He never wrote down any orders, and each was precisely prepared as it was requested, no matter how detailed. *No onions, mustard only, easy on the chili. Extra onions, mayo only, extra chili.* Two separate orders prepared and delivered with precision, speed, and accuracy. Amazingly, he had the ability to remember the uniqueness of each order without writing it down or asking the customer to repeat it. Each customer was completely confident that his food was prepared precisely as ordered. Even more amazing was the fact that Uncle Sonny Boy never used an adding machine, calculator, or cash register to accurately total up a customer's order (including tax) and give correct change. It was fun to watch this masterful math whiz, who had no more than an 8th-grade education take multiple orders, fill and deliver them without a single mistake, total the bill, and give correct change, completely in his head.

Despite having to work in an establishment that required black and white customers to dine separately, Uncle Sonny Boy hated this

Jim Crow arrangement that regarded his friends and family unworthy to sup in the presence of white people. In his mind and heart, he had to remind himself every day that this was a job to him and above all, it kept his family fed. My own dilemma paralleled Uncle Sonny Boy's when it came to eating at Jack's Café. While I felt that something was not right about my having to go to the side entrance instead of the front entrance, I think I rationalized that it was just a hamburger, and after all, I had to eat. I must admit that an added perk that made the separate dining easier for me to swallow (literally and figuratively) was the fact that Uncle Sonny Boy always gave me a family discount that ranged from 10% to 100%.

Uncle Sonny Boy looked like a white man and was often mistaken for being white by some of his new white customers or by some of his old ones who became so inebriated that they did not bother to self-censor their racial epithets. He told me many times that some white customers, after a couple of beers, would forget that he is not white. They would gradually lose their inhibitions and feel perfectly comfortable sharing with him racial jokes or freely using the "n" word in describing black people. Nothing made Uncle Sonny Boy angrier than to hear a white person say something insulting and racist toward him or some other black person in his presence. In fact, on one occasion a white customer felt it was okay to freely and unabashedly make reference to a black person as a "nigger." Uncle Sonny Boy lit in to him with a vengeance, telling him that he didn't appreciate him using that term. We are not "niggers", he told him. I will not allow you to come into this café and insult me and other black people with your racist remarks. To further make his point, Uncle Sonny Boy ordered the man to leave the café, immediately. The gentleman complied and left, stunned, I'm sure, that someone actually called him out on something he routinely remarked to his friends, co-workers, and family members. However, several days later, upon further reflection on his stupidity, he returned to the café and offered a heart-felt apology to Uncle Sonny Boy, which he accepted. Uncle Sonny Boy, whose real name was Harold, steadfastly maintained his dignity despite having to earn his living working in a segregated café and having to listen to insults from narrow-minded bigots. To his credit, he didn't just take those insults. He was not afraid to confront customers who said things that offended him. The regular white customers understood and respected Uncle Sonny Boy's stance on racial epithets. The new ones, like the one who was ordered off the premises for his use of the "n" word, had to sometimes learn the hard way. But everyone who was a regular customer, black and white, had nothing but the utmost respect for him. Some of them, undoubtedly, because of his sincere graciousness and some because he looked more like them than black customers. For those of us who really knew him for his engaging personality, his wit and wisdom, and his unselfish generosity, we respected him because we truly loved him.

Despite the acuity of his steel-trap mind, he was not able to avoid the assault on his mind and body brought on by Alzheimer's disease. His older daughter, Debbie Ann, began to notice the classic symptoms of forgetfulness and tendency to repeat himself; and she asked me to be aware of them during my conversations with him. I felt a blow to my gut when I, too, began to notice those same symptoms on several occasions. One such occasion was a conversation I was having with him at his home. Although he had been retired from Jack's Café for nine years, he told me that he had to go to the café the next morning to prepare the hamburger meat. To him, that had been his routine for decades: up at 4:30 in the morning, drive to the café, prepare the hamburger meat, stock the coolers with beer and soft drinks, and take care of other various and sundry details before opening for business. It was heart-breaking enough to hear him say that he was still working at Jack's Café and still responsible for performing those early morning tasks. The heart-break that I felt that evening went deeper than I expected as he repeated that statement no fewer than ten times. I was trying to reconcile this confused mind I was in the presence of with the mind of the math whiz. There was the confused Uncle Sonny Boy who believed that he was still working at Jack's Café. And there was the Uncle Sonny Boy whose steel-trap mind kept multiple food orders straight without writing them down and never used a calculator to compute the cost of a food order. Sadly, I could not find a way to reconcile the two disparate minds of this dear, gentle man who was more like a second father than an uncle to me.

Dementia was rapidly advancing and taking over his mind and body, and there was nothing I or anyone else could do about it. Like everyone else who loved him, I could only pray that his suffering would be short and that his family – Aunt Dora, Debbie Ann, Carol, and Bruce would find the strength to endure the pain and misery of watching a loved one deteriorate in such a heartbreaking way. When Uncle Sonny Boy passed away, the world lost a precious angel. Hundreds of men and women, black and white, young and old turned out for his funeral to show their respect for one of the truly good guys. I was privileged to speak briefly at his funeral. In my remarks I reminded everyone of Uncle Sonny Boy's keen sense of humor and his knack for creating phrases and sayings that were special and had a way of sticking with you for a lifetime. One of his favorite sayings was a greeting that he used with people he knew intimately: *How you was?* Another one, after greeting someone he knew, was: *Glad you could see me.* And in an act of humor-filled kindness, he would frequently ask me to let him hold something. That was a euphemism for, can I borrow some money? Uncle Sonny Boy knew full well that he really did not want me to give him money, and he also knew full well that I did not have any money to give him. Like a well-rehearsed dialogue, I would say, *Uncle Sonny Boy, I'm flat broke today.* His reply was always, *Here, boy. This will keep the haints off of you.* He would then very pleasingly slip a twenty dollar bill into my hand. I had no doubt that he got as much or more from that act of love and kindness as the thoughtful giver as I did as the grateful recipient. But it was not about the money. Money comes and goes. It was about the love and the strong familial bond between us, both of which endure forever. Like everyone who knew and loved him, I miss him every day. I miss his wisdom, his humor, and his impeccable model as a father and husband. If I have been able to internalize and adopt just a few of his many fine qualities, I will have become a richer person for it.

A short drive from Jack's Café, on north Main Street, was the medical clinic of a white doctor, Dr. Bethea, whom my grandparents faithfully patronized their entire lives. In fact, a large portion of his clientele was black elderly patients. As with all white doctors in town, he too practiced Jim Crowism in addition to practicing medicine, requiring all of his black patients to use a side entrance to his clinic and to sit in the colored waiting room, which was no more than an oversized broom closet. My visceral reaction to sitting in the segregated waiting room, at the time, was that this was so normal and so routine. It was no different from sitting in the "colored" section at Jack's Café or being served at the "colored" window at the Bouie Street Ice Cream Parlor or drinking from the "colored" water fountain or relieving myself in the "colored" restroom or waiting in the "colored" section of the Greyhound Bus Station, or riding in the "colored" section of the city buses, or reading the "colored" births and deaths in the newspaper. Although I was just a child, I understood and accepted the fact that racial segregation *was* the norm in Hattiesburg. I knew from years of observation that the centuries-old southern tradition of keeping the races separate and unequal dictated the way I would live my life as a "citizen" of Hattiesburg. But I also believed that somewhere in the deep recesses of my soul and spirit I knew that, ultimately, I would not let racial segregation conquer me. At some undefinable point in my young life, and throughout the rest of my life, I decided to reject the notion that Jim Crowism would define my personhood and my station in life, as it had done to my grandfather. Whenever I have needed to fortify my resolve to not allow racial discrimination to consume me, I discovered a convenient and useful way of maintaining an advantage over Jim Crow and other isms designed to keep me "in my place." I discovered that "my place" is actually a quiet place in my soul where I go when I need to be comforted by a power greater than Jim Crowism. When I go to "my place," I sometimes go with a heavy heart, but leave with a satisfied spirit. When I go to "my place," I sometimes go with doubts but leave with certainty. When I go to "my place," I sometimes go with anger but leave with contentment. Whenever I go to "my place," I am reminded that God's grace and mercy are not doled out based on skin color or income. His grace and mercy are mine, gifts granted to me through His blood. I also have learned to internalize the words and meanings of that inspiring and unflinching freedom song, *'Ain't Gonna Let Nobody Turn Me 'Round*. I have allowed that soulful and spiritually liberating song to become the perfect counterweight to the enormously successful efforts by the adherents to and devotees of Jim Crowism to keep me in "my place."

To keep me mentally in a perpetual state of inferiority and to keep me physically in my place – colored only – represented both the means and ends to Jim Crowism. I believe I knew, even at an early age that, despite its potency and ability to regenerate itself, racial segregation could not and would not stand forever. I also knew that I was not the sole proprietor of such optimism. My optimism came from the heroic and sacrificial efforts of my mother and the scores of other civil rights warrior, who refused to allow themselves and their children to believe and behave as though they did not belong in America.

I also have memories of the notorious drake stands (This is the pronunciation that I remembered hearing as a child. I never bothered to ask anyone how to spell it.) Drake stands were gathering sites for unemployed black men who were looking for work. The stands were scattered throughout the black sections of town and generally were in areas where there was heavy traffic, such as an intersection. Drake stands operated 24 hours a day, 365 days a year. In cold weather, there was always a fire in a trash barrel to keep the men warm. In the dog days of summer, a shade tree was more likely to serve as the gathering place of these determined men who desperately wanted to work. There was no fee to stand at the drake stand, no one was in charge, and generally there were 8-10 men at any one stand. Typically, a white farmer or some other white employer seeking temporary day laborers would drive by one or all of the stands. At each stop, he would either step out of his vehicle or remain seated inside, and then carefully inspect the group for individuals who appeared to be physically strong, reminiscent of the slave trader inspecting the goods before bidding on them. Depending on the needs of the employer that day – picking cotton, picking up trash, or picking cucumbers -- the men would either make themselves conspicuous by raising their hands and making eye contact with the prospective employer or they would become incognito by keeping their heads down and avoiding eye contact. When the employer saw someone he thought would fit the bill, he would say, "Come on, boy. You wanna work? Git in!" The men would jump into the rear of the truck, more often than not with a huge smile that revealed the joy of finding work, at least for that day. Typically these men were paid "slave" wages or with liquor and cigarettes.

Jim Crowism also manifested itself in the ubiquitous scenes around Hattiesburg in which black workers assigned to the city's sewage and utility departments dug trenches with shovels and picks, sweating profusely, while their white bosses stood over them with hands on hips, hardly breaking a sweat, carefully inspecting the work of their black underlings. Such scenes were reminders of the powerful white overseer on the plantation supervising the work of his black field hands. Adding to this classic image of white supremacy was the fact that only white workers operated the bulldozers and other heavy equipment that were on site to help with the digging, while the black workers worked only with shovels and picks. Operating heavy equipment was strictly reserved for whites, thus helping to preserve and perpetuate one of many cornerstones of Jim Crowism – racial division and separatism based on perceived superior physical strength of blacks and perceived superior intellectual strength of whites.

My mom and dad also recall the time in the early 1960s when two teenage brothers, Willie and Tommie Townes, were selling newspapers on the corner of Seventh and Main Streets. A white man drove up to where Willie and Tommie were standing and demanded a newspaper. For some reason, Tommie did not respond to the driver as quickly as the driver wanted. Without warning the driver bolted from his car and proceeded to curse, kick and beat Tommie. He was overheard warning Tommie to be quicker next time a white man tells him to do something. He continued his berating of Tommie by telling him that niggers seem to have forgotten their place and were trying to be too damn uppity. They needed to be reminded, he said, with a good ass-kicking that they ain't equal to a white man. The confrontation ended with a dare. The white man dared Tommie to retaliate. If he tried, he said he would blow his f--king brains out. This scene was played out in the full view of black and white witnesses. The idea of someone intervening on Tommie's behalf or calling the police was completely out of the question. Black witnesses knew that doing so would not have ended well for them. And white witnesses very likely felt that Tommie was probably getting what he deserved, even though they had no idea why he was being attacked in such a violent manner. In either case, Tommie endured the pain and the humiliation. After all, what else could he have done and still lived another day?

Chapter 4

The Birth of Jim Crowism

Growing up in Hattiesburg, I suppose I never gave much thought to how Jim Crowism came about and how it came to represent the legacy of not only Mississippi but the entire South. For most of my upbringing, surrounded by the pervasive signs and symbols of segregation – colored/white water fountains, colored/white restrooms, colored/white laundromats, colored/white entrances to the movie theater, colored/white entrances to doctors' offices, colored/white service windows and counters at restaurants and ice cream parlors, colored/white seats on public buses, colored/white birth announcements in the newspaper, colored/white obituaries in the newspaper – I subconsciously reasoned that such was just the normal way of life in Hattiesburg, Mississippi. That is precisely why Jim Crowism was so successful in achieving its goal, which was to establish and reinforce the inferior status of black people and to do the same regarding the supremacy of white people. I had known nothing else but life under Jim Crowism. I learned overtly and covertly the rules of the Jim Crow game. My grandfather taught them to me early on, not because he believed I was inferior to whites, but because he feared what could happen to me if I failed to follow the rules. The insidious nature of Jim Crowism was such that following the rules became second nature to me. I did not have to think about them; and I was not allowed to question them. Just obey them. Stay in my place. Maintain the natural order of things, and everyone would be just fine. Homeostasis was achieved and the universe was in balance.

It never occurred to me to even wonder, let alone ask, whether black people everywhere had to obey Jim Crow laws as I was required to do. In retrospect, I suppose that there were glimpses and hints that life in other parts of the country was not quite like it was in Hattiesburg. One such glimpse occurred when my brothers and I visited relatives in Chicago. My Chicago cousins, who were in my age range, understood that things in the south were different than they were in the north, although not all of them had ever spent any time in the south. The adults knew full well the pain of living in the south and the pleasure of living in the north. After all, it was Jim Crowism that prompted many of them to leave the south to make a better life for themselves and their families in the north, where there was far less *overt* racism. One of my cousins brought the point into focus regarding the actual and perceived differences in the south and north for black people. Cousin Jackie asked my brothers and me one day, "Do you guys have the same kind of money in Mississippi that we have up here?" She was not trying to be facetious or insulting. She actually thought that Mississippi must be like another country, not remotely tied to the rest of the nation by currency or culture. The question made me wonder. Is Mississippi really a part of the United States of America? Does it indeed have a different currency? After all, I was beginning to notice discernible differences in the north and south, at least as represented by Chicago and Hattiesburg. I noticed, for example, that black people in Chicago could sit anywhere on a bus they wanted. Also, the absence of *coloreds only* or *whites only* water fountains helped me understand why my Uncle Richard, Uncle James, Uncle Eugene, and Uncle Floyd fled Mississippi as soon as they could. And to my delight, when going to a restaurant, we did not have to enter through a separate door, as I routinely did in Hattiesburg without giving a second thought. Why would there *not* be differences in the currency, I wondered to myself? Of course, after showing Cousin Jackie a few coins and a folded up one-dollar bill, we were all satisfied that money was not one of the things that distinguished the north from the south.

Years later, prompted by an insatiable curiosity about the origins of Jim Crowism, I decided to conduct my own research. In doing so, I learned some new things and recalled some past learning from my history and social studies teachers that have been verified multiple times through personal experience: Although every person born in this country possesses certain unalienable and constitutionally guaranteed rights as humans and as citizens, Jim Crowism, through its unchecked and unmitigated cruelty and inhumanity ensured that black people were treated as though the United States Constitution and the Laws of the Land did not exist. (The name Jim Crow comes from an antebellum era minstrels' show in which black-faced white minstrels intentionally portrayed blacks as inherently and immutably inferior to whites. A sample of the lyrics is:

Come listen all you gals and boys I's jist from Tuckyhoe,
I'm going to sing a little song, my name's Jim Crow,
Weel about and turn about and do jis so,

Eb'ry time I weel about and jump Jim Crow.) For example, despite the passage of constitutional amendments, federal laws and landmark court decisions making it illegal, Jim Crowism did not permit black kids and white kids to attend school together; denied black citizens their full rights as registered voters; disallowed black people to ride in the front of city-owned buses; and prohibited black children from using the public library and visiting the public zoo. Jim Crow's omnipresence and omnipotence overwhelmingly shaped and reflected racial attitudes, which, in turn, determined the manner in which blacks were regarded and treated by the white power structure and vice versa.

For decades, such conditions were the norm in a country whose founders possessed the ingenuity and forethought to carefully craft a magnificent document that promised the blessings of freedom, justice, and equality for all of its citizens. At some point in my life an epiphany occurred, maybe several. I came to believe and appreciate that there was a resounding emptiness and hollowness in that promise when black people were added to the conversation about justice and equality. The fact of the matter was that Jim Crow, not the U.S. Constitution, was the chief determinant of the citizenship status of black people in Hattiesburg. Prior to that epiphany, I was acutely aware that it was the Jim Crow laws that were responsible for creating and maintaining a two-tier structure of citizenship – top of the ladder for whites and the bottom of the scaffold for blacks. And that such a structure was the way it was supposed to be, no questions asked.

Jim Crowism was rooted in laws passed by southern states following the Civil War and provided the "legal" basis for a massive and sustained violent backlash against the gains made by blacks during the Reconstruction Period. After the passage of the 13th and 14th Amendments to the U.S. Constitution, which, respectively, ended slavery and granted full citizenship rights to black people, southern legislatures sought to codify their belief in white male supremacy in southern society by enacting laws (so-called Black Codes) that deprived black people of rights granted under those amendments. Incidentally, Mississippi did not ratify the 13th Amendment until 1995. Black Codes were the offsprings of the Slave Codes which were enacted during slavery to codify the practice of treating black slaves as property and not as human beings. For example, the Slave Codes forbade ownership of land by blacks, group assembly without the presence of a white person, and marriage. The Slave Codes also served as the basis for determining the race of a newborn slave, with the mother's race being the primary determinant. If, for, example the father was white and the mother was a black slave, the baby was considered black. Actually, if the father were black and the mother were white, more likely he would have been lynched.

After the end of slavery, the Black Codes were enacted in order to perpetuate and preserve the continued subjugation of the "free" slave as the Slave Codes had done with the "unfree" slave. Black Codes, for example, stipulated that blacks could not sit on juries, testify in a trial against a white person, bear arms, or meet in unsupervised groups. In addition, the Black Codes contained a vagrancy clause that made it illegal for a free black person to be unemployed and without a permanent residence, an obvious ploy to re-enslave the newly freed slave.

With the passage and enforcement of Jim Crow laws and the introduction of the Black Codes, the newly ratified 13th and 14th Amendments essentially became null and void in the South. Moreover, with U.S. Supreme Court rulings in 1883 that the Civil Rights Act of 1875 was unconstitutional and in the *Plessey Decision* in 1896, reaffirming separate but equal, southern states became even more emboldened in their efforts to mandate racial superiority of whites.

The beginning of the Jim Crow era was also accompanied by the continuation of clandestine and terroristic acts by the Ku Klux Klan whose primary mission was to enforce Jim Crow laws, both written and unwritten. *Unwritten* Jim Crow laws were a set of racist practices, behaviors, and social mores that governed the way blacks and whites interacted. For example, if a dispute arose between a black man and a white man, the word of a white man was considered more veracious than that of a black man, even if the facts indicated otherwise. If a black man looked at a white woman in a way that indicated even the slightest hint of lust or physical attraction, he could be killed, with no questions asked. *Unwritten* Jim Crow laws reinforced the underlying intent of the written laws – the subjugation, disenfranchisement, and oppression of black people. Under Jim Crowism, black people were marginalized to the point that they were regarded as not fully human, physically revolting, intellectually inferior, and socially incapable of living among whites as equals. Of course, interpretations of biblical scripture that addressed the relationship between slave and master were used by ministers, policy makers, and politicians as means for justifying racial segregation and maintaining the institution of slavery.

Jim Crow's marginalization of black people reached new heights and became institutionalized throughout the country as early movies and black-faced minstrel shows of the 1920s and 1930s such as Al Jolson's *Mammy* and the silent film production of *Birth of a Nation*; and television shows of the 1950s such as *Amos-n-Andy*, portrayed black people in extremely stereotypical ways. In most of those productions black people were reduced to mere caricatures, lacking in the basic human qualities of civility, intelligence, and industry. Images that the media presented to the public portrayed black people as lazy buffoons, brutes, mammies, pickaninnies and sambos. The real tragedy of these stereotypes was not only in the intentional debasement and misrepresentation of the true nature and character of black people, but also in the fact that they came to represent reality in the hearts and minds of many whites, particularly those in the north whose opportunities to actually observe and to accurately know black people were virtually non-existent.

The worth of a black person's life during the Jim Crow era was measured strictly by how much physical strength he/she possessed and how well he/she could perform manual labor. Proponents and supporters of Jim Crowism found it remarkably convenient and without a twinge of guilt or remorse to routinely diminish the full humanness of black people, to concoct immoral and unjust laws and to shamelessly engage in repressive behaviors that were evil in both intent and outcome. This was the progenitor of the period from Reconstruction to the modern Civil Rights movement. This period of time greatly influenced my life, from my childhood to my adulthood. Everything I did, every decision I made, every thought I had, and every emotion I felt were influenced by, if not dictated by, Jim Crowism. If left to the architects and advocates of Jim Crowism, dreams of freedom and equality would have remained just that – dreams.

Ultimately, however, I developed a fervent belief that evil cannot stand forever. Ultimately, good triumphs over evil and in the final analysis, the evildoer is the loser. That belief was instilled in me by my parents, my pastor, my black teachers at Mary Bethune Elementary School, and by the scores of civil rights warriors who demonstrated to me how not to let anybody turn me around. I was taught that I had worth and dignity, which could not be diminished or destroyed by racism. I was taught that a person cannot ride your back if you are standing straight and strong. My grade school teachers, Mrs. Jackson, Mrs. McGowan, Mrs. Lewis, Mrs. Fowler, Mrs. Harris, and Mrs. Lee collectively taught me three very valuable lessons, frequently reinforced with a paddle. 1) Never settle for mediocrity, 2) No excuses for not putting forth maximum effort, and 3) You cannot be just as good as your white counterparts, if you expect to excel. The racism factor will knock you down a few notches if you are just as qualified, just as capable, or just as educated. Instead, strive to go at least three levels above the norm so that when the racism factor knocks you down a few notches, you are still in the game, regardless of the pursuit.

A review of past and contemporary history reveals numerous acts of government-sponsored atrocities, in this and other countries, similar to Jim Crowism. Their similarity to Jim Crowism is that they were all born out of a deep hatred toward individuals and groups of people who were regarded as expendable, lacking in full humanness, and the convenient scapegoat of all of society's ills. Such acts include, but are limited to, the following: 1) Scores of Indian nations were destroyed in this country because the value and worth of the lives of Indian people were diminished by those who wanted to possess their land, 2) Hitler found it extremely easy to commit genocide against Jews and Gypsies because he was able to disregard their humanness, 3) Ethnic cleansing in Bosnia-Herzegovina and Kosovo occurred because powerful people with evil intent so callously disregarded and diminished the humanness of the Muslim population. 4) The White minority in South Africa, for generations, was able to subjugate the black majority, until Mr. Nelson Mandela and Bishop Desmond Tutu showed the world that eventually good triumphs over evil. 5) The slaughter of 200,000 Hutus by the Tutsi army in Burundi in 1972 and the genocide in Rwanda in 1994 in which Hutus murdered a million Tutsis in three months.

Chapter 5

Freedom Day

Other memories of growing up in Hattiesburg move into my consciousness as I recall the many remarkable events, people, and circumstances that established Hattiesburg as one of several epicenters for civil rights activities in Mississippi in the 1960s. During that time, a unique and powerful social revolution was beginning to take place in the Hub City and I, along with my mom, brothers, and scores of other brave pioneers were about to bear witness to and help bring about the diminution if not the demise of Jim Crowism in Hattiesburg, Mississippi.

Wednesday, January 22, 1964, was an important day in the history of the civil rights movement in Hattiesburg. The day was officially known as *Freedom Day*. This special day is regarded as the official beginning of the active, large-scale, high-profile civil rights movement in Hattiesburg and would eventually become the largest and most active civil rights movement in the state of Mississippi. Although small-scale, low- profile efforts had been under way for years, this was the actual beginning of something big.

In the days and weeks leading up to January 22, hundreds of black and white ministers, rabbis, and priests arrived in Hattiesburg from points all over the country. The National Council of Churches sponsored their sojourns to Hattiesburg and to other parts of the south in response to God's unambiguous call to them to lend their support to His divine plan to end racial segregation. Representing a cross-section of religious faiths and denominations, these courageous men were welcomed and warmly received into private homes of local black civil rights activists, including my family's. Incidentally, if someone were not already a civil rights activist, by boarding civil rights ministers, they automatically became one. The Reverend Bob Beach, a white minister from Ohio, was one of two ministers who lived in our home. I thought he was an oddity because he was a white man who wanted to help end segregation in the south. I never had reason, before then, to believe that such a person even existed. His presence also stood out because he drove a curious car that had some interesting hydraulics that allowed him to raise and lower the car with the push of a button. The highlight of my morning was when he gave me a ride to school in his car. My buddies were impressed. And there was nothing cooler than being able to impress my buddies.

Whether hosts or guests, Freedom Day participants never knew exactly what to expect, but always knew to expect the worst. Operating, with impunity, inside and outside the power structure of Hattiesburg, the anti-civil rights forces were determined to thwart if not destroy the civil rights movement. They used all of their resources and proxies to threaten, intimidate, and terrorize anyone who dared challenge the traditions and practices of Jim Crowism. Jim Crow proxies and surrogates were often law enforcement officers who, despite their oath to uphold the law and to protect all citizens, had no qualms at all about using the power of their positions as peace officers to mete out punishment to those who challenged Jim Crowism. Such was the case with the Reverend L.O. Bradford, a black Freedom Day minister from Cleveland, Ohio, who lived in our home during his stay in Hattiesburg. Not long after arriving in Hattiesburg, Reverend Bradford was shockingly introduced to the risks and threats inherent in participating in the civil rights movement, notably risks and threats from law enforcement officers. While driving from a mass meeting at Priest Creek Baptist Church in Palmers Crossings late one night with Reverend Bradford and her three sons, my mother was pulled over by a county deputy sheriff. She was not speeding and had not violated any other traffic laws. Typically, officers would park their cars near churches while mass meetings were in session. As people left the meetings in their cars, it was fairly routine for someone to be followed by an officer, who was not necessarily interested in ensuring the safety of the driving public. Rather, he would typically do what he was about to do with my mother.

The ear-piercing sound of the sirens and the circling blue lights from the officer's car wildly bouncing off the darkness of the night was a sobering reminder that DWB (Driving While Black) was sufficient reason for an officer to pull over a black motorist. As soon as my mom knew that she was about to be pulled over, she reacted in an instinctively protective and maternalistic fashion and tried to reassure all of her nervous passengers that things would be okay. Although well-intentioned, those words just were not making me feel any safer. If her heart was pounding as fast and as loudly as mine, it had to be beating like a raucous, erratic bass drum in a marching band gone awry. Despite her gallant efforts to reassure us that we would be okay, I knew that our being okay was not up to her or to anyone else in the car. That would be strictly up to the officer who had just pulled over our car. Nevertheless, she warned us to answer the officer with a respectful, "Yes, sir" or "No, sir," if he asked anything and to not show any disrespect. As the officer approached the car, I turned in my seat to look through the rear window and saw that he was a tall, lanky man whose silhouette against the bright headlights of his car made him look like Marshall Dillon walking down the mean streets of Dodge City. Fear and tension continued to mount as we prepared ourselves for the worst. My palms were sweaty. My mouth was like cotton. The pounding of my heart was mounting with each beat. My breathing became heavy. And butterflies were flying all over my insides. When the officer finally arrived at my mother's window, he stood for awhile, intentionally prolonging the agony and fear that he must have known was present within the confines of my parents' white Ford station wagon. Adjusting his holster and placing his hand on the handle of his pistol, he leaned into her window and got so close to her that I'm sure she could smell his breath. The next few moments were some of the tensest I had ever experienced in my young life. As though someone had fed him an overdose of mean pills, he decided to boost everyone's fear to a totally new level. With nasty black spit from his chew tobacco running down the side of his mouth he looked over at Reverend Bradford seated in the passenger seat and shouted, "Another goddamn outside nigger preacher agitator, with your fancy collar and all!" He then slowly shined his bright flashlight in everyone's face, one by one, back and forth. To each question or remark he directed at my mother – "You got a license to drive this goddamn car? This nigger preacher your husband, gal? – she slowly and demurely answered, "Yes, sir, I got a license; and no, sir, this ain't my husband." He posited one more question, "Your old man knows you out with this nigger?" Not waiting for an answer, the officer continued. "Git these young'uns home and git em to bed. Reckon I ought to haul all ya'll black asses off to the jailhouse. Sick and tired you uppity-ass niggers running 'round with these outside agitators, stirring up all this mess that goes agin the laws of the sovereign state of Mississippi. I ought to just take this nigger preacher on a little ride with me. Bet that would convince him of what I'm talking 'bout. Wanna go on a little ride, nigger preacher?" Obviously not wanting to bring Reverend Bradford into the conversation, which would have surely escalated the officer's tirade, my mom quickly responded. "Sir, can we leave now? My boys are tired, and I need to put them to bed." After a few more terrifying moments of silence to let the full effect of his taunting interrogation sink in, the officer allowed us to leave, but not without a final insult. "Git yo' black asses on outta here and don't let me catch this agitatin' nigger sittin' over there 'round here again!" No doubt, he knew and we all knew that he had accomplished his only goal during that encounter – total and complete harassment and intimidation of everyone in that car.

Freedom Day itself, while originally intended to be only one day of marches, was actually a series of marches coordinated by the Student Nonviolent Coordinating Committee (SNCC), the Congress of Racial Equality (CORE), and the Council of Federated Organizations (COFO). The marches, held daily for about two weeks, began on Mobile Street, which, at the time, was a haven for black-owned businesses and home for a large segment of the black middle class in Hattiesburg, and after about an hour, ended at the Forrest County Courthouse. The purposes of the marches were to draw attention to the repeated refusals by Circuit Clerk Theron Lynd to allow black people to register to vote and to actually attempt to register black citizens. For refusing to register black citizens, Mr. Lynd was enjoined by the U.S. Justice Department in April 1962 and ordered to cease and desist from discriminating against black citizens who wanted to register. In July 1963 he was convicted of civil contempt in federal court for refusing to register black citizens, and to no one's surprise, he ignored both the injunction and contempt conviction.

As a regular participant in the Freedom Day marches, I remember such notable civil rights leaders as Aaron Henry, Fannie Lou Hamer, James Forman, and Bob Moses being present for many of the marches. The local NAACP chapter was not openly supportive of the marches, believing that confrontation was not an acceptable strategy in the struggle for civil rights. The tradition of the NAACP was to seek legal remedies and to avoid direct confrontation and public controversy. The first round of marches took place in cold, rainy weather conditions with dozens of curious bystanders, black and white, looking on. Despite the inclement weather, hundreds of brave men, women, and children showed up at COFO headquarters bundled up in overcoats, headscarves, rags, gloves and anything else that would shield us from the blistering wind and cold of the morning. Marches were well organized, orderly, and peaceful. But despite the orderliness of the marches, hundreds of heavily armed, red-faced, police officers with their snarling German Shepherd police dogs leashed at their sides kept a menacing vigil throughout the hour-long rituals, no doubt itching to spring into action at the slightest transgression. I also remember seeing dozens of city firemen, in full fire-fighting gear perched atop their bright red, shiny fire engines. To me, they appeared to be not only like firefighters prepared to put out a full-alarm fire, but also like machine gunners, in a scene from *Combat,* standing in an open-air army jeep, at the apex of a hill overlooking enemy territory and itching to engage the enemy at the least provocation. Although there was no hint or threat of fire at any point along the march route, scores of battle-ready firefighters were there, nevertheless, to carry out attack orders with their high-pressure water hoses as weapons, in the event of any disorderly conduct among us marchers.

Despite the visible and intentionally threatening show of force and weaponry from the police and firemen, there were no incidents. Instead, a deep and abiding commitment to the civil rights struggle in Hattiesburg by masses of black folk was born that Wednesday morning. This and subsequent marches further emboldened the black community of Hattiesburg to continue the fight to be free citizens in our own country and to do so through peaceful means, as exampled by Mrs. Rosa Parks and Dr. Martin Luther King, Jr., during the successful Montgomery Bus Boycott in 1955, by the four brave North Carolina A&T College students who were so severely and publicly beaten by vigilante whites for attempting to desegregate the F.W. Woolworth lunch counter in 1960 in Greensboro, and by the bravery and immeasurable courage displayed by scores of black and white Freedom Riders in 1961 who attempted to desegregate the nation's interstate bus and train systems.

Freedom Day was extremely successful, not so much in its goal to register more blacks, but rather in its efforts to get the attention of city officials to let them know that a new day was dawning and that business as usual was no longer acceptable to black people in Hattiesburg. As winter turned into spring and spring into summer, civil rights activities in 1964 began to gain momentum.

A sleeping giant had been awakened in Hattiesburg, Mississippi, on January 22, 1964. From that day forward, Hattiesburg would undergo an irreversible and massive transformation in race relations that would irrevocably turn Jim Crow on his pointed head. Thanks to the relentless and courageous work by local black citizen-warriors and clergy allies from the North, that long overdue transformation was now under way and would segue into an unprecedented civil rights movement in the heart of Dixie. The movement was destined to bestow upon black people in Hattiesburg the courage and willingness to demand their rights as free citizens in their own country. Time and history would show that that transformation was frequently painful and always fraught with peril; but like the faith that reassured us that joy comes in the morning, black people of Hattiesburg knew that a new day was on the horizon. They knew just as Moses and the Israelites knew that in order to be free of Pharaoh they had to have faith that the Almighty would protect and keep them despite the difficulties that lay ahead.

Chapter 6

Freedom Summer

Freedom Summer in Hattiesburg was a natural extension of Freedom Day. The momentum that had been created by the successes of Freedom Day carried over into Freedom Summer. However, despite the movement getting off to a great start and being buoyed by the momentum of Freedom Day marches, it was clear that an enormous amount of work was still needed in Hattiesburg. Black men and women were still denied the right to register to vote. Black people were still legally required to use separate drinking fountains, to sit on the back of city-operated buses, and to attend segregated schools. Jim Crow was still alive and well, but he was about to undergo a massive transformation. The unambiguous message from the black community to Jim Crow and all of his supporters was that in Hattiesburg, Mississippi, black people were no longer willing to accept second-class citizenship and furthermore, were willing to go to jail, risk physical assaults, and even die. To their credit, Freedom Day and Freedom Summer caused the local black community for the first time ever to become galvanized and mobilized to move to the next level in the struggle. Overwhelming fear, uncertainty, and apprehension, however, were all still present within the fledgling civil rights movement in Hattiesburg. But the metaphor of the train leaving the station was quite apropos. There was no turning back because the train to freedom had left the station and under no circumstances would it turn back; and the only reason it would even slow down was to take on more passengers.

Spiritually and physically supporting the gallant and galvanized local black community was a fresh cadre of ministers, rabbis, and priests, from the North. Also, for the first time, hundreds of mainly white college students from the North descended on Hattiesburg, along with a host of celebrities and entertainers from California and New York, in a symbolic and substantive display of support and solidarity for the efforts to improve the plight of thousands of Hattiesburg's black citizens.

Freedom Summer represented the first massive infusion of white people from the North and from the nation's northern colleges into the movement, thus giving form and substance to the notion that the struggle for civil rights was not an issue of which only poor, uneducated, southern black people should have sole ownership. If lasting progress were going to be made in the cause of civil rights, neutrality would not be an option; and all racial, ethnic, and cultural groups would have to buy into the principle of group ownership of the problem of institutionalized racism. More importantly, every racial group would have to do something profound and meaningful to heed the call for action. In the case of hundreds of northern college students, ministers, and entertainers, coming south in the summer of 1964 was their response to the call for action.

Placed in a larger historical context, Freedom Summer was one of many notable and unprecedented domestic and international events that would make the decade of the 1960s among the most dangerous in the history of the world and the United States of America. The Bay of Pigs incident (the unsuccessful attempt by the United States to invade Cuba and overthrow Fidel Castro's government) occurred in April 1961, which triggered a potentially apocalyptic event between the world's two Super Powers – the United States of America and the Union of Soviet Socialist Republics, which was a staunch supporter and ally of Cuba. Cuban-based Soviet missiles, armed with nuclear warheads, were pointed in the direction of the United States, as President Kennedy and Soviet Premier Nikita Khrushchev played a dangerous game of nuclear chicken. Backed by the might of its vast military arsenal, the United States responded by insisting that not only the missiles not be pointed in the direction of our country, but also that all Soviet missiles be immediately and permanently removed from Cuban soil. As a result, tension, fear, and anxiety prevailed throughout the United States. An eerie sense of impending doom permeated every small town and large city from coast to coast. Fall-out shelters and bomb shelters sprang up everywhere like mushrooms. Fortified buildings with basements were designated as fall-out shelters, which were designed to protect occupants from the fallout of an atomic bomb. I recall seeing attached to these buildings the ever-present 10-inch by 14-inch steel, fall-out shelter signs. They were all uniformly designed with black and yellow triangles, positioned equidistant inside a circle, with the ominous words, **FALL OUT SHELTER** printed beneath it. Air-raid drills in the nation's schools were conducted almost daily, in preparation of a nuclear bomb being dropped on the United States by the Soviet Union. I have very vivid memories of hearing the shrill sounds of the drill alarm interrupting the task of the moment at Mary Bethune Elementary School. As a grade school student, no matter what I was doing at the time – spelling, reading, arithmetic, or recess, I knew to respond as quickly and as compliantly as possible to the instructions I came to know and to fear. I dutifully took my place underneath my desk in a sitting fetal position with my hands covering my head. Not sure how the hands covering my head were supposed to protect me from a nuclear bomb, but I knew the drill. Not certain if this were a drill or an actual attack, all talking ceased; and I am sure prayers by our teachers replaced whatever was in their lesson plans for the day. Thank God, no missiles were fired and no one had to spend time in a bomb shelter. The Cuban missile crisis ended with no loss of life or property. Eventually, school children safely returned to the rigors of learning the 3Rs instead of learning how to safely crouch underneath a desk or table.

Next, staunch segregationists and racists in Mississippi displayed to the nation and to the world their penchant for exhibiting unmitigated hatred and oppression of black people as news of the assassination of NAACP Field Secretary Medgar Evers was broadcast to the nation on June 12, 1963. A white supremacist, Byron De La Beckwith, who would not be convicted of this act of supreme cowardice until decades later, shot Evers in his back in the driveway of Evers' home in Jackson, Mississippi.

Coming on the heels of the averted Bay of Pigs crisis and the wake-up call from the assassination of Medgar Evers, the Great March on Washington took place in August 1963, which brought to the attention of the nation the shameful plight of black Americans in the South. During that historic event which attracted over 200,000 people, Dr. King singularly changed the direction of the civil rights movement when he delivered his signature speech, *I Have a Dream.* He was able, through his powerful oratory, to simultaneously put the nation on notice that black people were prepared to go to extraordinary lengths to be free and to provide inspiration and hope for millions of black people who so desperately needed a messiah figure to lead them to the promised land.

Three months later, the nation was forced to face another crisis when an assassin's bullet took the life of President John F. Kennedy in November 1963. I remember being in Mrs. Harris' fifth grade class at Mary Bethune Elementary School when the announcement was made that President Kennedy had been killed. The school principal, Mr. Stegall, piped the live radio broadcast of the news of the President's assassination to each classroom over the school's PA system. Whatever class instruction that was going on at the time ceased immediately. We all sat silently listening to those shocking words from the radio reporter that President Kennedy had died in a Dallas hospital. It was like the energy in that classroom had been sucked out by a giant vacuum cleaner. Pretty quickly, sobs and sniffles could be heard not only in my classroom, but also from adjoining classrooms and from the hallway. My classmates and I were only ten years old, but we understood the tragedy of the moment. We knew that a friend of the *Negro* was dead. We could see and hear the sadness that our teachers were experiencing, and in turn we students became sad. I recall thinking, as we were leaving school for the day, about the prophetic nature of those ubiquitous billboard signs along Highway 49 between Hattiesburg and Jackson that carried the phrase, *KO the Kennedys.* Following President Kennedy's assassination, it seemed that *KO* no longer referred to *Knock Out the Kennedys.* Instead, it seemed to refer to *Kill Off the Kennedys.*

Seven months later, June 1964, the nation was shocked once again by news of the tragic murder of the three civil rights workers — James Chaney, Andrew Goodman, and Michael Schwerner — in Philadelphia, Mississippi. After being released from jail on bogus charges, the three civil rights workers were stopped once again by the police. This time, they were not arrested. Instead, they were driven to an isolated area of Neshoba County and executed by law enforcement officers and their Klan buddies.

By August 1964, the Gulf of Tonkin incident had occurred (the sinking of a U.S. Navy vessel by the Viet Cong in South Vietnam), which triggered the signing of the Gulf of Tonkin Resolution and marked the "official" beginning of the United States' involvement in Vietnam. Protests against the war were just beginning to take shape in a number of cities around the country. And the nation's attention was now divided between an escalating war abroad and an escalating social revolution at home. The stage was now set for increased public reaction – for and against the war; and for and against the civil rights movement. Even before the magnitude of these five historical events could fully unfold, and before the decade of the 1960s could come to an end, the nation would live through three more assassinations – Nation of Islam Leader, Malcolm X in February 1965, Dr. Martin Luther King, Jr., in April 1968 and Senator Robert Kennedy in June 1968.

And of course, the chaos that evidenced itself in the brutal clashes between Chicago police and anti-war demonstrators at the 1968 Democratic National Convention in Chicago contributed enormously to the sense that the decade of the 1960s was indeed dangerous. Adding more fuel to the fires of tension and controversy that characterized the 1960s were the protests by John Carlos and Tommie Smith at the 1968 Summer Olympics in Mexico City when they each raised a clenched black-gloved fist and bowed their heads during the playing of the *Star Spangled Banner*. And to top it all off, the United States put a man on the moon in August 1969.

Few events in America's history would be as divisive and as defining as the two major events of the 1960s – the Vietnam War and the Civil Rights Movement. And as history has consistently judged during the intervening years, the legacy and influence of those two events still remain indelibly emblazoned in the psyche of the nation.

During the summer of 1964, my family had the pleasure of hosting two white college students, Paula Pace from New York City and Beth Moore, from St. Paul Minnesota, in our home for the summer. Their stay with us was as memorable for them as it was for us, not only for the work they did in the movement, but the fact that their stay in Hattiesburg provided each of them some unforgettable and novel experiences. Neither had ever been south of the Mason-Dixon line. And neither had ever been around black people for any appreciable length of time. The three months that they lived in our home provided a unique perspective for them and for my family on how persons from a different culture and a different part of the country live. One of the novel experiences that illustrated the gulf in life and cultural experiences between them and us occurred when Paula and Beth jumped from their beds early one morning in utter fear. Although foreign to them, the sound that jolted them from their beds was so familiar to my family and me that we barely noticed. The two of them quickly leaped to their bare, pale feet, looked out the window in genuine astonishment and fear, called out to my mom, and asked what that noise was and what was causing it. Of course, my mom could not control her laughter as she reassured them they that it was just the neighbor's rooster. Feeling safe again and joining my mom and the rest of the family in floor-rolling laughter, they both confessed that they had never seen or heard a real chicken before.

My mom also recalls the night Paula and Beth first arrived in Hattiesburg and accepted my mom's invitation to attend church with her that night. Despite her busy schedule with the civil rights movement, my mom never missed church and was a pianist for several church choirs. Paula and Beth sat in the back of Star Light Missionary Baptist Church and after about 30 minutes had passed, beckoned for my mom to come back to where they were sitting. When she went to where they were sitting, my mom, with great patience and curiosity, quietly asked, "What do you want and why are you sitting so far in the back of the church? And why do you keep staring at the church door?" They both answered back, "We want to sit back here to be close to the door so we could see the Holy Ghost when he comes in! How long do you think it will be before he gets here?" Holding her laughter, my mom tried to explain. "Honey, the Holy Ghost is already here and he didn't come through no doors. You see, the Holy Ghost is something you feel, not something you see with your eyes or touch with your hands. You feel it with your heart deep down inside;

and when you feel it, child, you know it. That's when you know that the spirit of the Lord is with you. It's when you pat your foot when the choir is singing. It's when you shout amen when the preacher is preaching. And it's when the deacon is praying, you just feel like the burdens of the world done been lifted off your shoulder. That's the Holy Ghost, honey." "Oooh!" they said in unison with both relief and disappointment. Obviously, this was Paula's and Beth's first experience with the black church. Luckily for them it was also an opportunity to dispel some myths and stereotypes in a relative safe and humorous manner.

Beth and Paula also experienced a first when they ate a plate full of grits that only Daisy Harris could make. (Note: You make grits. You don't cook or prepare them!) Not only were they curious about the manner in which grits are made and how they taste, they were also curious about the strange sounding expression my mother customarily used when she told them she was going to the store. She told them the same thing anyone in Hattiesburg would have said when going to the grocery store: "I'm going to make groceries." Of course, Paula and Beth fell into the same trap many non-southerners (or non-Mississippians) still fall into today. They tried to figure out the logic of that phrase, and, of course there is none. It makes no sense. No one makes grocery. One buys groceries. It seems it is one of those southern idioms that have been passed on through the generations. The only time I think about the missing logic in that phrase is when I say it and someone reacts with curiosity and laughter as Beth and Paula did.

Freedom Schools

One of the many responsibilities of the volunteer college students and celebrities during Freedom Summer was to help set up and teach at Freedom Schools. The Freedom Schools' curriculum was designed to give black, school-age children a jump-start and a head start on the regular school curriculum we would face in the fall. Not only were academics – math, reading, and science - stressed in Freedom School, but enrichment activities were also an important part of the Schools' curriculum. In fact, I took guitar lessons from the renowned (even though I had never heard of him) folk singer, Pete Seeger. Noted black folklorist, Julius Lester, author of *Black Folktales*, also shared his spellbinding, story-telling talents with the children of Hattiesburg Freedom Schools.

Freedom Schools were all housed in churches and were free to attend. I attended the Mt. Zion Freedom School, which was located about five blocks from my home. Other Freedom Schools were housed at True Light Baptist Church, Priest Creek Baptist Church, St. John A.M.E. Church, and St. Paul United Methodist Church.

Freedom School teachers were all volunteers and most were black and white college students, ministers, priests and rabbis from the north and entertainers from New York and California. For the members of the clergy and for some of the college students, the primary source of motivation for participating in not only Freedom School but all of the Summer 1964 activities was their belief in the Judeo-Christian principle of resisting evil and responding to God's call to fight injustice wherever it appears. Given the interplay between religion and the civil rights movement, it is no surprise that so many persons of faith found it a natural fit to participate in Freedom Summer.

Each Freedom School teacher was genuinely concerned about making sure that all the Freedom School participants experienced success and would be able to demonstrate that success in the fall when regular school started. Admittedly, trying to get young people to be serious about academics during the summer was no easy task, no matter how committed the volunteer teachers were. However, those among us who were serious about our studies and, more importantly, cared if our parents knew we were goofing off, found the academic work beneficial, but sometimes lacking in any semblance of fun and stimulation. For example, I was able to improve my own 6th grade writing (not penmanship) and spelling skills because I had worked on the Mt. Zion Freedom School's newspaper. There were also debate teams that featured debates among the various Freedom Schools. Freedom School was where I first learned about Dr. Seuss's The Cat in the Hat. I had never heard of the author or his book.

Reading that story was like waking up on Christmas morning with a toy you did not expect to get. It was indeed a gift. It was made even more of a gift when, after reading the book, we actually acted out scenes from the book. One scene that I remember involved standing on a chair with a big hat on my head, and at some point, falling down to the floor.

While attending Freedom School, I was part of a group of students that attempted to desegregate the Hattiesburg Public Library. Of course, consistent with the practice of separate and unequal, the black library was a one-room dilapidated converted storage closet at the East Sixth Street Community Center that contained a paltry quantity of tattered hand-me-down books that were once brand new when they were at the white-only Hattiesburg Public Library. One afternoon, following normal activities at Freedom School, several of us students piled into the car of one of the white teachers – Sandra Adickes – who drove us to the Hattiesburg Public Library on Main Street to attempt to utilize some of the more advanced and modernized services of that library. As a white person, Ms. Adickes would have had no problem entering the library or using any of its services. However, because she was with a group of black kids, that was not to be the case on this visit.

In order to enter the library it was necessary to climb a set of concrete stairs that formed one side of a dual set of spiral staircases that led to the main entrance on the second floor. The gravity of our impending exploit did not fully sink in as we slowly climbed the stairs. I knew we were attempting something profound, something that had never been attempted before in Hattiesburg; but the major unknown was how the white library staff would treat us once we entered the front doors. Led by our white Freedom School teacher, we walked quietly in single file through the front door of that impressive two-story, brick edifice that, despite having the word PUBLIC prominently inscribed in its signage, and being supported by taxes paid by black and white taxpayers, was off limits to black people. It was not until we actually entered the library and were there for a few minutes that I realized that what we were doing was going to result in something unusual and totally unexpected. Once inside, I remember being in eye-popping awe of the magnificence of this building, with its vaulted ceiling, shiny, tiled floor, long, sturdy wooden tables, high-back chairs, and rows of steel shelves stacked with thousands of books and magazines that looked to be in perfect condition. In contrast to what I was accustomed to seeing at the East Sixth Street Community Center library, this was like another world altogether. It even smelled different. After inspecting one of the long rows of books, we each took seats at one of the long tables. Shortly afterwards, a tall, redheaded, bespectacled lady came to the table. I sort of knew that she was not coming over to welcome us to the library from the serious scowl imprinted on her beet-red face. She stood at the end of the table with her arms folded and announced in a nervous library-soft voice that was just loud enough for nearby white patrons and each of us to hear her every word. "I'm sorry, but you people are going to have to leave this building, and right now." When she was asked why, she said, " Well, well, because the library is closing and you have to leave so we can lock the doors." When told that the posted library hours indicate that the doors should remain open for several more hours, she nervously repeated her refrain, "You people are just here to cause trouble. Now I told you the library is closing. Besides, y'all are supposed to go to the colored library anyway if you want to use any books. Now if you don't leave right now, I'm gonna have to call the police to get them to remove you." Not wanting to be responsible for causing any harm that might result if the police tried to remove us, Ms. Adickes told us to get up from our seats and to follow her out the door and back to her car. We followed her instructions and somehow I knew, as we were leaving through the glass front doors of the Hattiesburg Public Library, that our young group of pioneers had both won and lost. We won because we were able to physically go inside a building that had always been closed to black kids. We lost because we were forced to leave the public library for no other reason but our race. I also left with a feeling that this would not be the last time I would go inside this library. Indeed, several months later, my friend Benton and I applied for and were issued official turquoise colored library cards with our own names embossed on a silver tab affixed to the front of the card.

Free Southern Theater

In addition to the fun that I had in Freedom School, writing stories in weekly newsletters, acting out Dr. Seuss stories, and hanging out with Pete Seeger, I had the opportunity to watch live stage plays presented by a group of professional actors known as the Free Southern Theater. Founded in New Orleans in 1963 by Gilbert Moses, Tom Dent, and John O'Neal, the Free Southern Theater operated on a simple but noble mission – to bring to black people of the south, black stage plays performed by professional black actors. The only actors that most of us had ever seen were the stereotyped caricatures on television and in the movies, such as Amos and Andy, Rochester on the *Jack Benny Show*, and Stepin Fetchit. These talented but financially and organizationally challenged thespians from the Free Southern Theater, however, were nothing at all like the caricatures to which we had grown accustomed and which had helped shape our individual and collective self-images. The Free Southern Theater attempted to portray black life in a positive, yet realistic manner, unlike what we were accustomed to watching on television or seeing at the movies.

While on its summer tour in 1964, the Free Southern Theater came to Hattiesburg, August 2-4, to present, *In White America*, a play by Martin Duberman about the struggle for civil rights in America. Attending such an event was a first for us black children, and I am sure that fact was apparent to the cast members. But they were extremely understanding and were quite patient with our sometimes inappropriate laughter and ill timed applause. One incident in particular illustrated our lack of manners, maturity, and couth. At one point in the play, a slave was being auctioned. The auctioneer was barking out for bids "...$100...who will offer $100 for this buck?" Not surprisingly, someone in our group yelled, "I'll give a $100 for that buck!" Naturally, that was a very inappropriate remark. Some of us knew that it was not right for black people to bid on slaves, even if it was just make believe. Others thought it was funny and laughed. To my surprise, the actor playing the part of the auctioneer stopped the play and took advantage of a teachable moment. He admonished us about bidding on a slave. He said that it was wrong for anyone to willingly buy another human being. And it was even worse for a black person to even pretend he was buying another human being. For those who did not already understand the inappropriateness of pretending to purchase another human being, his aside brought the point home in a very dramatic and impactful manner. I was glad he made the point and the play continued. At the end of the play I knew I had witnessed a profoundly breathtaking event. I was deeply moved by the superb acting skills of a cast of extremely talented black actors who enabled me to feel even better about being black. These characters did not fit the caricatures and stereotypes to which I had become accustomed when watching television. After watching those live stage plays, featuring exceptionally talented actors portraying black people in a non-stereotypical manner, I felt liberated because I now had a choice. For the first time, I was able to see myself in these black actors and the characters they portrayed. I no longer had to see myself *only* through the actors and characters portraying Amos and Andy, Stepin Fetchit, and Rochester. What a contrast - proud or pitiable, strong or stereotyped! For my money, I opted for proud and strong over pitiable and stereotyped.

On their second tour through the south in the fall of 1964 and winter of 1965, the Free Southern Theater made a stop again in Hattiesburg, January 23-24, 1965, thanks to the efforts of COFO's Hattiesburg Director, Sandy Leigh. I remember the excitement of attending St. Paul United Methodist Church the first evening of the performances to watch the Free Southern Theater's production of *Purlie Victorious*, a comical satire, written by Ossie Davis, about life on a southern Georgia cotton plantation. I recall being mesmerized by the wonderful acting, dancing, and never-before-heard soulful and rhythmic songs, such as *The Harder They Fall, God's Alive, and Big Fish, Little Fish*. August 18-21, 1966, the Free Southern Theater returned to Hattiesburg for its presentation of three additional black plays: *Roots* by Gilbert Moses, *I Speak of Africa*, a one-act play by William Plomer, and *Does Man Help Man?* by Bertolt Brecht.

I recall that the actor Robert Hooks, who later starred in the television series in N.Y.P.D, was in *Purlie Victorious* and that Gilbert Moses, was the director and Gilbert's then-wife, Denise Nicholas was an actress in each of the plays. Ms. Nicholas would later go on to have a starring role in the television series *Room 222*, and more recently was a regular on the television series, *In the Heat of the Night*. Gilbert Moses went on to a successful career as a director of several Hollywood movies, including *The Greatest Thing That Almost Happened, The Fish That Saved Pittsburgh,* and *Ghostwriter – Ghost Story.*

Voter Registration

Freedom Summer was also significant because it launched a massive voter registration drive that permanently altered the political landscape in Hattiesburg and indeed in the entire south. For the many decades from Reconstruction to the start of Freedom Summer, the history of black voter registration in Hattiesburg was characterized by futility, intimidation, and unrelenting efforts by the white power structure to enact laws and engage in practices that not only discouraged, but also penalized black participation in the democratic process. For example, payment of poll taxes – actual monetary fees charged by the Circuit Clerk, and the mandatory administration of a literacy test – verbal interpretations of a selected passage from the U.S. Constitution were required in order to register to vote. Because money to pay poll taxes was scarce, coupled with the fact that many blacks felt intimidated by the idea of having to read and interpret something as unfamiliar as the U.S. Constitution, many prospective black registrants simply refused to even attempt to register to vote.

So the stage was set to embark upon a long-overdue and much needed attempt to repair the breach between America and its exploited and disenfranchised black citizens in Hattiesburg and the entire South. The rallying cry for voter registration drives was *One Man, One Vote*, which reflected the updated intent of the framers of the U.S. Constitution to ensure that each eligible person possesses the one vote to which he/she is entitled. The original version of the intent of the framers of the Constitution purposely omitted black people, along with women and poor whites, from the list of eligible participants in the fledgling democracy. Interestingly, poor whites and women won the right to vote far sooner than black people.

Voter registration drives, therefore, embraced the notion that the fundamental ingredient of a viable democracy is the right of all of its eligible citizens to register and to freely vote for ideas and individuals of their choice. Within the civil rights movement, we embraced and lived by the principle that until the right to vote could be freely claimed and fully exercised by every citizen regardless of race, the ability of our democracy to live up to its true meaning and spirit would remain unfulfilled. So, in a sense the efforts by the civil rights movement to ensure that black citizens obtained their constitutional rights as registered voters was one of the most patriotic acts that any group of citizens could possibly perform.

Although I was much too young to register, I willingly responded to the call for volunteers to seek out unregistered black citizens and to encourage, coax, or beg them to become registered voters. Voter registration drives had to be well coordinated and were quite labor intensive. A successful voter registration drive involved door-to-door canvassing by at least two individuals. In a town the size of Hattiesburg, that required a critical mass of dedicated people – young, old, male, female, black, white, local, northern college student.

Black sections of Hattiesburg were assigned to pairs of voter registration workers who visited the homes of people assigned to them. As in most southern towns, the black community in Hattiesburg was divided into Quarters as they had been done during and after slavery to designate black sections of town, i.e. Arledge Quarters, Newman Quarters, Meridian Quarters, and East Jerusalem Quarters. My family lived in Arledge Quarters. Other black sections of Hattiesburg were called the Park, Graveline, and Red Line. Workers would knock on the doors of hundreds of black homes to ask two important questions: Are you a registered voter? If you are not, will you make the effort to become registered? We only asked adults who were at least 21 because at that time in the State of Mississippi, no one under the age of 21 could vote. We would invariably receive a mixture of responses from people, including slammed doors in our faces, refusals to answer the knock, and occasionally a heart-felt and tearful expression of courage on the part of an elderly person who was willing to risk everything to register.

Massive black voter registration is perhaps the most significant accomplishment of the civil rights movement in Hattiesburg. It not only provided a sense of accomplishment for civil rights activists, but it instilled an enduring source of pride for previously disenfranchised black people. Indeed, as the voter registration rolls swelled with increased numbers of black registrants, white politicians began to actively seek out black voters, which provided a collective sense of power. The drive to register more blacks eventually led to black candidates seeking public office, locally and statewide. Beginning with the 1968 session, Robert Clark of Ebenezer, Mississippi, became the first black man since Reconstruction to serve in the Mississippi Legislature. Although most other black candidates, initially, were not successful, the effort to run for public office did represent a significant attempt at political self-empowerment. With such notable progress, albeit, slow and uneven, I began to believe that maybe, just maybe, the movement's promise was becoming manifest. I even allowed myself to engage in hopeful thinking. I began to think that by the time I was old enough to register to vote, all the work that was presently being done, would make it much easier for me to

Another notable attempt at black political self-empowerment occurred during the 1964 Democratic National Convention in Atlantic City, New Jersey. As they had been for decades, white democrats from Mississippi continued not to oppose any efforts to integrate its convention delegation, but also to oppose the National Democratic Party's position on racial inclusiveness.

The opposition to the National Democratic Party's position on civil rights by southern white democrats started as far back as 1948, when southern states formed the Dixiecrat Party. To demonstrate their displeasure with both political parties, the Dixiecrats attempted to throw the presidential election into the House of Representatives by refusing to support the Democratic candidate, Harry Truman, or the Republican candidate, Thomas Dewey. Instead, they ran their own candidates, Governor Strom Thurmond of South Carolina (He later switched to the Republican Party and became Senator Strom Thurmond.) for President and Mississippi Governor Fielding Wright for Vice President. The Dixiecrats failed in their efforts to upset the

1948 presidential race, but they refused to give up the battle cry of white southern racists – "Segregation today, segregation tomorrow, segregation forever!"

The all-white Mississippi Democratic Party brought that same battle cry and reactionary attitude to the 1964 Democratic National Convention where they assumed there would be business as usual – decades of successful efforts by powerful reactionary white southern politicians such as Mississippi Senators John Stennis and Jim Eastland and former Senator Theodore Bilbo, who once filibustered anti lynching legislation, to maintain their control of the heart and soul of the Democratic Party. Present at the convention, however, was the Mississippi Freedom Democratic Party (MFDP), an insurgent group of black and white Mississippians, headed by Fannie Lou Hamer, that sought to be certified as the official Mississippi delegation. Representing Hattiesburg in the MFDP delegation were Peggy Jean Connor, George Harper, and J.C. Fairley. The MFDP's chief argument for being certified and seated as the official Mississippi delegation was that the integrated MFDP, not the all-white delegation, was more representative of Mississippi. Although the MFDP was on solid moral and legal ground in asserting such a claim, Democratic Presidential and Vice-Presidential running mates Lyndon Johnson and Hubert Humphrey, in the view of many, betrayed the Mississippi Freedom Democratic Party by refusing to support efforts to unseat the regular Mississippi Democratic Party. Instead, they chose political expediency over moral correctness. Johnson knew that if he were going to defeat Barry Goldwater, the Republican nominee for President, he would need the South – the white South that is. However, a shallow victory did occur: a compromise was reached that gave voting and speaking rights to two delegates from the MFDP and seated the others as honored guests. Nonetheless, the all- white delegation was certified and allowed to represent the State of Mississippi, despite the fact that it supported the continued disenfranchisement of black people in Mississippi. Convention delegates agreed that in the future no delegation would be seated from a state where anyone was illegally denied the right to vote.

Paternalism and Sexual Encounters – Tension Within the Movement

Despite the commitment and exceptional sacrifices from white college students who worked in the voter registration drives and with the Freedom Schools during Summer 1964, tension was evident between some white college students and some of the seasoned black veterans of the civil rights movement. There appeared to be at least two sources of tension. One source was the paternalistic attitude that some white students exhibited towards blacks in general in the South. Ironically, some of the white students regarded black people in the South in much the same way as southern whites did – people who should be pitied, not respected. Along with the display of pity, some white college students were somewhat self-righteous in the way they responded to southern white racism. Many foolishly viewed themselves as non-racist simply because they were not from the south which led to condescending remarks and attitudes that were indeed racist. For example, it was not unusual to observe some white college students snickering at the broken English of elderly black men and women as they expressed themselves in the only way they knew. Phrases such as, *This is us house*, or *Let's go sit on the gary* (porch) were considered funny and something to be mocked by some white students. Also, some would attempt to mimic the speech patterns, dialects, and slang of black people as though they were some novel or hip way of speaking.

In addition, some of the white college students possessed a know-it-all attitude that was based on limited experience in the south and with the civil rights movement. Some, unfortunately, believed that intellectual ability translated into a street-wise ability to organize and manage a voter registration drive or to plan and carry out a march. Such an attitude ran afoul of the hard-earned wisdom of seasoned black civil rights activists who rightfully believed that their experience on the front lines earned them the right to have their views respected, especially by individuals who had been present for only a short period of time and whose remaining time was even shorter.

Another source of tension between white college students and black civil rights activists was the issue of sex, although I was too young at the time to remotely comprehend what that meant. Years later, when doing research on Freedom Schools and talking with individuals who were old enough at the time to comprehend the issue, I began to think more about the subject myself. Apparently, an unexpected dynamism was created with the mixture of young white college coeds and young black men in Hattiesburg, resulting in a number of romantic and sexual encounters. Some theorize that the source of the tension over sex was the mutual curiosity about the other group's interest in romantic and sexual relationships. Such situations created resentment, jealousy, and distrust regarding the motives of some of the white coeds and some of the young black men of Hattiesburg. Some black women involved in the movement felt particularly resentful and angry toward some white coeds because of the belief that some white women operated with a set of sexual mores that ran counter to those long ago established and adhered to in southern black communities. Beginning with slavery and continuing throughout the ensuing decades, interracial sexual encounters in the South were quite common and generally regarded by blacks and whites as ordinary. Except, such encounters almost always involved white men and black women and were rarely openly discussed by anyone in the neighborhood. Nearly everyone in my neighborhood, for example, including youngsters, was aware of a white insurance agent, Charlie, who routinely slept with black women in my neighborhood when he called on them at their homes to collect their insurance premiums. Everyone knew about Charlie's escapades, but they were not regarded as taboo or unusual. Nobody felt anger or judgmental, and no one ever confronted Charlie or his women customers. It was just something that happened, typically several times a week.

However, with the arrival of Freedom Summer and the active participation by white women, the rules of sexual engagement suddenly changed. Black men and white women started having sex with each other, which was in conflict with the normal operating rules, and in turn, sparked strong emotional responses from many black women involved in the civil rights movement. Incidentally, fear of real and imagined black male/white female sexual encounters was also a source of constant irritation and grave consternation for racist southern white males and was also the primary reason for their fierce and violent opposition to the involvement of white women in the civil rights movement. Some black women believed that some promiscuous white women, most of whom had little or no contact with black men prior to coming south, were using sexual encounters with black men to demonstrate their unqualified acceptance of black people and to satisfy their curiosity about black male sexual prowess. Sexual encounters based on racial stereotypes, they believed, were a distinction without a difference, as far as racist activities were concerned.

For black men and white women involved in such sexual encounters, part of the motivation was the added excitement and titillation of challenging the long-standing southern taboo of no sexual contact between black men and white women. Also, there was the whole contentious debate over whether white women were taking black men from black women.

I was aware that a young black man who was actively involved in the movement married a white northern coed who was a Freedom Summer worker; and both immediately fled the state and the movement. They obviously knew they could no longer remain in Mississippi and remain married to each other. Whether it was true love or true lust, their not-so-secret tryst resulted in the loss of two valuable soldiers in a movement that so desperately needed every single available civil rights worker. Further, their relationship greatly reinforced the belief by many that some white women and some black men were in it (the civil rights movement) only for the sex. In any case, there was no doubt that the issues of interracial romance and perceived or real paternalism created noticeable tension within the leadership and the rank-and-file of the civil rights movement; but not enough to cause any long-term deterioration in efforts by everyone to remain focused on the task at hand – providing assistance, support, and reinforcement in the battle to gain equal rights and justice.

Chapter 7

When the Village Was Strong and Kids Were Kids

As the civil rights movement was shifting into high gear in Hattiesburg during the summer of 1964, I was cognizant of other events going on in my little world in Arledge Quarters, U.S.A., as well as in the larger world outside Mississippi. As important as the civil rights movement was, there were other things going on that occupied my time and attention such as television, movies, sports, and music. These outlets provided convenient and familiar means of temporarily forgetting the ugliness of racial segregation and permitted me to experience the joy and excitement of being a child. Moreover, they created a much needed sense of normalcy in my small, segregated world in Hattiesburg, Mississippi.

The ongoing struggle for civil rights in Hattiesburg created a reality that both contradicted and confirmed what I observed through television, movies, and sports. When viewed through my only window to the world – the entertainment and news media, I came to understand that in some ways life outside the South was far better than the one I was living in Hattiesburg and that in other ways, it was no better. For example, I watched numerous television shows, commercials, and movies that were completely devoid of any characters who looked like me. Further, due to the absence of black actors in commercials, it was easy to believe, for example, that black people did not use shampoo, drink soft drinks, or buy automobiles.

Most of the handful of early black television and movie characters, unfortunately, were gross stereotypes and caricatures that perpetuated the notion of black inferiority. Television shows such as *Amos-n-Andy* and movies such as *The Birth of a Nation* were particularly effective in perpetuating the image of black inferiority. If one believed, for example, that black women were domineering, bossy, and lacking any hint of sex appeal and that black men were lazy, violent, and sexual predators, viewing some of these shows and movies would assuredly reinforce that belief. Other movies, however, such as *To Kill a Mockingbird, To Sir with Love, Nothing but a Man, and A Raisin in the Sun*, while acknowledging the devastating and even fatal consequences of racial discrimination, attempted to portray black characters as proud people with the same hopes and dreams as white people. I recall, as a child, reading Harper Lee's *To Kill a Mockingbird* and years later watching the movie version of her novel. In both instances, I remember being so angry that the black character, Tom Robinson, was falsely accused of rape, but heartened by the fact that a white lawyer, Atticus Finch, defended him. The fact that a black man was being falsely accused of raping a white woman was nothing new to the south. And in the end, Tom did lose his life, which was consistent with the customary way of dealing with such violations of Jim Crowism, regardless of guilt or innocence. What was such a departure from the norm of life in the south was the fact that, at least in the movies and in the book, a white man was on the side of a black man.

Many of those television shows, movies, and commercials simply mirrored, and in some cases contradicted, the reality that was present in Hattiesburg for decades under Jim Crowism. As was attempted by the producers of these stereotyped and caricatured movies and television shows, public officials and business owners in Hattiesburg who subscribed to the tenets of racial segregation and Jim Crowism attempted to instill in the minds of black people that we were innately inferior to whites. They attempted to do so by creating and maintaining an educational, political, and economic system that placed black people at the lowest rung of the socioeconomic ladder, where they foolishly believed black people would always remain. As with the producers and writers of racially stereotypical movies and television shows, the producers and sponsors of Jim Crowism failed to understand that the perpetuation of racial stereotypes was more of a statement about their own humanity than about that of those whose humanity they attempted to reduce through grossly and intentionally racist caricatures and stereotypes. Further, they failed to understand a basic principle of human interaction – one cannot hold down a man in a ditch unless one gets in the ditch with that man! In other words, by attempting to oppress black people in Hattiesburg and throughout the south, the perpetrators of Jim Crowism, i.e., government, caused all of its citizens, black and white, to suffer from the devastating effects of poverty and poor economic conditions. What else but racist attitudes caused the state of Mississippi to create the infamous Mississippi Sovereignty Commission for the expressed purpose of thwarting efforts to end racial segregation, particularly in the public schools? In the process of carrying out its vindictive actions against its black citizens through its historical efforts of socially, politically, economically, and educationally marginalizing and oppressing such a huge segment of the population, the entire state suffered. In other words, a funny thing happened on the way to racial segregation. The immense suffering caused by racial segregation was not restricted to black citizens, who were, of course, the sole targets of the Jim Crow oppression. Poor white citizens, who possessed limited educational and economic opportunities due, in part to, intentional economic and educational decisions made by elected officials, also suffered. Mississippi, for example, passed laws that allowed school systems to close in opposition to the *Brown Decision*. The racial climate in Mississippi did not engender a positive view from the rest of the nation toward the state's leadership, its educational system, and its economic practices. As a result, businesses were reluctant to build or relocate to a state that stood in such strong opposition to basic human rights. The fact that Mississippi ranks last in so many measures of health, economic, and educational well-being, bears a direct relationship to its history of racial oppression.

Paradoxically, the notion that life outside segregated Hattiesburg was better also came via television, especially through variety, action, and comedy shows, news reports, and sporting events. Shows featuring non-stereotypical black entertainers and actors were few, but black people heavily watched most of them. Shows such as the *Nat King Cole Show* in the late 1950s, although it stayed on the air for only one year, *I Spy*, starring Bill Cosby in the mid 1960s, *Julia*, starring Diahann Carroll in the late 1960s, and *Room 222*, starring Lloyd Haynes and Denise Nicholas in the late 1960s enabled black people to feel proud of how we were being portrayed on television. These shows also allowed white viewers who believed in the caricatures of *Amos-n-Andy* to challenge some of their stereotypical thinking about the characteristics and abilities of black people.

Watching the local and national news was a nightly ritual for my family. In fact, we probably watched every newscast that Chet Huntley and David Brinkley ever did during their 15-minute broadcast from 5:30 – 5:45 on the local NBC affiliate, WDAM. My mother believed it was critically important for us to watch the national news every night so that we could be informed and conversant about what was happening in the world, although most of what was broadcast was unpleasant and depressing. The Vietnam War was developing into a daily headline grabber and lead story on the nightly Huntley-Brinkley Report. As the first televised war in U.S. history, it made undeniably clear the madness, destruction, and death that were part and parcel of war. There were also nightly broadcasts of civil rights demonstrations in which scores of black demonstrators were viciously attacked by police dogs, beaten by out-of-control, hate-filled police officers, and sprayed with high-powered water hoses by angry firemen. Particularly disturbing was viewing the merciless, brutal and unprovoked attack by white police officers on demonstrators at the Edmund Pettus Bridge in Selma, Alabama, in 1965 and the continuous violent attacks on black demonstrators by the notoriously brutal Director of Public Safety, "Bull" Conner and his violent police officers in Birmingham. Watching such scenes, as despicable as they were, created a stronger resolve in many black people to remain committed to the struggle and to feel a sense of camaraderie with others who were experiencing the same pain we were experiencing in Hattiesburg.

Television, particularly network news programs, played a major role in bringing to the attention of the nation not only the poverty, squalor, and segregation under which black citizens in the south were required to live, but it also showed the nation images of relentless and violent reaction by bigots to the struggle for basic human and civil rights. These detestable images, broadcast nightly into homes all across the country, resulted in collective anger, guilt, and embarrassment in the nation, which in turn, put additional pressure on politicians to bring an end to legalized segregation. In my view, three notable events, in particular, represent critical points in the civil rights movement, and television was key in bringing each of them to the attention of the public and politicians: 1. Rosa Parks's refusal to move to the back of the bus in Montgomery, Alabama in December 1955 and the resulting success of Montgomery Bus Boycott introduced Dr. King to the civil rights movement as one of its more dynamic leaders. 2. The rousing and emotional appeal of Dr. King for freedom and equality in his famous *I Have A Dream* speech at the March on Washington, August 1963. 3. The televised assault of black demonstrators by white police officers at the Edmund Pettus Bridge during the first attempt to stage the Selma-to-Montgomery March in 1965 triggered such an outcry from the nation that Congress and President Johnson were forced to enact and sign the Voting Rights Act of 1965.

The popularity and novelty of television shows were still around in my neighborhood in the summer of 1964. Shows such as *Bonanza*, *The Fugitive*, and *Combat* were among my favorites. No matter how much fun I was having with my friends, especially at 6:30 on Sunday evenings, I would put all that fun and play aside, plop myself down in front of our old black and white television to enjoy my favorite show – *The Wonderful World of Disney*. Cable or satellite television was not available, of course, so only the strength of a finicky rabbit ear or roof-mounted antenna could determine the number and type of television shows we could actually watch.

Nevertheless, the mass media served a useful purpose and permitted me to believe that despite what was going on in the civil rights movement, movies and television shows were being produced and watched, records were being recorded and sold, and my favorite sports teams were either causing me great joy or great sadness. Despite its many shortcomings, the media, in its varied forms, including the movies, reminded me of the more enjoyable parts of life as a child.

Because of the strangle hold that Jim Crow had on all forms of entertainment, going to the movies was an inimitable experience for black people in Hattiesburg. There were five movie theatres in town – Star Theatre on Mobile Street, which was owned by whites but catered to an all-black clientele. The Saenger Theatre located in downtown

Hattiesburg was owned by whites and catered to blacks and whites; however, blacks were required to enter the theatre through a side door that could only be accessed from a narrow, congested alley; and of course, we had to sit in the balcony. The Lomo Theatre, also located downtown, was for blacks and whites, but like the Saenger Theatre, blacks were required to sit in the balcony. And the Rebel Theatre also downtown, which as the name would suggest, catered to whites only as did the Rose Theatre also located downtown. There were two drive-in theatres – the Beverly Drive-In and the Broadway Drive-In, that were completely off limits to blacks. Personally, I preferred the Star Theatre because it specialized in my favorite form of escapism by primarily showing "B" movies, of the Western and Horror genres. I have only one unpleasant memory of the Star Theatre. While standing in line to purchase popcorn at the concession stand, a friend of mine named Larry (actually he was more like an acquaintance than a friend) hauled off and punched me in the stomach after I told him I did not have enough money to buy popcorn for him. It was a pretty solid punch causing me to bend over and momentarily gasp for air. As I righted myself, I saw loony Larry bolt through the front door and head up Mobile Street. Larry and I never talked to each other after that incident I have no clue what ever happened to him.

Nevertheless, I remember sitting on the edge of my rickety theatre seat, gobbling handfuls of popcorn, and being mesmerized by such movies as *Hercules Unchained, King Kong Versus Godzilla*, and numerous "shoot-em-ups" featuring my favorite cowboys – Roy Rogers, Gabby Hays, Hopalong Cassidy, and Gene Autry. I was so infatuated with cowboy movies that one of my most memorable gifts from Santa Claus was a Roy Rogers double holster with two six-shooters.

Sports were also a means of escaping and forgetting the frightening times in which I lived and reminded me that some things in the country were operating with a degree of normalcy. My father and grandfather (Daddy) were avid sports fans and their enthusiasm rubbed off on me at an early age. They were particularly interested in baseball and boxing, two sports in which blacks were beginning to play prominent roles. Daddy even coached a black semiprofessional baseball team in the late 1930s that was owned and operated by his employer, Hercules Powder Company. Because major league baseball's first black player, Jackie Robinson, played for the Brooklyn Dodgers, my family tended to be Dodgers fans, even though they were no longer in Brooklyn. So, naturally, there was slight disappointment in my family that the pennant races in 1964 involved the Philadelphia Phillies and the St. Louis Cardinals in the National League and the New York Yankees and the Baltimore Orioles in the American League, although we rooted for Lou Brock, Curt Flood, Bob Gibson and the rest of the Cardinals in the World Series.

The year 1964 also saw a range of reactions to the emergence of Cassius Clay (Muhammad Ali) as a dominant figure in the boxing world. The younger generation tended to admire Clay and his cockiness – *Float like a butterfly, sting like a bee; I am the greatest and the prettiest!* – while many in the older generation like my grandfather who remembered the humbleness and humility of Joe Louis, did not like Clay very much. Nevertheless, many of us were proud that he had become such a popular fighter, especially after winning the heavyweight crown from Sonny Liston in February 1964. Some of us became even prouder of him when he refused induction into the military three years later.

Besides my father's and grandfather's influence on my becoming an avid sports fan, one other individual had an equal or greater influence. Bobby Ray "Fat" James further cultivated my decades-long love for football, basketball, and baseball. Although he was never an outstanding player in any of those sports, he was a walking encyclopedia regarding sports trivia, sports records, and sports personalities. He could speak for hours about a range of sports topics from his beloved Southwestern Athletic Conference (SWAC) to the pandemonium whiz kids lineup of the 1950s Philadelphia Phillies. He could spin such a spell-binding yarn about the famous "catch" Willie Mays made in 1954; championship games between Bill Russell and Wilt Chamberlain; electrifying touchdown runs by Gale Sayers; and a spectacular game-winning interception or punt return by Lem Barney that I thought I was actually witnessing the action he was describing. He could name the starting lineup for every World Series team for the previous ten years and cite the statistics of each player. He could do the same for the National Basketball Association (NBA), the National Football League (NFL), and the American Football League (AFL) and Super Bowl championship games, going back decades. To enhance the excitement of hearing about famous sports stories and sports personalities, Bobby Ray would often pretend to be a play-by-play announcer, with up-to-date statistics and background stories on the players. In the days before the merger of the National Football League and the nascent American Football League, Bobby Ray and I were the few sports fans in the neighborhood who rooted for the new league. Because of Bobby Ray, I developed a life-long interest in professional football, beginning with my favorite AFL teams and players, such as Cooke Gilchrist of the Buffalo Bills, Charlie Toler of the Houston Oilers, and Speedy Duncan of the San Diego Chargers. Bobby Ray was a very gentle and well-liked individual, who never got the chance to live his dream of being a professional play-by-play sports announcer. Nevertheless, he was my hero, not only because of his passion for sports, but also for his compassion and passion for people. He spent much of his time visiting the sick and home-bound, offering them conversation and company, which no doubt was a great comfort to them. He was a humble man, although he has forgotten more than most will ever know about the history of sports in the United States. He was a generous man, often buying toys and food for children and adults who could not afford them. He was a simple man, not needing or wanting much in the way of fancy clothes, the latest gizmo or gadget, and other material things. Nothing gave him more pleasure than simply talking sports and giving to and visiting with someone in need. And if the person with whom he was visiting wanted to talk sports, that was more of a special moment for him. If I were to list the names of everyone who has had a profound and lasting influence on my life, the name of Bobby Ray "Fat" James would be near the top of that list.

On the local sports scene, my attention was focused mostly on wrestling or rasslin'. I watched Mid-South Wrestling faithfully on the local television station every weekend and went to live matches at the Greater Hattiesburg Baseball Park and the Wade Kennedy Livestock Arena. At the baseball park, black wrestling fans sat in the left field side of the stadium, clustered together in an area half the size of the section for white fans. In those days, there were no interracial wrestling matches at either arena. I attended my first-ever wrestling match at the Greater Hattiesburg Baseball Park with my grandmother, Mama Mag. Whether the action was staged or real, it was great entertainment for black and white fans alike. Mama Mag was absolutely convinced that the action inside and outside the ring was real, and she would become fighting mad if she heard anybody say otherwise. Of course, she is also the same woman who once called up the local television station to complain to the station manager that the police had arrested the wrong person for murder on her favorite soap opera. Mama Mag is what her grandchildren called her, except for my cousin Barb, who always called her Big Mama. Her given name was Maggie, and depending on who her husband was, her last name was either Harris or Henry. I always knew her as Maggie Henry, married to Burke Henry, who I barely remember. She and Daddy Herman divorced when my dad was a teenager.

Daddy Herman was also a very interesting man. He had several missing fingers from both hands, which usually were gripping a glass of Old Charter. Despite his fondness of a little nip, as he called it, he had some pretty likeable traits, as I recall. One of those was generosity, albeit seemingly begrudgingly so. Whenever he visited us at our home, he always gave my brothers and me a nickel, which we typically used to go to Preacher's Store to buy a sack full of two-for-a-penny cookies. Having that many tasty coconut cookies, all to myself, was pure nirvana. In my own little prepubescent, cookie-loving world, I came to associate Daddy Herman with the indescribable joy of gorging myself with the delectable taste of coconut cookies. His gifts never went above a nickel, which really riled my dad. He thought Daddy Herman was being a tight wad by giving us only a nickel, but in my little cookie-loving world, a nickel was like manna from heaven. On the dark side, Daddy Herman enjoyed watching my baby brother Harold smoke cigars. Not edible, candy cigars – real Tampa Nugget stogies. The drill was always the same. He would call Harold to his side and place the compliant five year-old on one of his knees. He would next pull a fresh cigar from his shirt pocket, remove the label and sleeve, bite off the tip, moisten the entire cigar, and place in his own mouth. He would flip out his well-used Zippo cigarette lighter and set fire to the end of the cigar. He would take a few drags to make sure the cigar was completely fired up before offering it to Harold, who willingly accepted it and placed it between his tiny lips. Harold would take a drag form he cigar, and as if he were imitating Daddy Herman, he would blow several well-formed smoke rings into the air. A gut-busting laugh from everyone present, children and adults, quickly followed. He and his audience repeated the sequence until the cigar was completely consumed. Harold finally stopped smoking cigars and entertaining Daddy Herman and others when he became very ill after finishing off one of the stogies.

Mama Mag could easily be mistaken for a white woman. She was very light-skinned, and in her youth, she was a very attractive slender woman with long black hair that fell below her shoulder (based on an old photo in my home). Her grandfather was a white man named Morgan Lindsey, who was an overseer on a plantation in Alabama, where her family lived. After learning that Mr. Lindsey had impregnated her grandmother, her family was forced off the plantation and fled to Mississippi with only the clothes on their backs. Regardless of her skin tone or last name, Mama Mag was an enigma. I have no doubt that she loved her sons, Sonny Boy, Junior, Woofie, Leon, and her daughter Helen, who died before I was born. She also loved her grandchildren, but she could absolutely drive all of us up the wall. One of her ways of driving me up the wall, as a kid, was whenever I was in grabbing distance of her, she would put me in a mama-bear hug, pull me close to her in a very tight embrace, and punctuate the moment with a peck on my cheek. I dreaded that. The peck on the cheek was awful, made even more awful as her porcupine-like chin hairs scraped the side of my face as she landed one of her infamous juicy globs of spittle that constituted a peck on the side of my face. I did not know which discomfort to address first – dry off my face or check to see whether I was bleeding. She was also a serial hypochondriac. Her chief ailment always concerned her heart. At least once a week she would complain that she was having a heart attack. My dad and I went to check on her one evening after one of her complaints about her heart, which I believed was her way of asking for attention. Obviously, neither of us was a doctor, but it did not require a medical degree to diagnose her "heart" problem. After observing a pot of collard greens on top of the stove with no lid, my dad asked how long the greens had been out, and if she had been eating them. She said they had been out a couple of days and yes, she had been eating them. "Well, Mama, if you eat food that's cold and been on the stove uncovered for two days, you are supposed to be sick." He bought her some Alka-Seltzer, and her "heart" problem went away. Despite her quirkiness, she tried to be a good grandmother. She would slip a quarter or two into my pant pocket while dispensing one of her slobbering kisses, which only partially compensated for the dread of having to wipe my cheek and check for cuts (Out of respect for her as my grandmother, I wiped off my cheek only after she turned her head, of course. As much as I disliked having to wipe my face, I knew she meant well.). She appreciated my visits. She always had something nice to say about how I was dressed, how I wore my hair, or how I smelled. During one of my visits with her when I was a college student, my hair became the topic of discussion or derision for one of her friends, who was also visiting her. Her friend observed my huge Afro; and she lit into me with a double dose of vim and venom. After observing the size of my Afro, she proffered her matter-of-fact views of my hair and my salvation. With the conviction of someone who daily reminded herself of her piousness, self-righteousness, and the correctness of her biblical interpretations, she informed me that I was going straight to hell. Stunned, I asked why was I going to hell and how could she be so certain. She told me it was because I was allowing my hair to grow too long. If I ever hope to go to heaven, I would have to cut my hair. She told me in a very authoritative manner that it was a sin for women to cut their hair and for men to let theirs grow too long. I asked her how she knew, and she said it is in Leviticus, and as far as she was concerned that was good enough for her. I had never heard that before. I knew Moses warned Aaron and his sons not to allow their hair to become unkempt. But my hair was anything but unkempt. I would spend at least ten minutes every day shaping my Afro – raking it out, putting a silk scarf over it, and smoothing out any unevenness. No way was my `fro unkempt. I had known some pretty judgmental bible-thumpers in my day, but I had never had one of them to tell me that I was going to hell because of my Afro. I thanked her for her concern for my salvation and exited the premises before she could find more reasons for my guaranteed appointment with Lucifer.

But despite Mama Mag's many acts of kindness toward me, it was hard for me to feel that same kind of maternal love for her that I felt for Mama, my mom's mother. I am sure that is because I spent more time with Mama, especially during the early parts of my childhood.

When I attended wrestling matches without Mama Mag, it was at the Wade Kennedy Livestock arena, where there were bleachers on both sides – one for whites and one for blacks. My favorite wrestlers were Oni Wiki Wiki, Mario Galendo, Cowboy Bob Kelley, Lee Fields, and Bobby Fields. Whenever I saw any of these wrestling icons at Wade Kennedy, sometimes with my dad, I was in hog heaven. Unlike Mama Mag, my dad insisted that wrestling was fake, but I always sided with Mama Mag because I wanted to believe that it was real. Whenever my dad saw me becoming overly engrossed in a wrestling match, he would try to bring me back to reality by reminding me that if someone were actually hit in the face with a closed fist, he would be swollen and bruised. Actually, he was right, but that did not matter to me. After all, my dad had also tried to convince me that I would have severe mental health issues if I continued playing Solitaire. He believed that playing such a frustrating game would surely lead to insanity.

At any rate, I remember going to the restroom during a wrestling match one night at the livestock arena and witnessed something that just completely convinced me even more that wrestling was *not* fake. Cowboy Bob Kelley had just finished his match and had gone to his dressing room, which was located next to the restroom. His dressing room door was open, and I could see him and hear every word he said. He had real blooding flowing profusely down one side of his face from a kick in the face by his opponent. And he was cussing up a storm about how he was cheated out of the match. I did not think he was faking it all, no matter what my dad said. However, the wisdom that comes with time and maturity has since allowed me to see the error in my thinking about the authenticity of professional rasslin'! In a way, that was a big disappointment for me, on par with learning the truth about Santa Claus.

I also enjoyed going to venerable Black Sox Park on Sunday afternoon to watch the Hattiesburg Black Sox, an all-black semiprofessional baseball team that played its home games in the black community of Palmers Crossing. This team reminded me so much of the barnstorming teams featured in the movie, *Bingo Long and the Traveling All-Stars*. They epitomized the mantra, "Brothers who played but never got paid." My brothers, my dad and I usually went to a game when the Black Sox played one of their chief rivals -- the Laurel Black Cats, Mobile Buckeyes, New Orleans Travelers, Jackson Cubs, Homestead Grays, Meridian Braves, or the Birmingham Black Barons. In the heyday of the Negro Baseball Leagues in the 1940s and 19950s, the Black Sox hosted teams that featured such future major league players as Hank Aaron, Tommy Aaron, and Tommy Agee.

All seating at Black Sox Park was behind the screen. There were no outfield seats. What I remember most about the seats at Black Sox Park was that they were all bleacher-type seats constructed of wide wooden planks, some of which splintered from being weather worn. If I were not careful when sitting, I could easily get a splinter stuck in my behind, which happened more than a few times. Despite being occasionally attacked by a menacing splinter, I was very impressed with the playing field itself, which was always in exceptional condition. The team, owned and coached by Milton Barnes, was outstanding; and rare was the season when they did not win most of their games. In fact, during the 1966 season, the Black Sox earned a perfect season, going 33-0. The list of players who plied their skills over the years with the Hattiesburg Black Sox is a Who's Who of local baseball talent. That list includes: Willie Sanders, Dean McCullum, Willie McCullum, Willie Conner, Howard Doss, Troup Chatman, Perry Doss, Shelby Tatum, Willie "Pig" Stokes, Alvin Eatman, Darrell Doss, John Jackson, John Lee James, Johnny Owens, William Revies, Dave Gray, Tobie Martin, A.W. Watson, Tommie Dukes, Bobby Ray Thompson, Scott Jones, Excell Moore, Felder "Bo" Tatum, Dave

Gray, Melvin Marshall, Cecil Marshall, Charles Marshall, and Cliff Marshall. Three of the players – Perry Doss, Willie Sanders, and Tommie Dukes played in the Minor Leagues with the Kansas City organization.

Mr. Barnes was known not only for his ownership of a successful semi-professional baseball team, but he was also noted for his ownership of a successful dry cleaning business, and a home building/contracting company. However, my memory of Mr. Barnes is much more personal. It seems that one day as a small child, maybe six or seven years old, I was outside my house having so much fun and absorbed so deeply in my playing that I became completely oblivious to the fact that my bladder needed emptying. After I finally decided that I had better heed nature's increasingly urgent call, I should have gone inside the house to use the restroom like a normal human being. Instead, because of sheer laziness or just not wanting to interrupt my fun for too long, I decided to go around to the side of the house to relieve myself. I finally finished and could only think about hurrying up so that I could get back to having fun again. But in the haste to zip up my pants – yikes - my penis got stuck in the zipper. Ouch! is all I could yell and pain is all I could feel. I was off like a light and scurried around the house to the front porch where my mother was sitting. She immediately espied my embarrassing quandary and could hear from my yelling that I needed quick relief. She took at closer look at my agonizing dilemma and quickly determined that she had no idea how to extricate me from this untidy and delicate situation. I think she was torn between laughter and tears; and bless her heart, she tried, but there was very little she could do except to try to reassure me that things would be okay. But my increased yelling and escalating pain challenged and contradicted that belief to the point of making it utterly groundless. So, as we were sitting there on the front porch with no clue as to how to get me out of the zipper, Mr. Barnes drove past by the house, and in utter desperation my mother flagged him down. He got out of his car, walked over to me, and immediately figured out I was in a real mess here. But I guess there was something about a man being on the scene that just seemed to calm me down a bit; so Mr. Barnes gently maneuvered the zipper in just the right manner and in no time I was free at last! For being in the right place at the right place, Mr. Barnes will always occupy a special place in my memory bank and I will always remain in his debt.

Also, during the 1960s, Berry Gordy's monstrous creation known as Hitsville, U.S.A., or Motown Records, began to emerge on the recorded music scene. This was the beginning of what today is called old-school music. Motown's vast array of talented artists created a unique style of rhythm and blues that captured the attention of music lovers everywhere and became a source of pride for black people. In sharp contrast to many of the "singers" of today, artists from the old-school had to have excellent singing voices in order to have a hit record. Sadly, many of those old-school artists, despite having excellent singing voices did not come close to making the type of money that today's far less-talented artists earn.

At any rate, a talented group of Motown stars, in the summer of 1964, released a smash hit that literally had everyone dancing in the streets. Martha and The Vandellas' *Dancing in the Streets* quickly moved to the top of the charts. I knew nothing about charts; I just knew that it was a great song. Also, other Motown emerging stars had hit songs in 1964: The Supremes' *Baby Love*, The Four Tops' *Baby, I Need Your Loving*, and The Temptations' *The Way You Do the Things You Do*. Although on a different recording label, The Impressions also had a smash hit during the summer of 1964, *Keep On Pushing*, as did the Drifters, *Under the Boardwalk*. I had collected 45 and 8-track recordings of some of those songs but had to rely on radio to hear most of them. Few, if any, local radio stations played R&B music, however one station, WXXX, devoted an hour a day to playing only R & B music. So, I relied on two white Disc Jockeys, John "R" (Richburg) and Hoss Allen, both of whom I thought were black, on WLAC Radio (1510 AM) in Nashville, Tennessee, for a nightly fix of soul and R&B music. Although Nashville is over 400 miles from Hattiesburg, the clarity of the broadcast signal from WLAC was great, especially on rainy nights. I did not even mind the obligatory sales pitch to buy the records of the artists that were playing. All I cared about was that I was enjoying some really good music, which replaced, at least for the moment, the unpleasant reminders of living in segregated Hattiesburg.

During the summer, music was a staple at the Country Club (later named Pineview Park and changed again to Dahmer Park), which was actually the former white-only country club that was passed on to the black community by the City of Hattiesburg after whites abandoned it due to the "frightening" trend of neighborhoods surrounding the country club became increasingly black. The Country Club was a spacious outdoor recreation park consisting of a swimming pool, several little league baseball fields, and a food grill that blasted Motown hits all over the park. Music coming from the grill's PA system was like a magnet that attracted the young and old alike to the concrete dance floor for nonstop dancing. One fellow in particular, during the summer of 1965, attracted a lot of attention when a certain song played. Whenever Frank Brown heard the Four Tops' *I Can't Help Myself*, no matter what he was doing -- playing ball or swimming -- he would immediately stop, race to the dance floor and dance wildly by himself until the song ended. He did not care about any other song but that one. And Frank was not the only person to race to the dance floor when that song was played. The rest of us would race there to watch Frank dance. In fact, once Frank got really wound up, everyone would just stop dancing to watch Frank who was not bashful at all about dancing in front of a big crowd. I thought he was cool, and I think he liked the attention he was getting. When the song ended, Frank and the rest of us in the crowd would then go back to what we had been doing, until the song was played again and then the scene would be repeated. Frank later had a serious and debilitating emotional breakdown and ended up spending most of his life in a mental institution.

Despite the unpleasantness of living under the harsh rules of racial segregation, as a youngster in Hattiesburg I had quite a normal, at least by standards that existed then. Measured against today's standards, however, none of us should have even made it out of our adolescent years. We did things at that time which seemed safe and normal, but would be considered dysfunctional and even life threatening today. For example, when I was a child it was common practice to play outside, unsupervised by adults, at all hours of the night without fear of being abducted or molested. Such fear was non-existent because the village was strong. Neighbors knew each other, talked to each other, and most importantly depended on each other. Whether children needed protection or punishment, parents and children could count on others in the neighborhood to do what was necessary to make sure that children were safe or if need be, make sure that we got a "whuppin" if we messed up. Mrs. Trotter, who lived up the hill from my house, was notorious for intervening when boys made the mistake of fighting near her home. Whenever a fight started in or near her presence, she would grab her "licking stick" and start swinging at the combatants, sometimes making contact, not so much to hurt anyone, but to make them believe that they should fear her more than each other. After arriving home, the boys would be greeted by their belt-toting parents who would make an additional installment on their punishment. In contrast to the prevailing climate of today, parents never threatened Mrs. Trotter with a lawsuit or even threatened to harm her for what she had done. Instead, they thanked her and expressed their gratitude to her because everyone understood that she was only doing her job as a loving and caring member of the village who simply accepted her responsibility to help rear the children.

The village was also strong because of the consistent and enduring love, commitment, and care given to us by our black teachers. Although, relegated by the school district's central administration to second-class status vis-`a-vis their white counterparts, these proud, competent, and committed men and women refused to allow such disparagement to stop them from giving us their very best. In turn, they expected nothing less than the very best from us. As a grade school student, I thought that most of my teachers were the meanest people in the world. That thought especially occurred on those unwelcome and dreaded occasions when they would whip my behind if I did not perform up to my pedagogic abilities. One such unforgettable occasion occurred when I was in Mrs. Imogene McGowan's second grade class. I was a fairly bright child, who was assigned to her *Double A* class, which meant that I was in the "smart" class – good old ability grouping! The groupings were designated AA, A, and B, in descending order of perceived ability. Each of the 30 plus children in her class was issued a workbook, from which Mrs. McGowan routinely gave assignments that we were to complete at home and bring back the following day. One of those assignments will forever remain imprinted in my mind for the rest of my life. Before I could begin working on the assignment at home, I somehow managed to spill a glass of red Kool-Aid on my workbook, which caused several of the pages to stick together. Unfortunately for me, those stuck pages were the ones I was supposed to work on; so I did not do the assignment. The next day, after checking roll, collecting lunch money, and listening to the morning announcements on the PA system, she predictably ordered everyone to open his or her workbooks to the assigned page. In the midst of workbooks being plopped down on desks and pages being frantically turned, the bespectacled, deep ebony-hued Mrs. McGowan slowly opened her middle desk drawer, which sent shivers up my spine. I knew that she was not opening the drawer to take out a pencil or a piece of chalk. No, she was slowly removing from the desk drawer her preferred means of getting her students' attention, especially those who had not done their homework or who had not done it correctly. As she walked up and down each row and paused at each child's desk, she would ask to see the completed *and* correct homework assignment. Depending on what the student produced, she would either nod and verbally express approval or would rear back with her very effective attention-getter—a two-foot long black fan belt – and whack the student across the back, accompanied by a stern warning, "Don't let me have to tell you again!" I had observed this scene many times; and up until then I was always a recipient of an approving nod from Mrs. McGowan. But on this particular morning, however, I was full of dread because I knew that I had not done my homework. Moreover, I knew that the Kool-Aid laden pages in my workbook would not engender any sympathy from her or suspend or postpone the inevitable. So, as she left Lewis' desk and gave him a couple of whacks, I began to brace myself. I was eerily aware that I had never before paid attention to how loud Mrs. McGowan's footsteps were, all the time hoping that she would just pass right on by my desk, or at worst, trip over her own clunky feet and decide to not check anymore workbooks. Even so, I felt the tears well up inside me and slowly flow from my eyes. And as the beaded-up tears trickled down my face, across my top lip, I began to taste their distinct saltiness as they entered my mouth. "Harris, where's your homework, son?" She did not expect an answer, and I did not attempt to provide one. I knew that no answer or excuse would stop what was about to happen. Besides, I was so frightened I don't think I could have said anything anyway. I just continued to feel the wetness on my face and the salty taste in my mouth from the gushing tears flowing from my eyes. I closed my eyes as tightly as I could, gripped the top edge of my desk, and took a deep breath. The next sound was that of Mrs. McGowan's thick black fan belt landing with the force of ten men on my back, which caused me, instinctively, to thrust my upper torso forward, and to try to make my shoulder blades touch one another. I then let out a barely audible, "Ouch!" and continued to tighten my grip on the desk. As I opened my eyes I noticed that I was producing even more tears. I had silently counted each lick that found its mark on my seven-year-old back – one…two…three, and was aware of the piercing pain and the pulsating throbs that seem to cover my body from head to toe. There was no feeling of embarrassment, just unbelievable pain. No one turned in their seats to laugh and make fun of me because everyone knew Mrs. McGowan would have given the laugher the same or worse treatment. Because of my aversion to pain, however, from that day on I never again forgot to do my homework and above all else, I made certain that the Kool-Aid remained a safe distance from my workbook. When my mother saw the condition of my back, she was concerned. But she also concluded that I must have done something to justify those raised red welts on my back. She never threatened to sue the school district or attempt retribution directly on Mrs. McGowan. As I looked back on that incident decades later, I realized that Mrs. McGowan's intent was not to sadistically inflict harm on me, but instead to instill in me, by force if necessary, the notion that I must excel academically. Failure and mediocrity were simply not options. She and other teachers of that era believed in and constantly reinforced the idea that not only *could* all their students excel, but also that they *would* excel. The Mrs. Jacksons,

McGowans, Lewises, Fowlers, Harris, Clarks, Chambers, Sandifers, Hopsons, Perrys, and Lees and the Mr. Lucases, Boykins, Picketts, Clarks, Johnsons, McGees, Suttons, and Stegalls had been out in the world, and they knew that if their young charges were to be successful in life, they would have to be serious-minded, high-achieving students. Moreover, because they had been out in the world, they all knew first-hand the challenges that black people faced in the south. Education, a good solid education, was the only way to level the playing field, they believed. Further, they attempted to impress upon all of their students, without necessarily being explicit, the notion that that we could not settle for being just as capable as our white counterparts. I got it. And I appreciated the attempts they made in trying to bring that view to my consciousness.

At some point in my young adulthood, I visited Mrs. McGowan at her home to give her a gift. Not a physical gift, but a gift of my deep appreciation of her successful efforts to instill in me a belief in my ability to achieve. I reminded her of the incident with the workbook and the thoughts and feelings I had at the time when the backside of my torso became very familiar with her quite effective attention-getter. We chuckled briefly as she told me that she really did not mean to hurt me. I told her that I understood. If fact, I told her, as an adult I am so thankful for that whipping. I told her that years later, with an adult's perspective, I understood the message behind the whipping. Indeed, it was not to wantonly inflict pain on me. Instead, the message was, *Harris, no excuses, no matter how convenient. I will not allow you to take the path of least resistance and give in to your laziness. You **will not** accept mediocrity. You **will** excel, even if I have to beat it into you.* And I told Mrs. McGowan, who had long retired from teaching, that teachers today cannot mete out punishment as she and others did when the village was strong. We both agreed that times have changed and what teachers did back then worked for that time, with those students, and with those families. We both lamented that so many of our youngsters today will never know the love, guidance, and devotion that she and others of her era attempted to share with us. She smiled and her eyes gleamed as she said, Harris, thank you for dropping by and telling me that story. With a gentle squeeze of my hand as I rose to leave, she said, *as the saying goes, it is better to get your flowers while you can enjoy them, not when you are lying in a casket.*

While I did not have the good fortune of being one of her students, Mrs. Marjorie Chambers probably had the single greatest impact on students at Royal Street and Rowan High Schools, especially seniors. An example of her impact on students was her requirement that all of her senior students memorize the lyrics to the *Star-Spangled Banner.* She was prompted to impose such an unusual requirement after watching Aretha Franklin forget some of the words to the National Anthem during the 1968 Democratic National Convention. She told my brother and other seniors that she was going to make sure than none of her students would ever embarrass themselves by forgetting the National Anthem. She saw Aretha Franklin's memory lapse as an egregious offense that should never be repeated, ever, especially by any of her current or future social studies students. So, every student who wanted to graduate in 1969 had to recite or sing the lyrics to the *Star-Spangled Banner.* Anyone refusing to sing or recite the National Anthem could forget about graduating. In those days, graduating seniors were required to secure the signature of each senior class teacher in order to graduate. Mrs. Chambers announced to her students that she would not sign the graduation sheet for anyone who refused to sing or recite the National Anthem or was unable to do it correctly. Even a stuttering student was not given an exemption to her graduation requirement. Reportedly, he was told that he could sing it like he was Mel Tillis, if he had difficulty in speaking the words. Such a graduation requirement today might be considered unfair or even illegal. But during the era when black teachers were held in high esteem and took seriously their sense of responsibility and accountability sans high-stakes testing or character-building curricula, such a requirement was rather routine and non-negotiable. Those black teachers and administrators doggedly subscribed to the view espoused by Dr. Martin Luther King's mentor, Dr. Benjamin Mays, who said that the boy who starts out behind in a race has to run faster to catch up and even faster to win. Those brave men and women deserve special acknowledgement for their patience, love, and commitment in helping me realize that I could run faster than I ever thought I could.

Time for a little fun

The unpleasantness of having to live under the oppression of racial segregation was also blunted by playing games with friends in the neighborhood. One of my favorite games was hide-and-seek – *Last night, night before, 24 robbers at my door. I got up and let one in. Hit him in the head with a rolling pin. 5-10, 15--20, 25-30, 35-40, 45-50, 55-60, 65-70, 75-80, 85-90, 95-100. All around my base ain't got no hundred. Ready or not, here I come.* That was our version of the start of the game whose object, of course, was to hide in the most obscure place possible and to remain hidden until it was safe to stealthily return to base. If the counter caught someone before returning to base, that person was "out." The last one to be caught would become the counter in the next round. Being the counter was not nearly as much fun as hiding. When my friends, brothers and I played this game, we did not restrict our hiding to safe and logical places such as a nearby ditch or a row of hedges at a neighbor's house. It seemed that hiding that close to base was much too easy and not any fun at all. So, we routinely expanded the hiding area to include several miles that easily extended to the entire Arledge Quarters, and the nearby projects, although there were risks in going anywhere near the projects. Jimmy Watts and his Project Boys were known to beat up boys who came around the project and did not live there. Nevertheless, we would hide and seek for hours on end until well into the night. On school nights, of course, we had to be home before the street lights came on. Our only concern was trying to avoid being caught by the counter or being caught too close to the Projects – not being kidnapped or sexually molested by some child predator.

When we grew bored with hide-and-seek, we would have foot races. These foot races did not take place on a track or on some other smooth running surface as they might today. Instead, by necessity and circumstance, our foot races took place on the only running surface we had available -- an unpaved, gravel street next to my home. Side streets in my neighborhood were not paved until years later, which was the norm for most black neighborhoods at that time. The races always took place at night in order to reduce interference from passing cars; but it also increased the likelihood of running into something, like a clothesline. That actually happened to me while playing at night in my back yard when I narrowly escaped being blinded in the right eye when an unseen, sharp, rusty, piece of the wire clothesline cut a deep gash just below my right eye. Typically, most foot races were impromptu events and took place when everybody present boastfully claimed to be the speediest in the group. Some had a basis for making such a claim, but others, like me, did so just to irritate the faster guys. And of course, the only way to settle such an important argument was to actually have a race. Typically the race, a full sprint, not a jog, would start at the corner next to my house and the finish line would be a couple of blocks away or at whatever spot the losers would just stop running from exhaustion. After catching our breath, we would run again and again, each time hoping to dethrone my next door neighbor, Charles Ray (his first and middle name) who usually won each race, which was really amazing considering he always ran with no shoes.

If we did not have school the next day, we would begin the morning with a game of baseball or football, depending on the season. In either case, the games were always played in the same gravel street next to my house that served as the track field the night before.

My house was a modest, plain wood frame, 3-bedroom house that served as the local gathering place for all the neighborhood boys. In fact, there was so much gathering at my house that grass never grew in the front yard because of all the standing, stomping, and slam-dunking of a worn-out bicycle tire rim nailed to the pecan tree that served as our basketball goal and stand. The neighborhood was working class, and most of the other houses were also wood frame, some with paint, but most just had a natural wood finish that had turned unnaturally ashy gray from exposure to the elements. And we had to be careful when playing around those houses because of splinters from the unfinished and jagged edges on the wooden boards. I certainly received my share of splinters, which had to be carefully removed by a steady hand with a needle or straight pin that had been heated over an open flame. Some houses even had inexpensive faux-brick siding. Such houses were considered fancy, almost pretentious, and the faux siding actually was a pretty inexpensive way to make them stand out from the others. Tin roofs were pretty much the norm when it came to housetops, which caused rather loud, rhythmic, and hypnotic poundings on the top of most houses during heavy rainstorms.

Whenever it rained or was about to rain, however I would rather be anywhere in Hattiesburg than at Mama's (my maternal grandmother) house. Ordinarily, I loved being at her house, especially on those mornings when she made grits for Daddy and me. Those were special times when Daddy, Mama and I sat around the breakfast table enjoying the best tasting grits anyone could make. And Mama's grits seemed especially delicious when, following Daddy's lead, I would put a couple of teaspoons of apple butter, a scrambled egg, and a couple of crispy strips of crumbled-up fried bacon in the grits, stir them all up, and feast on the mouth-watering concoction with a couple of slices of hot buttered toast and a cold glass of milk. But when it rained, apple butter, bacon, grits, eggs, and toast were not enough to make me want to be at Mama's house. She had this incredible fear of bad weather; and whenever it rained this gentle sweet woman amazingly turned into a dreaded prison warden. When rain clouds were gathering or God forbid, there were lightning and thunder, everyone in the house was ordered to sit perfectly still; and the fan, television, radio, and anything running off electricity had to be turned off. No one was allowed to talk, walk, sneeze, cough, use the bathroom or make any sounds at all. I could only sit there in complete darkness, motionless, hot, scared to go to the bathroom, and scared to breathe too loudly. She believed that the slightest movements and sounds inside the house would automatically become magnets for lightening and surely cause someone inside to be struck. Since no one inside the house was ever struck by lightning, I guess she figured she must have been right in insisting on complete silence and no moving about. She would even go through the entire house and cover every mirror with a bed sheet because she also believed that mirrors attracted lightening. Since none of her covered mirrors ever attracted lightening, she had to believe that she was doing the right thing. I loved that woman, but she sure could do some strange things when the weather got bad. After the bad weather passed, it was again safe to go back to playing, watching television, or better yet go down to Mr. McCullough's house, call my mom on the telephone, and ask her to come pick me up before it started raining again.

There were several interesting "establishments" in my neighborhood that operated on the fringes of the law but were extremely popular among adults. I recognized, by sight, most of the adults who patronized one of the establishments; and some I knew only from frequently observing their fancy cars driving slowly down my street, casing the establishment for signs of danger or for faces that might disrupt their attempts at being incognito. One of those establishments was located at Mr. Wiley's house, which was separated from our house by a narrow ditch and a narrow gravel street. At all hours of the night and day, including Sunday, people parked on the road next to and in front of Mr. Wiley's house to "visit" him. At least that is what my dad told me when I first asked him why so many people came to Mr. Wiley's house all the time. However, I learned the truth one day when my oft-intoxicated Uncle Junior sent me to Mr. Wiley's house with a folded up slip of paper with something written on it that I was told in no uncertain terms not to read. I was both frightened and curious about this mysterious mission. The fear and the curiosity both came from not knowing what really went on inside Mr. Wiley's house. What could be going on in that house that so many people would want to "visit" Mr. Wiley's house so much? I was afraid because I could only imagine what I would see once I went inside – someone dead, someone scary, or something that I had never seen before in my young life. The curiosity came from the fact that I was really wondering what was going on inside Mr. Wiley's house so I could tell all my friends, who also had never been inside before. So, I slowly walked up the three concrete steps that led to Mr. Wiley's large, bright, red-painted concrete porch. I tapped lightly on Mr. Wiley's wooden screen door and peered inside hoping to see some thing or someone that might give me some hint as to what in the world was going on in that house. All the time I was vacillating between hoping and not hoping that someone would hear the faint sounds of my knocks on the door. I could hear the blaring sounds of B.B. King streaming through the front door blasting my eardrums, so I figured that everyone inside must be having a real good time; but because the music was so loud I had to call out Mr. Wiley's name while knocking on the door a little harder. I was somewhat relieved but still felt the butterflies flying around inside of me when Mr. Wiley finally appeared at the door. With his familiar half-smoked cigar stuck in the side of his mouth, Mr. Wiley greeted me with the normal greeting he used whenever he saw me on the street. "Hey Ant. How you been?" This time he added, "What can I do for you?" I handed him a slip of paper that my Uncle Junior had given me when he sent me on this mysterious mission. After reading the slip of paper, Mr. Wiley said with a slight grin, "Come on in, son." He then walked out onto the porch, looked up and down Fredna Avenue as he gently pushed my shoulder and motioned me to go on inside the house. He did not stay long on the porch because as soon as I crossed the threshold, he was standing right behind me. He told me to have a seat on the sofa, and he hurriedly walked into what I thought was the kitchen. While sitting there on the sofa, I could not take my eyes off the numerous black and white photographs on display underneath the heavily smudged piece of glass that fit perfectly atop the rectangular coffee table. I did not recognize anyone except Mr. Wiley, his wife and son. Before I could examine each photograph as closely as I wanted, Mr. Wiley quickly rounded the corner from the kitchen with a large brown paper bag that gave no immediate hint of its contents. He handed the bag to me and walked with me to the door. He opened the door, walked out onto the porch, looked left and then right, and then told me I could go. As I stepped off the porch, I realized that I was cradling something wet inside the bag. I then took a look inside the bag and saw a big wet bottle of cold beer. That was when I realized that Mr. Wiley operated one of several illegal bootleg houses in the neighborhood and that was why my Uncle Junior sent me on this mission. Hattiesburg and Forrest County were both dry, which meant that the sale and consumption of liquor were illegal. I later learned from my dad and Uncle Junior that Mr. Wiley specialized in selling three types of alcohol – beer, stoop or corn liquor, and name brand unsealed (untaxed) whiskey. Periodically the police would raid his house, primarily to shake him down for hush money and to give the appearance they were enforcing the ban on the sale of liquor. Routinely, after one of those sham arrests, Mr. Wiley was back home within a couple of hours, open again for business.

Mr. Wiley had regular customers who seemed to be right out of central casting. Most of them were always nice to us kids, sometimes flipping a quarter or fifty-cent piece to one of us as we played in the street next to Mr. Wiley's house. Some of them were downright entertaining. There was one man in particular who seemed to command the attention of most of us kids whenever he came by to "visit' Mr. Wiley. The only name I ever heard anyone call him was Eagle Eye. Eagle Eye talked all the time, profanely and loudly most of the time, and always to himself. He walked constantly, from one end of Fredna Avenue to the other, staggering from one side to the other. Whenever Eagle Eye was passing by while we were playing ball, we would stop playing because we knew he was good for a few good laughs. He allegedly did some really amazing things, according to my dad, like chewing and swallowing broken glass. As Eagle Eye passed, we could not resist the temptation to start searching the ground for pieces of broken glass. When he got near enough to hear us, but far enough away in case he started chasing us, we would yell to Eagle Eye to show us how he ate glass. To our disappointment, each time he would just ignore us, let out a few of his choice expletives and go straight to Mr. Wiley's house. My dad told me that Eagle Eye was "shell-shocked" from the Big War and that he did not have all of his senses. He had spent some time at the VA Hospital, but that did not seem to do much good.

There were many characters with odd-sounding nicknames who gathered at my house after school and on weekends to just hang out and talk about what was going on in the world; and of course, there were no better experts on worldly topics than we. Guys with nicknames such as "Bark-o-lot," "Fat," "Peanut," "Stank," "Devil," "Speedy," "Pistol-head," "Dog-head," "June-Bug," and "Freight-Train" would pontificate on the events of the day. Most topics, however, centered on sports – who was the greatest prize fighter – Joe Louis, Cassius Clay or Floyd Patterson; who was a better NBA center – Wilt Chamberlain or Bill Russell; or who was the best running back in football – Jim

Brown, Lenny Moore, or Gale Sayers. No decision was ever reached about who was best at anything, and none was expected. Instead, these pontification sessions were more like rituals or rites of passage for us younger boys. Older, more experienced-in-life guys argued their points; and they were either accepted or challenged. These sessions represented ways of learning – yes about sports, but importantly about how to hold your own in a heated debate or how to yield to the greater wisdom of someone older and wiser.

The more forceful orators (not necessarily wiser), especially ones who would get so carried away that they would start spraying us with their spit, seemed to command the most attention. Bobby Lee or "Stank" was notorious for spraying anyone who was within two feet of him. So, when he started talking, everyone would just step back a few yards to give him plenty of room. I don't know whether he thought we stepped back because of the true meaning behind his nickname or because we did not want to be showered with his omni-directional spittle.

When pontification sessions ended, it was then time to get down to some serious baseball or football. When playing sandlot football, I always preferred to play wide receiver and was pretty good at it, especially when my brother James was the quarterback. He had a rifle arm and was accurate with most of his throws. When it came to baseball, the sandlot version was more to my liking. I did not play organized ball because I was not good enough and because of my fear of being hit by a wild pitch, which seemed to happen a lot when I was batting and Charles Ray was pitching. In sandlot baseball, we typically played with a tennis ball or a rubber ball that was about the size of a tennis ball. Broken brooms or mop sticks, or a right-size tree limb were transformed into Louisville Sluggers. We simply made do with what we had without the benefit of regulation gloves, balls and bats. What we lacked in equipment, we more than made up in pure unadulterated fun, often pretending to be Willie Mays or Hank Aaron, standing at the plate, in the bottom of the ninth, tie score, and belting a game-winning homer into the next block. There were some moments in some games that will live in my mind forever. One such moment involved my brother Harold, who was as tough as nails and enjoyed playing baseball. But like me, he preferred to play sandlot ball rather than organized team ball. One afternoon, Harold was playing three-man baseball – a pitcher, catcher and batter, when he was hit in the mouth with a rubber baseball, causing a front tooth to become loose. True to his nature, he calmly called timeout, ran home, found a pair of pliers and yanked the dangling tooth completely out of his mouth. Without any concern for the pain he must have been feeling, he then returned to the game and carried on as though nothing out of the ordinary had happened. Not long after that incident, Harold broke both arms while engaging in some pretty rough horseplay with one of his friends. He was known in the neighborhood for his death-defying antics such as climbing onto the top of our house, taking a running start down the roof, jumping, and while in mid-air, turning a summersault and landing on his feet.

Charles Ray (the barefoot runner) was also an interesting character. He lived next door to me and was about a year older than I was. Actually, he didn't know for sure how old he was because when he was born he was delivered by a mid-wife at his grandmother's home and a birth certificate was never recorded and filed to indicate an official date of birth. Grade-wise, however, he was one grade ahead of me, although he never finished high school. Hanging out at Charles Ray's house was one adventure after another. One of the more memorable adventures was a weekly ritual initiated by Mrs. Tressie, his grandmother – ring the neck of a plump chicken, de-feathering it, and boiling it in a huge black pot in her front yard in preparation for the next evening's meal. She was extremely skillful at selecting just the right chicken, gripping its neck in just the right spot and using the proper technique in rendering the helpless animal completely lifeless in a matter of minutes. Actually, the most challenging part of preparing a chicken for dinner was catching it, which she left to Charles Ray. He proudly claimed the title of the best chicken-catcher in the neighborhood, although in order to perfect those formidable skills, he usually required a partner to help corner the doomed yard bird. No. I was never his partner, just a spellbound observer. Cleaning up and taking a bath after working frantically trying to catch a frightened chicken or just being filthy dirty from playing hard all day was another adventure for Charles Ray. He did not use a conventional tub because his grandmother did not have a conventional bathroom. Instead, he had to use an outhouse and a #3 tub to bathe, which was placed on the back porch and was just large enough for him to fit in.

Charles Ray and I did some things that today seem really bizarre, but at the time they were perfectly normal, if not a little scary. For example, about once a week, always after dark, Miss Tressie would send him on a special errand for her. This errand was special because it was always done at night and always involved money. And he would always ask me to go with him, mainly because he was too scared to go anywhere at night by himself; although he was so fleet of foot that he could out run his own shadow. Every Monday night at the same time, he would knock on my front door or yell for me from the front yard. In either case, he would say, "Ant! Come go with me to pay the 'barrel' lady!" I would ask my mom if I could go; she would say go ahead but come straight back home. We would head off in the direction of the "barrel" lady's house, which was about 4 or 5 blocks from my house. This errand would quickly turn into an adventure that only Alfred Hitchcock could appreciate. I think because he was so frightened of the dark, Charles Ray tried his best to make me feel the same as he did, and more times than not, he was successful. This thoroughly frightening, Hitchcockian adventure would start when we reached the house of the "ball-team" lady (Actually, it was "ball teeth" lady, but it always sounded to us kids like "ball-team."). Her dark-brown, wood frame house had a dark, rusty screen across the front porch that sat behind a thick row of towering oak trees that always seemed to make noises whenever we were near them. During my entire childhood and during hundreds of day-time and night-time trips past her house, I never saw a light on in the "ball-team" lady's house; and the darkness and eeriness of her house were made even more so because there were no street lights to illuminate our pathways or reveal the presence of some creature lurking behind one of the oak trees, just waiting to pounce on one or both of us.

While cautiously strolling past the "ball-team" lady's house, we heard the rattling and rustling of the leaves and limbs in the trees, which sounded like someone was actually up in the trees shaking them. Our curiosity and fear put up a fierce battle with each other, until Charles Ray said, "Ant, don't look up in them trees, man. The 'ball team' lady up there and she might spit in your eye." As if that was not enough to cause our hearts to pound even harder, I shouted, "Charles Ray! Run! There she is standing on the front porch." We would then take off like we had a couple of jet engines strapped to our backsides. We never looked back for fear that we would see someone or something that we really did not want to see. This time, fear won out over curiosity, which probably accounted for my being able to run as fast as Charles Ray. Once we made it past the "ball-team" lady's house, our fear slowly turned to mischief. We took the path that ran alongside Mr. Shane's house. Mr. Shane was a very nice elderly gentleman who did a lot of handy work around the neighborhood. He lived alone and was a very kind-hearted man who always seemed to have a smile on his face. As we passed his house, Charles Ray and I would scratch the window screen on his bedroom window loudly enough to awaken Mr. Shane. He would yell in a justifiably angry voice, "You boys get on away from here 'fo' I git my gun!" Not knowing how serious Mr. Shane was about getting his gun, we took off again, this time not stopping until we finally got to the "barrel" lady's house. Charles Ray would knock on the "barrel" lady's door and shortly afterward, a short, stout, dark-skinned lady dressed in her Sunday clothes came to the door. Charles Ray announced to her, "I'm here to pay the barrel." Tucked neatly in a small white envelope in Charles Ray's front pocket were several wrinkled dollar bills. He handed the envelope to the "barrel" lady who cheerfully accepted it; and after being away for a few minutes she came back and handed Charles Ray a small piece of paper with writing on it. He would say, "Thank ya, mam. Be back next week." It was not until I reached adulthood that I finally figured out who the "barrel" lady was, why Mrs. Tressie sent us to her house every week, and what was on that piece of paper the "barrel" lady gave to Charles Ray. The "barrel" lady was the lady to whom Mrs. Tressie paid her burial insurance premiums. She was the burial insurance lady; but to our ears and understanding, she was the "barrel" lady. And the slip of paper handed back to Charles Ray was the receipt.

Not as frequently, but just as mysteriously, Mrs. Tressie would send Charles Ray to collect red clay dirt in an area near the Projects that had mounds of dusty, red powdery dirt. I often went with him and would ask why we were going to get red-clay dirt. He was not really sure, but he thought somebody was going to eat it. Yuck! I thought. Who in the world would eat red-clay dirt? As Mrs. Tressie later explained to us, it was for one of her pregnant daughters, Dixie Lee or Peggy. She said women who were carrying needed the dirt because it helped them with delivering the baby. Seeing as how she helped deliver babies all the time, I figured she knew what she was talking about. Later, I figured it was the iron in the dirt that was helpful to Dixie Lee and Peggy. Actually, eating red clay was common among many black families because of its perceived medicinal benefits. As a unique delicacy and the object of intense cravings, many people regularly ate oven-baked red clay dirt patties mixed with vinegar. The unbaked patties were also used to help heal broken bones.

When the kids in the neighborhood would finally settle into a much anticipated ball game, frequently the game would be interrupted by mischief, often instigated by the Means brothers who lived a block from my house. The three Means brothers – Robert, Ray and Frank – did not play football or baseball with us, mainly because they were not very good, and they were not in our little clique. Instead, because of where they lived, they hung out with the Ruby Avenue boys who were nice guys and except for the Means brothers, excellent baseball players. When the Means brothers watched us play ball from their street corner, I think they felt left out. But they always knew what to do to get noticed and at the same time how to disrupt our game. They would challenge us to their "power" game – rock throwing or chunking. These boys could stand fifty yards from a utility pole, or telegram pole as we called it, and hit the middle of that pole with a rock 9 times out of 10. Their most impressive throws were with a curve rock (a flat rock). Their accuracy with a curve rock was exceptional and without knowing it, they possessed a deep understanding of the principles of aerodynamics and physics better than most teachers did. They knew just how much arc, thrust, power, and angle to use to cause that rock to curve enough so that it would hit its target dead on. My friends and I knew baseball and football, but we were out of our league when it came to rock-throwing. The Means brothers were undisputed champs.

It would seem, however, that being challenged to a rock-throwing contest would simply involve seeing who could hit a pole, tree or a tin can the most number of times from the greatest distance. But no, that would have been too easy and would not have been as much fun. Instead, the Means brothers would declare "war" on us in the middle of our games by launching carefully aimed rocks in our direction. They were like in-coming missiles launched from behind enemy lines. Well, when the rocks landed near our feet, we knew two things. One, we knew that they intended for the rocks to land at our feet and not on our heads. If they wanted to hit us, they could have easily done so. Two, we knew that the only way to get on with the game was to accept the challenge, even though we knew we were outclassed. So, as more incoming rocks landed closer to us, we would stop the game, gather up rocks in our pockets and hands, and quickly find cover. The "war" was now on. Charles Ray was not only our fastest runner, but he was also our best rock thrower. So, instead of wasting energy throwing rocks and missing our targets, the rest of us who would just keep Charles Ray supplied with all sizes of rocks. He liked the big curve rocks and more times than not he would come pretty close to hitting one of the Means brothers or the tree or pole that shielded them. Invariably, there would be a momentary pause to allow cars to go by, but that just gave the Means brothers more time to gather more rocks and to improve their advantage over us. After a few more minutes of hurling rocks at each other, but never hitting anyone to the point of injury, we stopped. The Means brothers would declare victory, which they duly earned. We would then go back to playing our game – at least until the Means brothers felt left out and bored again. That was fun and like running from the "ball-team" lady, enjoying music, movies, television, and sports, it made us forget for a while the ugliness of Jim Crowism.

Chapter 8

White Reaction to the Civil Rights Movement

The Death of Mr. Vernon Dahmer

As with any great movement for social justice, the civil rights movement engendered a great deal of hatred, violence, and resistance from those who felt threatened by changes to the status quo. Chief among those to respond to the movement with violence and hatred was the Ku Klux Klan, which was notorious for its special brand of clandestine and cowardly acts of terror against anyone they considered an "agitator."

Hattiesburg was not spared the wrath of the Klan as it brought the city of Hattiesburg to the attention of the nation in one of its many displays of terrorism and spinelessness on January 10, 1966, in the small rural all-black community of Kelly Settlement, on the outskirts of Hattiesburg. On the previous night, confronted with the cacophonous sounds of rapid-fire gunshots, the pungent smell of thick, billowing black smoke, and the bloodcurdling sight of an out-of-control fully involved fire engulfing their home, Mr. Vernon Dahmer, wife Ms. Ellie, and children Dennis and Betty were awakened from what started out as normal evening of rest. Blindly navigating their way through broken glass, collapsing walls, crashing ceilings, and frantically dodging flying bullets and deadly firebombs, the family managed to get through the smoldering timbers that represented their haven just a few hours earlier. However, while struggling to defend his family and his home, Mr. Dahmer lost consciousness and died the next morning at the Forrest General Hospital from severe burns and smoke inhalation.

Not only was the death of Mr. Dahmer itself a senseless tragedy, but adding to that tragedy was the cruel irony of his having four patriotic sons serving in the U.S. military, defending rights that their own father could not enjoy. The gunshots and firebombs were the handy work of the local chapter of the White Knights of Mississippi, regarded as the most violent Ku Klux Klan group in the south. Members of this notorious, terrorist group were involved in the murders of the three civil rights workers – Andrew Goodman, Michael Schwerner, and James Chaney in Philadelphia, Mississippi, in June 1964.

Mr. Dahmer, owner of a small grocery store in the Eatonville Community and among the handful of blacks who were registered voters in Forrest County, received numerous threats on his life after he made it known that he was willing to assist other blacks to register to vote and to assist them in paying their poll taxes. He was fully aware that such activities were major violations of Jim Crow law and were punishable by death. Nevertheless, Mr. Dahmer's unshakable commitment to social justice and to helping his disenfranchised black brothers and sisters of Forrest County become registered voters prevailed over whatever fear and trepidation his persecutors and executioners wanted him to feel.

Mr. Dahmer's death was a wake-up call for black and white citizens of Hattiesburg. For whites, this tragic event was a massive embarrassment and forced many of them to more closely examine their own racist beliefs and behaviors. Mr. Dahmer was well-known by many white business owners and bankers in town who, as much as white people could, held him in high regard, primarily because he was a successful business owner and he did not represent an economic threat to any of them. Consequently, some of these business owners felt personally affronted by this deadly attack on Mr. Dahmer and his family. In an unprecedented act of humanity, a local bank, First Mississippi National Bank, set up a relief fund for the Dahmer family. Dr. Ralph Noonkaster, President of all-white William Carey College in Hattiesburg, directed a community-wide fund-raiser for the Dahmer family.

For most of us black citizens, this tragic event, while intended to frighten us into submission, only served to strengthened our resolve to work even harder for our freedom. Black citizens of Hattiesburg struggled, individually and corporately, to deal with the loss of Mr. Dahmer. In the midst of our grief, we were left to wonder, *how many more lives would have to be lost? How much more blood would have to be shed? How many more beatings, jailings and insults would we have to put up with before we would be allowed to live as free citizens in our own country?* We had already lost several prominent leaders and supporters of our struggle for freedom to the assassin's bullet— President Kennedy and Mississippi State Field Secretary Medgar Evers in 1963, and Nation of Islam leader Malcolm X in 1965. But as much as we revered these men and mourned their premature deaths, the death of Mr. Dahmer hit close to home and affected everyone in ways unlike the deaths of President Kennedy, Malcolm X, and Medgar Evers. Mr. Dahmer was one of us. He shared a hometown with all of us. Vernon, Jr. was my mother's schoolmate in high school. Mrs. Dahmer was a highly regarded schoolteacher in the community of Bay Springs. Mr. Dahmer was not an outspoken man and did not seek publicity. He was not confrontational. He did not fit the profile of a charismatic fiery civil rights leader that was the typical target of racist assassins. So, because he was such an unlikely target for KKK action, his death served as a sobering reality check and as an unambiguous wake-up call for the rest of us.

The grief process in senseless deaths like Mr. Dahmer's requires appropriate, decisive and quick responses so that the grief does not become debilitating and destructive. In the case of Mr. Dahmer's death, the keys to dealing with this overwhelming grief were prayer, a surprisingly responsive legal system, and a much needed public response to not only the tragedy of his death, but also to the scores of other tragedies that had already occurred all across the south. We also wanted to respond to the totality of injustices and indifferences that had created a climate of hatred, bigotry, and reckless disregard for the value of a black person's life. Of course, prayer was never in short supply. Black churches all over the city of Hattiesburg and surrounding areas offered up special prayers for the grieving Dahmer family. The legal system apparently was working, as District Attorney Jimmy Finch decided to prosecute the men charged in Mr. Dahmer's murder.

And finally, for a public response to Mr. Dahmer's murder, on January 15, 1966, a march to the Forrest County Courthouse was held. The march provided participants an outlet for expressing grief and outrage at the forces of evil that were directly and indirectly responsible for Mr. Dahmer's death. There was discernible tension, excitement, and anxiety in the crowd that day. Hundreds of black faces, laced with war-weary frowns and deep-seated expressions of anguish, faithfully revealed the intense fear and anxiety that only soldiers must experience just prior to going into combat. The obligatory chatter and the sense of urgency among the crowd derived their energy and momentum from sheer nervousness and the frightening realization that no one knew for sure how the day would go. We could easily become the victims of trigger-happy police officers, or some nutty Klansman could shoot into the crowd and hurt someone. We simply did not know what would happen. We only knew that something greater than our fear was present with us. We knew that God's faithful presence and divine guidance would lead us beyond the fear and uncertainty of the moment.

The chatter was intermittently punctuated by moments of individual and group silence in which the memory of Mr. Dahmer as well as those of other fallen leaders was invoked. As a signal that it was time to begin the march, a corporate prayer would be offered: *Lord, we want to thank You for being with us today. We just want You to move among us here today, Lord, and show us what You would have us do in Your holy name. Guide and keep the leaders of this march today, Lord. Touch their hearts and lead them according to Your will. Lord, we also pray that You will touch the hearts of these racist, mean-hearted, hate-filled, white folks who need to know Your saving grace. They just need to know, Lord, that we are all your children. They just need to know You made us different, Lord, but in Your eyes, there ain't no difference in Your children. Help them to hear Your divine message of love and forgiveness and to resist Satan's evil and divisive message of hatred. Although we've been on the battlefield for so long now and our hearts are hurting mighty with the grief of the loss of Mr. Dahmer, we pray that You will help us maintain our commitment to nonviolence and help us to stay committed to the cause that You have laid out for us. Bless the Dahmer family. Bless the families of all our fallen brethren who have made the ultimate sacrifice for justice and equality. Bless the leaders of this march today, O Lord. Keep us safe and keep us in the right spirit as we prepare ourselves for this march. We know that You told us that where two or three are gathered in Your name, there too are You in the midst. So, be with us today Lord. We need Your guiding hand and the reassurance of Your everlasting arm. In the name of precious Jesus, Amen!*

The shaking and the shivering seemed to increase noticeably, caused, no doubt, by an amalgam of hearing the Word, feeling the bone-chilling cold, and thinking about the ever-present fear and uncertainty of what was going to happen next. For many that day, this was their first-ever march, and for others, sadly, this was not the first and would not be the last. Clearly, the outrage caused by the murder of Mr. Dahmer had forged a deep sense of solidarity and unity among black people in Hattiesburg. It was great to see such a display of unity, but sad to note that it took a man's death to make it happen.

With ministers and leaders of the movement out front, the march proceeded orderly up Mobile Street, picking up bystanders who agonizingly conjured up the nerves to join us. The route then turned right at a slight angle on to Batson Street and up a slight incline next to Sears on Main Street. We peacefully marched across Main Street to our destination – the Forrest County Courthouse. Police were present in full riot gear and clearly prepared to deal with any breach of the law they observed, no matter how minor. March leaders repeatedly admonished us to remain calm and not to retaliate against any type of attack, whether it was from law enforcement or from one of our misguided white brothers. The notion of nonviolence was the cornerstone of the civil rights movement. Dr. King was very prophetic in his adoption of that form of protest when he led the Montgomery Bus Boycott in 1955. No doubt, many in the anti-civil rights camp would have preferred a violent response to the segregation laws of the south. If that had been the case and the movement had chosen violence over nonviolence, there certainly would have been a precipitous, quick and violent end to the movement. But because the movement was patterned after other successful nonviolent peaceful protests, and was based on an abiding belief in biblical teachings that disapproved of violent reaction to other acts of violence. The Reverend James Lawson is credited with introducing the principles of nonviolent protest to Dr. King. Reverend Lawson spent three years as a Methodist missionary in India and was greatly influenced by the legacy of Mohandes Gandhi, who utilized non-violent, passive resistance techniques to help bring an end to British rule in India. Christ utilized it in the most perfect way, when he warned in the Sermon on the Mount: But I tell you, *Do not resist an evil person. If someone strikes you on the right cheek, turn to him the other also.*

Around 11:30 a.m., Patrolman James Owens started pushing people off the sidewalk, attempting to arrest a marcher who he claimed reached into his coat pocket, "possibly for a weapon," according to newspaper accounts. Given the fact that the weather was cold that day and lots of people placed their hands inside their coat pockets, Patrolman Owens' explanation was flimsy at best and completely bogus at worst. Witnesses to the incident reacted with predictable anger and outrage and began demanding that the officer release the man and that Owens, who had a reputation of brutality toward blacks, be fired on the spot. The crowd began to surge closer to Owens and the man whom he and, ironically, a black officer, Patrolman Willie McGilvery, were attempting to arrest. At any moment, a full-scale riot was about to begin. The officers in riot gear were prepared to join the fray and no doubt would have welcomed the opportunity. But NAACP President, Mr. J.C. Fairley, quickly intervened and helped diffuse a highly volatile situation. He held blunt and frank discussions with police Chief Hugh Herring as the crowd and police nervously looked on and listened. Standing toe-to-toe and eye-to-eye like two heavy-weight boxers about to go 12 rounds, Mr. Fairley spoke first, saying, "Owens pushed me and some of these other marchers off the sidewalk and pulled his blackjack on me trying to arrest Mr. Gaddis. I told Owens that I would take care of Mr. Gaddis. He's not bothering anybody. All Gaddis was doing was singing out of tune. Now you gotta do something about Owens." The crowd supported Mr. Fairley's remarks by yelling, "That's right! Get rid of the Klucker (Klansman). We ain't gonna take no mo' whuppins from Owens!" Mr. Fairley quieted the crowd and continued. " Owens is out of control and somebody's gonna get hurt if you don't get him outta here. And you got to fire him right now. He's gonna cause some big problems here if you don't do something about him." Chief Herring responded, "Now, Fairley, first thing we gotta do is get your people moving and break up this crowd. If anybody gets hurt, it's gonna be your people. You see all these other officers with weapons. If something breaks out, they will use `em." "Well, Chief, if that happens that blood's gonna be on your hands. Now what do you plan to do about Owens?" The Chief shifted his weight from one leg to the other, let out a loud and long sigh, and shook his head. "Fairley, the only thing I can do is take this to the Civil Service Board and in the meantime, I'll take him off patrol and put him on desk duty." Speaking with even more fervor and confidence, Mr. Fairley said, "Well, Chief, that will work, for now. We'll keep an eye on that civil service hearing to see what they gonna do. If they don't do the right thing, you gonna hear from us." Fortunately, the two of them were able to agree to a solution that caused the tension to ease a bit, but not go away. The crowd was pleased with what it heard from Chief Herring and that Mr. Gaddis was not going to be arrested. After a few speeches on the courthouse steps, the march ended with everyone proceeding back to march headquarters on Seventh Street. A few people lingered about, still angry and appearing more than willing to take on the police. Eventually, they were persuaded by march leaders to leave the area and to return with them to march headquarters. Patrolman Owens called Mr. Fairley the next day and apologized for his behavior at the march and asked Mr. Fairly to forgive him. Mr. Fairley believes that it was a transparent ploy on Owens' part to curry favors with members of the civil service board and thereby, avoid suspension from the police force. It did not work. He was indeed fired shortly after this incident and to the delight of the black community there was now one less police officer on the Hattiesburg Police force to threaten us.

Nevertheless, there remained a sense of loss, fear, and frustration among many of us who participated in that march. The near meltdown of the march that day was another chilling reminder of how dangerous the times were. Among all of us involved in the movement in Hattiesburg, there was the real - not imagined - fear that if the Klan could do that to Mr. Dahmer, they could do it to anyone at anytime. But our hope and faith in God remained unwavering and ultimately became our strongest weapons in resisting the evil of the Klan and their sympathizers.

In a totally unprecedented act on the part of law enforcement and the district attorney's office in Hattiesburg, several Klansmen were arrested and charged with arson and with the murder of Mr. Dahmer. As a young child of 13 years, I developed a keen interest in the trials of these men and was present for most of the proceedings. Of course, in keeping with the customs of Jim Crowism, all of the black spectators were required to sit in the crowded balcony of Circuit Judge Stanton Hall's Courtroom. I generally sat near the middle of the balcony next to a woman who, to my amazement, would regularly breastfeed her baby. She just whipped her breast out right there in front of everybody like it was nobody else's business. I am not sure what caught my attention more, the exposed breast and ravenous suckling by the baby or the drama that was taking place on the courtroom floor underneath me.

Nevertheless, a Hollywood screenwriter could not have better scripted an academy-award-winning scene that was unfolding in Judge Hall's courtroom. District Attorney Jimmy Finch was examining star prosecution witness Billy Roy Pitts, who had turned state's evidence. As Mr. Pitts was giving details of the plans hatched by him and his cohorts to murder Mr. Dahmer, there was hush throughout the entire courtroom. Even the nursing mother interrupted her baby's feeding to make sure she heard every single word from Mr. Finch and from Mr. Pitts. Dressed in a blue seer-sucker suit that sharply contrasted his red, ruddy complexion and wrinkled skin, Mr. Finch, after asking Mr. Pitts to state his name, address and occupation, turned to Mr. Pitts and asked, "Mr. Pitts, who was with you on the night of January 9, 1966, when you participated in the firebombing of the home of Mr. Vernon Dahmer? Are those men in this courtroom today, sir?" Dressed in a blue blazer and a red, open, collar shirt, with a receding hairline that revealed even more of his rosy-red complexion, Mr. Pitts responded, "Yes, sir." "Would you please point them out to the court," Mr. Finch replied. Watching Billy Roy slowly raise his trembling right hand and point to Cecil Sessum (a Baptist minister), Charles Wilson and William Smith was a scene that had never before been played out in the courts of Mississippi – an active Ku Klux Klan member, not an undercover operative, ratting on his fellow Klan members. There were tears of joy and a chorus of sighs and "yes, Lords" among our packed-in group of spectators in the balcony, prompting Judge Hall to momentarily halt his customary whittling, pound his gavel and issue a warning for us to keep quiet. Those of us in the balcony were as stunned as the Klan supporters and sympathizers sitting below were, but for much different reasons. We were stunned because a white man was finally coming forward with the truth after years of cover-ups, lies, and conspiracies. The Klan supporters and sympathizers were stunned because the code of silence that had been so strong for so many years and had been the glue that held the Klan together was broken.

The testimony of Mr. Pitts was very convincing to the all-white jury. Although Imperial Wizard Sam Bowers, Devors Nix, Charles Noble, and Henry DeBoxtel were also on trial for murder and arson, the jury deadlocked on their case. But to the delight of all right-thinking people, black and white, Sessum, Wilson, and Smith were convicted and sentenced to life in prison. Interestingly, one of the defense attorneys, William Waller, became governor of the State of Mississippi in 1973 and soon after taking office, commuted the sentence of his former client, Charles Wilson, to time served. The U.S. Office of Civil Rights later filed charges of civil rights violations against ten of the defendants. The all-white jury acquitted three and no verdict was reached for the other seven.

The leaders and other highly visible participants of the movement who daily placed themselves in harm's way (Mr. J.C. Fairley, Mr. George Harper, the Reverend J.C. Killingsworth, the Reverend John Cameron, the Reverend E.E. Grimmett, the Reverend L.P. Ponder, Mr. Charles Glen, Mr. Nathan Bourne, Mr. B.F. Bourne, Mrs. Lavada Jackson, Mrs. Pinky Hall, Mrs. Daisy Harris, Mr. Doug Smith, Mrs. Ruth Cameron, Mrs. Peggy Gould, Dr. C.E. Smith, Mr. John Gould, Mr. Horace Lawrence, the Reverend Milton Barnes, Jr., Mrs. Victoria Jackson Gray, Mrs. Alice Hall-Fluker, Mr. James "Sonnyboy" Fluker, Mr. James Magee, Mr. Charles McArthur, Mr. Charles Philips, Mr.

James Nicks, Mr. Major Pugh, and Mr. Benton Dwight, Sr.) felt particularly vulnerable after Mr. Dahmer's death because the Klan believed that if the leaders were frightened off or killed, the movement would quickly die.

The fear that the participants had for their own and their family's safety, and for their livelihood was very real and more than amply justified. Interestingly, for many adult activists, the loss of their jobs was actually more frightening than the loss of their lives. Deep religious convictions and an abiding faith in the divine providence that guided the movement caused many to simply regard death, as the will of God and that in the by-and-by things would be all right. The loss of a job, however, meant the loss of means to support one's family in the here and now. Except for the few individuals who were self-employed, everyone else feared losing their jobs if their white employer objected to their involvement in the movement. There were few things in Hattiesburg worse than a laid-off black man with a family who had been labeled a civil rights agitator and was unable to find another job with another white-owned business. If a white person chose to fire a black employee for participating in the civil rights movement, there was little or no recourse for that employee. There were no enforced labor laws to protect him. And there were not enough large black-owned businesses to absorb the black unemployed. So, many who wanted to be involved in the movement, i.e., school teachers, laborers employed at hostile white-owned businesses, and women who worked as domestics in the homes of hostile white families feared retribution if they actively participated.

There was another unprecedented murder trial in Judge Stanton Hall's courtroom that attracted lots of attention from both blacks and whites in Hattiesburg. In addition to the fact that the trial involved a rare black-on-white crime, this case attracted attention because the white man, "Cotton" Humphrey, was a local county deputy sheriff who had a much deserved reputation of brutality towards blacks in the Palmers Crossing community. After being pulled over in his car one night by Deputy Humphrey, a young black man named Claudies "Clyde" Shinall, apparently fearing for his safety, shot Deputy Humphrey at point-blank range and killed him. I attended the trial nearly every day and watched how Jimmy Dukes, the county attorney, vigorously prosecuted Mr. Shinall. While Mr. Dukes's prosecution of Mr. Shinall was quite ordinary, in the sense that he was very thorough and professional in his job, there was still something quite extraordinary and unusual about the whole trial: The fact that there was a trial at all. The usual manner of disposing of such cases was the immediate disposal of the suspect's body in the Leaf, Bouie, or Pearl River. Of course, Mr. Shinall was convicted and sentenced to death. Later his sentence was commuted to life at Parchman State Penitentiary.

Mississippi Sovereignty Commission

The reputation Mississippi earned for being hell-bent on maintaining its racist heritage was evident in so many ways. Of course, the overt acts of violence were the most visible and most egregious examples of that well-earned reputation. But that reputation was aggressively fortified by equally egregious state-sponsored acts of oppression and discrimination. Perhaps the most renowned and the most scurrilous efforts by the state of Mississippi to create, foster, and reinforce efforts to oppress its black citizens and to resist racial equality was the infamous Mississippi Sovereignty Commission. Legally established and sanctioned by the Mississippi Legislature in 1956, two years after the Brown Decision, the Sovereignty Commission's official mandate was to "protect the sovereignty of the State of Mississippi and its sister southern states from the interference of the federal government." In essence, lawmakers granted blanket and limitless authority to the 12-member commission and its agents to maintain racial segregation in the state, especially school segregation. Agents of the Sovereignty Commission utilized tactics of harassment, intimidation, surveillance, and exercised subpoena powers to investigate law-abiding citizens it regarded as agitators or communist sympathizers. Mr. Lee Cole was the Sovereignty Commission agent assigned to Hattiesburg.

He maintained a well-deserved reputation as an aggressive investigator who kept close surveillance on civil rights workers in Hattiesburg. The Sovereignty Commission collaborated with black ministers and informants along with various and sundry white supremacy organizations, including the White Citizens Council and local law enforcement officials to create and maintain files on over 87,000 citizens. In fact, from 1960 to 1964, the Sovereignty Commission gave nearly $200,000 in taxpayers' money to the White Citizens Council as payment for its assistance in carrying out its mission to spy on law-abiding citizens and resisting desegregation.

An example of the hostility shown to the civil rights movement by the Mississippi Sovereignty Commission is in a statement made by a Commission official following the murder of Mack Charles Parker, *If we set {sic} back and waited for the government to punish Mack Parker, it would never happen. So we did it ourselves.*

The legislation that established the Mississippi Sovereignty Commission required that all files related to the work of the Commission remain sealed and closed to public inspection forever. When Governor William Waller vetoed the Commission's authority and funding in 1977, the legislature passed a law requiring the Commission's records to remain secret for fifty years. The American Civil Liberties Union (ACLU), however, filed suit in federal court to force the state to release Commission records and files to the public before 2027. In 1989, U.S. Federal District Judge William H. Barbour, Jr., ruled in favor of the ACLU and ordered the records released immediately.

Mississippi Sovereignty Commission records are housed in the Mississippi Archives and are available for viewing by the public in person or via the internet. Commission records contain information on individuals the Commission considered "integration agitators," subversive, un-American, or a threat to the segregated way of life in Mississippi. The following files are examples of the attitudes and behaviors that exemplified the purpose, scope, and intentions of the State Sovereignty Commission.

the end only a few short paragraphs appeared in the press to the effect
that Kennard was withdrawing his application. Today, hardly anyone
outside of Hattiesburg knows what you are talking about when you mention
the Clyde Kennard case. An airing of this case in the press would have
increased the tension in the State and would not have aided in quieting
racial unrest. It would have also disclosed information of value to the
NAACP.

The State Sovereignty Commission might be likened to the FBI in
ferreting out information about communism and subversion; or the Army,
Navy, and Air Corps intelligence agencies during time of war seeking
intelligence information about the enemy and what the enemy proposes to
do. For all practical purposes, our enemy is the NAACP and any other
organization which is attempting to advocate integration and trampling
of our state rights. The State Sovereignty Commission obtains information as to what these enemies of ours propose to do and makes this
information available to our State authorities, and, in some instances,
to local authorities. Based upon this information, decisions are
reached and plans put into effect to block the attempts of the NAACP
and others to force integration in Mississippi.

The act creating the State Sovereignty Commission was passed at the
1956 regular session of the Legislature. It provides for four ex-officio
members, namely, the Governor, Attorney General, President of the Senate,
Speaker of the House; and three members, citizens to be appointed by
the Governor, two members of the Senate to be appointed by the President of the Senate, and three members from the House of Representatives

May 4, 1959

MEMO TO: Director, State Sovereignty Commission

FROM: Zack J. Van Landingham

SUBJECT: M. C. Parker
Civil Rights-Violence

On April 28, 1959, Mr. Purser Hewitt, Managing Editor of the Jackson Clarion-Ledger, telephoned the writer, stating that he was fixing to depart for the Mississippi Gulf Coast on a speaking engagement. However, he desired on the following day to come back by Poplarville to observe the operations and the investigation looking toward the apprehension of the mob who broke into the jail at Poplarville and took the Negro, M. C. Parker, and allegedly lynched him. Mr. Hewitt said he knew he would not be given any inside information, nor did he expect any such special treatment. However, he did desire to be able to observe operations without being given a "brush off" by the Agents. I told him I was sure he would be cordially received. I also told him I would be glad to telephone the FBI in New Orleans and inform them of his proposed visit to Poplarville. He said he did not feel this was necessary.

I did, however, telephone the New Orleans office and talk to ASAC Andy Dinsmore and informed him of Mr. Purser Hewitt's visit and the fact that he was the Managing Editor of the Clarion-Ledger. Mr. Dinsmore said he would contact Mr. Ralph Bachman, the Agent in charge of the FBI who at the time had his headquarters on the 2nd floor of the American Legion Building, Poplarville, and was directing operations in that locality. Mr. Dinsmore said he was sure Mr. Hewitt would be cordially received. However, he did not know that any particular information could be made available to him.

I also discussed with Mr. Dinsmore the fact that Attorney Dudley Connor, Hattiesburg, had informed the writer at the time of the investigation of Clyde Kennard in Hattiesburg, that if the State Sovereignty Commission wanted that Negro out of the community and out of the State they would take care of the situation, and when asked what he meant by that, Mr. Connor stated that Kennard's car could be hit by a train or he could have some accident on the highway and nobody would ever know the difference. I also informed Mr. Dinsmore that Governor Coleman had been advised of a remark by Connor within the past 2 weeks to the effect that what Mississippi needed was a real good lynching. I informed Mr. Dinsmore that Governor Coleman had previously made known this remark to ASAC Ralph Bachman.

Mr. Dinsmore thanked the writer for the above information and stated that the same would be passed on to Mr. Bachman.

STATE SOVEREIGNTY COMMISSION

MAY 6 1959

INDEXED
SERIALIZED
FILED

5-3-17

My Dad's Reaction to the Civil Rights Movement

My mother was the constant in my life when it came to the civil rights movement. She was passionate in her commitment to the movement and was willing to make whatever sacrifices needed to advance the cause of social justice in Hattiesburg. She instilled in her three boys the importance of being involved, being accountable, and being dependable when it came to our involvement in the movement. Whenever there was a march, demonstration, or mass meeting, Daisy Harris was present with her three boys in tow. I was not just along for the ride. I was physically present to lend myself to whatever a kid of my age was asked to do. That included handing out leaflets advertising meetings, leading freedom songs at mass meetings, and going out on voter registration canvassing trips in the community. I had a deep appreciation for the dangers of being involved in the movement. The images of both youngsters and adults being beaten by police officers, attacked by police dogs, and having high-pressure fire hoses turned on them were seared into my brain, as were the images of the four black girls killed by Klansmen while attending Easter church services at the 16th Street Baptist Church in 1963 in Birmingham, Alabama. The death of Medgar Evers and the scores of other black men who were murdered for standing up for justice were also burned into my memory. Fear was ever present. It was present whenever I distributed mass meeting fliers, led freedom songs, walked a picket line, or participated in a march. But the fear was mitigated by a mother who had a way of protecting her boys, and at the same time exposing them to the ruthless realities of being black in a southern town in the 1960s.

Now, with my father, it was a slightly different story. I was especially mindful of both his reaction to and his role in the civil rights movement. I knew that he was deeply troubled by the murders of civil rights workers and did not want the deaths of these brave warriors to be in vain. He witnessed the dehumanizing insults my grandfather had to endure. He witnessed a callous and unprovoked violent attack against an innocent young black man by an angry hate-filled white man. He saw the gruesome picture of Emmett Till's brutally beaten

111

body in *Jet* magazine. Interestingly, my dad had seemingly contradictory reactions to all that was happening in the civil rights movement in Hattiesburg, including the murders, marches, and demonstrations. On one hand, he refused to directly participate in marches or walk picket lines, and on the other, he was one hundred percent supportive of every aspect of the movement, including his family's participation. He proudly and unhesitatingly welcomed civil rights workers into our home and even provided transportation for marchers on his days off. His refusal to directly participate in the movement was based on his very strong conviction that he could not and would not abide by the principle of nonviolence. I heard him say many times that it is best he not walk a picket line because if anyone, cop or Klan, hit him or one of his family, he was definitely not going to turn the other cheek. Anyone who knew James Harris, Sr., or "Woofie" as everyone called him, knew he was being totally honest and would have done exactly as he said he would. "Woofie" Harris was not afraid of anyone, regardless of race.

One day, my mom's white boss telephoned our house and while speaking with my dad, called him a nigger and started cursing him. From what I could hear, my dad was giving as much or more as he was getting. After a few minutes of expletives, my dad angrily hung up the telephone and rushed out of the house. He jumped into his car and sped off to Mr. Kelsey's office to confront him – no – to whip him. As he entered the door to the office, Mr. Kelsey struck him in the back of the head with a pistol and my father passed out. Somehow, he managed to leave, dazed, but undaunted.

My dad believed he was as much a man (not more than) as any man, black or white, and he wanted desperately to instill that belief in his three sons. One of his more memorable attempts at instilling that belief in us was to threaten to whip us if he ever heard us refer to the local white grocer as *Mr.* Preacher. First, my dad did not care for the fact that the grocer was not actually a preacher, and did not seem to have any qualms about using that title. Such titles, he believed, belong to men who were truly called by God to minister to His people and who were actively doing so. In my dad's view, this "preacher" did not fit either of those two criteria. Second, my dad did not like the idea of his sons using the term Mr. because of the customary Jim Crow practice of white men being referred to as Mr. and black men being referred to by only their first names. Although he had a limited formal education, Woofie understood the complex dynamics of human interactions and was wiser than most Ph.D.s. One of his more unforgettable jewels of wisdom that he often shared with his three young boys was that respect and honor were earned and not bestowed on one simply because of skin color.

Although I was emotionally closer to my mom than to my father and took my cue from her when it came to civil rights activities, nevertheless I loved and respected my dad immensely; and like most kids in the neighborhood I had a very healthy fear of him. He had a well-earned reputation for not putting up with nonsense or mischief from kids or adults. One of his more dramatic displays of impatience with mischief came after I shattered a living room window from the outside with a hard rubber baseball. After seeing the damage caused by the errantly thrown ball, he ran outside to the front porch and stood there with both fists clinched so tightly, I thought his knuckles would break through his skin. There I was, standing there in utter fear and hopeless confusion, wondering how long it would take me to walk and run to California. He became so angry that I thought I was about to meet my maker. Instead, he chose a worse fate. He ordered me bring him not only my ball, but also my two brothers' balls. After he had all three balls, he took up a strategic position on the front porch, hollered to us, "I'll make sure y'all don't bust no more damn windows. Hell, I work too damn hard to be spending my money fixing windows." And as if to rid himself of both his anger and these terrible instruments of destruction, he flung all three balls across the street into a field of tall weeds. I was never sure if he got rid of his anger after throwing the balls away, but after seeing how far he threw them, there was no doubt at all that he had certainly gotten rid of all three balls.

My dad also had some pretty traditional beliefs about what constituted manhood and masculinity. He subscribed wholeheartedly to the notion, for example, that boys should not do housework, which I rather favored myself. He believed that was a woman's job and that if any of us boys dabbled at all in mopping the floor or washing dishes, we would somehow become gay. When he was not around, my mother would still make us do housework, even if we protested that it would make us "funny." My dad also strictly forbade any of his sons to play the piano, for the same reason he did not want us to do housework. It was okay to bang on the piano keys and make noise, as that was a boy thing to do, but playing chords was strictly forbidden. At the time, I thought he was right about housework and playing the piano, just as I thought he was right about everything. As an adult, however, I have learned to play the piano and regularly wash and fold clothes, cook, clean the house, all while remaining heterosexual.

Chapter 9

Resistance Movement

Boycotts

Aside from our everlasting and abiding faith in God as our principal strength in the quest for freedom, boycotts proved to be the most effective method of achieving our goals, particularly goals that involved the hiring of black people in white-owned retail establishments and ending the illegal practice of operating segregated facilities. Despite limited individual economic resources, the majority of black people in Hattiesburg understood the collective economic power we possessed. Moreover, we understood that we had no obligation to spend our money with businesses that refused to hire black people or required black people to be served in a separate area from whites.

The murder of Mr. Vernon Dahmer at the hands of the Ku Klux Klan in 1966 galvanized and emboldened the black community in Hattiesburg. Rather than allowing Mr. Dahmer's murder to intimidate us or to allow his death to be in vain, black citizens of Hattiesburg made a collective decision to seize the moment and press for more concessions from city leaders and white business owners. Mr. J. C. Fairley, president of the Hattiesburg Chapter of the NAACP, made public a list of demands that the NAACP wanted the city and white business owners to address. Those demands were: 1. "Hiring of Negro deputy sheriffs. 2. Early appointment of two Negroes to the city school board; election of one Negro to the county school board. 3. Negro policemen already on the city force be integrated into the department with full authority. 4. Hiring of Negro transit bus drivers. 5. Street improvements in Negro communities. 6. Hiring Negro firemen. 7. Desegregation of all city and county facilities. 8. Desegregation of both students and faculty in public schools. 9. Negroes on the city council and in policy-making positions in local government. 10. Desegregation of juries. 11. Desegregation of hospital facilities and staff. 12. Use of courtesy titles of Mr., and Mrs., or Miss, by shopkeepers and clerks when waiting on Negroes. 13. Compliance with the 1965 Voting Rights bill. 14. Elimination of health hazards by stopping an open ditch from the Hercules Power Co., (the town's largest manufacturing concern) that flows through the Negro community. 15. Elimination of police brutality, both verbal and physical." Thus, the gauntlet was thrown, and from that point forward a battle would ensue between the opponents and supporters of Jim Crow laws and practices. The stage was set for a series of direct actions by opponents of Jim Crowism after it became clear that the supporters of Jim Crowism were not willing to accede to the demands that Mr. Fairley had articulated.

Perhaps, the most ambitious and ultimately, most successful boycott was a comprehensive two-phase selective buying and riding campaign in the summer and fall of 1967. The first phase was directed at the City of Hattiesburg for its practice of requiring black passengers (the majority of its passengers) to sit on the back of the bus and for refusing to hire black bus drivers. Negotiation sessions were held between city officials and leaders of the movement when demands were made for the city not only to end its practice of forcing blacks to sit on the back of the bus, but also to hire black bus drivers. Naturally, the city officials refused such "radical" ideas, insisting they were within their legal rights to decide where black riders could sit, and to hire or not anyone they wanted to despite the passage of the Civil Rights of Act of 1964. And just as naturally, our leaders immediately called for an all-out, zero-tolerance boycott of the city buses in Hattiesburg. The strategy of ride-sharing, walking, and utilizing black-owned taxis -- undergirded by a fierce determination to maintain unity and solidarity -- became the foundation of a successful boycott. The boycott lasted several months and finally ended on September 6, 1967, with a letter signed by Arnold Burkhart, Regional Manager of the Hattiesburg Bus Lines: *As of today (September 6, 1967), Hattiesburg City Lines has employed four (4) Negro Operators. Three are in training today, and the fourth is to report for training on Thursday, September 7, 1967. There will possibly be a fifth Negro Driver employed next week when school starts and at the present time we are considering a Negro applicant for employment in our garage. As additional openings arise, these openings will be filled on the basis of qualifications, irregardless {sic} of race.*

Because of the adverse economic impact of the boycott on the Bus Line's income, many of the white bus drivers were either laid off or resigned. When agreement was reached between the boycott leaders and the officials of the bus line and the buses started rolling again, black bus drivers had replaced nearly all of the white drivers. Indeed, it was an incredible and satisfying sight to see black men in uniforms behind the wheels of city buses and black bus riders sitting in seats that were previously the exclusive domain of whites.

Buoyed by the success of the bus boycott, the second phase commenced in late September as boycott leaders began to identify retail establishments that had no black employees. Especially targeted were white-owned retail businesses whose major clientele was black people. This targeting included most downtown businesses. Before a store was targeted for action, however, someone would go to the business, ask if there were any openings, request an application, and finally, ask for an interview. Persons selected for such missions were qualified to do the work and were instructed on how to conduct themselves in the most exemplary manner possible, so as not to give the employer any excuses for refusing to hire them. Eventually several black people were employed at a handful of downtown businesses and the boycott ended after two months. Notable among the hires were Mr. Melvin Lamar, who was hired at Smart Shoe Store, and Mr. Barry Hullum, who was hired at Waldoff's Department Store. These two courageous young men are notable because soon after they began their new jobs and having gained some notoriety, locally, they were drafted into the military and sent to Vietnam. Tragically, Mr. Lamar was killed in action, defending rights that, as a citizen of the United States of America, he was unable to fully realize. Many wondered whether there were a connection between Mr. Lamar's and Mr. Hullum's decision to desegregate the downtown Hattiesburg workforce and the decision by the Selective Service to draft them. The local draft board, which was all white, was no doubt, responsive to the political climate of the times. That the board intentionally targeted these young men because of their civil rights activities was not outside the realm of possibility, as far as we were concerned. The draft lottery, which was designed, in part, to eliminate such practices, was not instituted until December 1969.

Another selective buying target was the white-owned Seventh Street Grocery Store, located in the Love Hall Building on the corner of 7th Street and Mobile Street. Ignoring requests to negotiate with boycott leaders and experiencing serious economic hardship resulting from the boycott, the owner stubbornly refused to hire any black clerks and in a matter of days, he closed his business. Other white-owned stores in the black community – Steelman's Grocery Store on Eastside Avenue and Lott's Grocery Store, on Country Club Road-- were also targeted for action, but unlike the owner of the Seventh Street Grocery Store, Steelman's and Lott's soon complied with demands to hire black checkers. The owner of Steelman's Grocery Store, however, initially responded to requests to hire black clerks by saying that he would shut his store down before he'd hire a "nigger" to work for him. After a week of lost revenue and mounting prospects for losing more, not only did he hire Ms. Peggy Fluker as his first black clerk, he even attended a mass meeting one evening accompanied by boycott leader, the Reverend J.C. Killingsworth and tearfully asked the black community to forgive him for his years of racist behavior. As an historically forgiving people, we promptly did so. Soon black customers resumed shopping at Steelman's Grocery store and eventually other black clerks were hired.

Grocery store boycotts were different from boycotts of the buses and the downtown stores. With both the bus and downtown boycotts, the most effective and ultimately most successful strategy was simply to declare the stores and the buses off-limits for black trade. Nothing else was needed, no marches, pickets, or demonstrations, primarily because of the prolonged period of time expected to achieve the objectives of the boycott. Direct action like pickets and demonstrations required a tremendous number of people to consistently show up for picket duty over a relatively long period of time. Getting that type and level of participation from large numbers of truly committed black people was not at all a certainty. Moreover, such activities in white sections of town would have surely invited retaliation from some whites and created the types of violent confrontations in which we were likely to not prevail. Also, the likelihood of picketing being effective or even adding any pressure to the storeowners was very remote.

With grocery store boycotts, however, the tactic of placing picket lines at those sites was utilized because of the anticipated short duration of such boycotts. A relatively small number of people, 5-10, was needed for grocery store picket lines. I took my place on the picket lines at several of the locations. I put a sign around my neck and took my place within the group of other picketers. I felt I was making a difference, although there was no guarantee that the store owner would give a rat's behind if we were present or not. In addition, the picket lines were also visible reminders to the storeowner and customers alike that we were serious about achieving the goals of the boycott. Because of years of neglect and harassment from white grocery storeowners who never felt compelled to hire black workers, along with the lack of alternative grocery shopping for black customers, there was strong initial resistance to the boycott from both customers and owners. So, the picket lines were a visible reminder to customers and storeowners that nothing less than complete compliance with the terms of the boycott would be acceptable. Another factor in using pickets at grocery stores was that those stores were in the heart of the black community; and we felt relatively safe and considerably more emboldened to assert our economic and political influence.

An interesting subplot evolved during the boycott that was not common knowledge. Following the bus boycott and prior to the end of the downtown merchants boycott, four members of the Executive Committee of the local NAACP chapter felt very strongly that the bus boycott ended prematurely and that the leadership was too passive. The Reverend J.C. Killingsworth, Mrs. Daisy Harris (my mom), Mr. J.C. Fairley, and Mrs. Alice Fluker formed a new organization, The Forrest County Action Committee (FCAC) and took over what remained of the boycott, buoyed by strong community support. The president of the local NAACP chapter, Dr. C. E. Smith, strongly objected to the continuation of the boycott and to the maverick executive committee members' formation of the new organization. Feeling betrayed by these individuals, Dr. Smith suspended each of them from the executive committee claiming their conduct was not in the best interest of the NAACP. However, all refused to resign their positions in the chapter. In a letter to Mr. Roy Wilkins, Executive Director of the NAACP, dated January 11, 1968, Dr. Smith requested assistance from the National Office to back the suspension of the four nonconformists. In response to Dr. Smith's letter, Mr. Wilkins, in a letter to my mother dated January 25, 1968, informed her that she and the other three executive committee members in question were temporarily suspended and that a hearing would be held to take final action. She received an air-mail, special-delivery letter, dated February 8, 1968, from Mr. Gloster Current informing her that she was to appear at a hearing at St. Paul United Methodist Church, February 17, 1968, at 11:00 a.m. to respond to charges of "conduct inimical to the best interests of the NAACP." I attended the hearing, which was held in the church's basement. What I recall most about the hearing is that neither side gave an inch, and Mr. Current upheld the suspension of the executive committee members. Although this action caused a split in the Hattiesburg leadership of the civil rights movement, the ability of people to deal with differences allowed the movement to continue. Actions by James Earl Ray less than two months later, however, would do more to affect the civil rights movement than the rift between the NAACP and the FCAC.

Mass Meetings and the "Spirit"

Mass meetings were gatherings of movement supporters and participants to discuss boycott goals, strategies, and most importantly to foster and reinforce solidarity and commitment to those goals and strategies. Mass meetings were generally held every night in a church, especially during the summer months and when boycotts were in progress. Our chief means of advertising meeting sites and dates were word-of-mouth, passing out leaflets to people on the street, and in some instances, through church announcements. It was not unusual, however, for some black church leaders to refuse to make announcements and to refuse to allow meetings in their churches. Among some of the reticent black church leaders, there was justifiable fear that the Ku Klux Klan would bomb their sanctuaries if they showed support for the civil rights movement. Others, however, were ordered by powerful white opponents of the civil rights movement to refuse access to their churches by civil rights "radicals" and "agitators" or anyone else directly associated with the civil rights movement. Those particular church leaders, while deeply committed to their religious beliefs, failed to understand that the greatest radical and agitator the world has ever known, Jesus of Nazareth, charged all of us to resist evil in all its forms, to challenge injustices whenever and wherever we witness them, and to always be concerned for the least of these. Of course, many white Christians seemed not to heed that message either, as their positions on the issue of civil rights ranged from indifference to outright support of racial segregation. Perhaps the most poignant and most effective challenge issued to the white faith community came in Dr. King's famous *Letter from a Birmingham Jail*. In that famous treatise written April 16, 1963, from a Birmingham, Alabama, jail cell to a group of white clergymen in Birmingham who had publicly criticized him for leading efforts to end segregation in Birmingham, Dr. King challenged them most eloquently and effectively: *I have traveled the length and breadth of Alabama, Mississippi and all the other southern states. On sweltering summer days and crisp autumn mornings, I have looked at her beautiful churches with their lofty spires pointing heavenward. I have beheld the impressive outlay of her massive religious education buildings. Over and over again I have found myself asking: "What kind of people worship here? Who is their God? Where were their voices when the lips of Governor Barnett dripped with the words of interposition and nullification? Where were they when Governor Wallace gave the clarion call for defiance and hatred? Where were their voices of support when tired, bruised and weary Negro men and women decided to rise from the dark dungeons of complacency to the bright hills of creative protest?"*

Yes, these questions are still in my mind. In deep disappointment, I have wept over the laxity of the church. But be assured that my tears have been tears of love. There can be no deep disappointment where there is not deep love. Yes, I love the church; I love her sacred walls. How could I do otherwise? I am in the rather unique position of being the son, the grandson and the great-grandson of preachers. Yes, I see the church as the body of Christ. But, oh! How we have blemished and scarred that body through social neglect and fear of being nonconformists.

There was a time when the church was very powerful. It was during that period when the early Christians rejoiced when they were deemed worthy to suffer for what they believed. In those days the church was not merely a thermometer that recorded the ideas and principles of popular opinion; it was a thermostat that transformed the mores of society. Whenever the early Christians entered a town the power structure got disturbed and immediately sought to convict them of being "disturbers of the peace" and "outside agitators." But they went on with the conviction that they were a "a colony of heaven," and had to obey God rather than man. They were too God-intoxicated to be "astronomically intimidated." They brought an end to such ancient evils as infanticide and gladiatorial contests.

Things are different now. The contemporary church is often a weak, ineffectual voice with an uncertain sound. It is often the arch supporter of the status quo. Far from being disturbed by the presence of the church, the power structure of the average community is consoled by the church's silent and often vocal sanction of things as they are.

Although some of the black church leadership in Hattiesburg capitulated to the movement's opponents, most rank-and-file churchgoers did not. Ironically, one of the most ardent and consistent supporters of the civil rights movement in Hattiesburg was a tall, gangly, chain-smoking, white Catholic priest named Father Peter Quinn. This man truly heeded Christ's call to defend the rights of the poor and the oppressed. He maintained a high profile in Hattiesburg through his participation in marches, transportation of marchers, and his tireless devotion to black youth. Thanks to Father Quinn, the Catholic Youth Organization (CYO) was formed in the mid-1960s and quickly became a safe haven for the black youth of Hattiesburg to channel their creativity, energy, and emotions in positive directions. Often, for example, CYO headquarters and the Holy Rosary Catholic Church were pick-up and drop-off points for youth who participated in marches and demonstration. Father Quinn not only opened his church and CYO headquarters to the civil rights movement, he also made sure that transportation was not an obstacle to youth who wanted to participate in any of CYO's activities, whether a march, mass, or a dance. It was quite common to see Father Quinn driving his blue station wagon all around Hattiesburg, filled with young black men and women going off to some event. Father Quinn had a special gift of building a much needed bridge among rival youths who lived on different sides of town. Gangs were not generally prevalent in Hattiesburg during that era, but there were some rather serious rivalries and clashes between individuals who lived on opposite sides of town. Father Quinn possessed a God-given talent for bringing them together and engaging them in activities that focused their attention on their common foe rather than on each other.

Mass meetings were open to the public, regardless of race or color, though with very few exceptions, only black people attended them. The exceptions were local media representatives and white college students who were in Hattiesburg to assist with voter registration drives and with Freedom Schools in the summer of 1964. We were justifiably suspicious of the local media because of our belief that they were collaborators with local law enforcement and the infamous Mississippi Sovereignty Commission. They also tended to report negatively about the civil rights movement, and were curiously silent on the harsh conditions created by racial segregation in Hattiesburg. We regarded their silence as tacit, if not explicit, approval of those conditions.

I remember contributing to some cause for alarm the day of one of the mass meetings and in the process giving myself an up-close and personal encounter with a couple of Klansmen. On a hot but otherwise normal summer afternoon, my friend Benton and I were distributing leaflets to homes and to people on the streets publicizing a mass meeting for that evening, a task that we had performed many times. As the two of us were walking along the side of a dusty, gravel road, alternately kicking and throwing rocks, I began to notice the increasingly loud sound of a broken muffler that warned of an approaching vehicle from the rear. As I reached down to pick up another rock, I noticed that the decibel level of the car muffler was still very high but no longer rising, indicating that the vehicle was slowly coming to a stop. By the time I stood upright, I spotted two young, grungy-looking, ruddy-faced white men in an early model beat-up pick-up truck rolling slowly next to Benton and me. It did not take long for the two of us to realize that we were in a spot here, especially when we noticed a rebel tag prominently displayed on the truck's front bumper. We had always been warned by adults in the movement to be wary of vehicles that displayed the rebel flag. Invariably, that meant that the occupants or owners were Klansmen. Our sense of fear and trepidation began to grow even more as we noticed several rifles and shotguns hanging from the rear-window gun rack. Then, as though on a film director's command, the truck's forward motion and ours came to a sudden halt at the same time. The loud and uneven base sounds of the broken muffler suddenly began to become even more noticeable as they seemed to match beat-for-beat the rhythm and loudness of my very own heartbeat, which was racing like a frightened gazelle. Benton and I looked at each other and then at the two occupants of the KKK truck and our first thought was, yes, we could indeed outrun them, if we needed to. But we decided not to run. Instead, we stood defiantly and waited for them to say something; and they quickly obliged. "What you boys handing out, there? Gimme one o dem papers, boys, so we can know what you niggers up to." Then a long pause as the passenger spat some nasty, chewing tobacco toward my feet missing, thank God, by a couple of inches. "Some nigger meetin' you tellin people 'bout, ain't ya?" Although we should have known better, we gave them one of the leaflets. They then shifted their stares from the leaflet to the two of us, then to each other and finally back to the leaflet. They spent so much time staring at the leaflet and at each other that I began to wonder if they could actually read. Between the two of them, they soon figured that their first hunch was right – a nigger meetin', which they again said to us as they balled the leaflet up and threw it at us. They quickly sped away causing their rear wheels to kick up a cloud of dust and send rocks and gravel flying toward our already dusty, sweaty, and frightened bodies. As I fanned my face to clear away the dust, I was aware that Benton and I were either feeling especially brazen or experiencing a temporary leave of our senses. We knew to be wary and suspicious of white men in pick-up trucks, especially pick-ups displaying a rebel flag and shotguns. This was the first time Benton and I had come face-to-face with real, life Klansmen during our leaflet distributing detail. No doubt, on many previous occasions we had seen Klansmen, who could have as likely been dressed in police uniforms and two-piece suits as in grungy t-shirts and blue jeans.

Later, after realizing that we may have made a serious error in giving those white guys a leaflet, we told one of the adult leaders who was part of the security detail for mass meetings what we had done. He reminded us of what we had already reminded ourselves – that was not a smart thing to do! Those white guys in the truck now knew when and where we would be meeting and it was quite likely that they would show up and cause some problems. So, he reported our crazy action to the head of security, a former Green Beret, who along with several other men from Hattiesburg, were trained by the Deacons for Defense, the renowned Bogalusa, Louisiana-based civil rights self-defense organization. Naturally, he and his fellow sentinels increased their vigilance, but nothing happened that evening. The training that the men received from the Deacons for Defense helped to ease the fear, somewhat, of being caught off guard by some lunatic Klansman.

Protocol at mass meetings usually followed a set of well-established procedures: first, there would be the singing of several freedom songs, a stirring prayer, a speech or two, followed by some plan of action, a closing prayer, and finally, the traditional singing of We Shall Overcome. Regardless of the time or the place, no meeting ever started until the congregation sang several emotionally and spiritually uplifting freedom songs. Songs such as *Ain't Gonna Let Nobody Turn Me Round, Eyes on the Prize, Wade in the Water*, and *Oh Freedom* were among the favorites.

Some of my friends, my older brother James, and I had a special role during mass meetings. We always sat in the front pew, and when it was time for the meeting to begin we would receive a hand signal or a nod from one of the adult leaders. On cue, I joined my brother and my friends in a slow ascent from our seats. In sync, as though we had rehearsed it, we slowly pivoted and faced the congregation. The congregants would become silent as all eyes became fixed on us. Everyone knew the drill and anxiously anticipated what was to come next. With the nod of a head as the downbeat, my brother, my friends and I would begin singing a freedom song, a capella, of course. Although a little nervous at first, we would soon settle into a nice, relaxed and soulful rhythm. That rhythm would become more defined and more intense as soon as we saw the faces of the people in the congregation light up and heard their voices joining in with us. In the tradition of singing in the black church, everybody in the congregation intuitively knew when to stand and join in. What a beautiful sight – a throng of black bodies standing, singing, sweating, swaying from side to side and clapping to the self-propelling and unique rhythm that freedom songs produced. The first song might have been *Old Freedom –Oh, oh freedom! Oh, oh freedom! Oh, oh freedom, over me. Before I be a slave, I'll be buried in my grave, and go home to my Lord and be free, and be free!* The chorus and melody would be sung at least three times with alternating verses: *No more moaning! No more moaning! No more moaning! Before I be a slave.... There'll be singing! There'll be singing! There'll be singing! Before I be a slave... There'll be shouting! There'll be shouting! There'll be shouting! Before I be a slave....*

By the time we finished the first song, everyone had worked up a good sweat and had found the right key and pitch. My friends and I would quickly huddle and decide what to sing next so as not to lose that exhilaration and spirit of the moment. As we were caucusing, we could feel the electricity and excitement growing in the sanctuary. Shouts of "Amen!", "Yes, Lord!", "Have mercy!", and "Come on with it!" could be heard throughout the church. No one was sitting and no one was standing still. Hand fans, compliments of Hall Mortuary or Century Funeral Home, most of which were bent in the middle, also seemed to keep their own rhythm as everyone furiously fanned their hot, sweaty faces. It was highly emotional and represented the strongest tradition of black worship in the south. In fact, we were having church!

Typically, someone from the congregation would shout out a request for the next song, which always seemed to be one of my favorites: *Eyes on the Prize* or *Ain't Gonna Let Nobody Turn Me 'Round.* The lyrics and rhythm melded together to create a melody that invoked the sacred memory of our ancestors and reinforced our dogged determination to gain our freedom – *Keep your eyes on the prize and hold on, why don't you hold on. Hold on! Hold on! Hold on! Hold on! Keep your eyes on the prize, and hold on, why don't you hold on! Paul and Silas were laid in jail. They had no money to go their bail. When they began to shout, the jail door opened and they walked out. Keep your eyes on the prize and hold on, why don't you hold on. I never been to heaven, but I been told. The streets are silver and the gates are gold.*

As I looked out over the crowd, striking images and melodious sounds became firmly imprinted in my mind, forever. An ocean of black bodies – all shapes, sizes, and ages – short, tall, skinny, big, old, young, healthy, infirm – were moving and swaying to the rhythm and the a capella sounds of the freedom songs like a well-rehearsed gospel choir. Sweat dripped profusely from tired faces that showed the strain of living for so long with the indignities and abuses of racial segregation and second class citizenship; voices belted out cries for freedom that spoke directly to the Creator; and hands clapped and feet stomped in the tradition of the ancestors who used similar, rhythmic claps and stomps to communicate messages of hope and yearnings for freedom.

Then we would sing the final song, *Ain't Gonna Let Nobody Turn Me 'Round*. As with the previous songs, my friends and I would begin singing in unison and the congregation would quickly follow our lead. They would again match our key, rhythm, and pace, and together we would all experience an unexplainable euphoria that only comes from singing songs about the struggle for freedom. *Ain't gonna let nobody turn me round, turn me round, turn me round; ain't gonna let nobody turn me round, I'm gonna keep on-a walking, keep on-a talking, marching up to freedom land. The Mississippi River is deep and wide. I'll get my freedom on the other side. Ain't gonna let no billy clubs turn me 'round, turn me 'round, turn me 'round, ain't gonna let no billy clubs turn me round, I'm gonna keep on a-walking, keep on - talking, marching up to freedom land!*

Not only did freedom songs help put all of us in the right frame of mind and help us focus on why we were there, more importantly, they reminded us, once again, that the spirit of our ancestors and the spirit of God were with us. Now the meeting had officially begun! A pastor would offer a prayer to the Creator for courage, determination, and wisdom as we continued on our path to freedom. He would ask for forgiveness for the oppressor and strength for the oppressed. He would close by invoking the imagery of Moses leading his people to the Promised Land. You did it for Moses and the Israelites, Lord, and we know you can do it for us.

On occasions, there would be prominent civil rights activists and supporters present at some meetings, such as Ms. Fannie Lou Hamer, Mr. Charles Evers, Mr. James Farmer, and Ms. Denise Nicholas. After being introduced prior to discussion of any business, these guests would typically express their support and solidarity for our common struggle for freedom and encourage us to "keep on keeping on." Ms. Nicholas and Ms. Hamer, I recall, were both at a mass meeting one evening together at Bentley Chapel United Methodist Church; and their mere presence made a big impression on me, especially Ms. Hamer. A sharecropper from Ruleville, Mississippi, with very little formal education, Ms. Hamer was able to speak to people's hearts and minds with passion, compassion, and sound logic. She came to symbolize the challenges and the rewards of the civil rights movement, through her Herculean efforts to get black people registered to vote in Mississippi and her semi successful challenge of the all-white Mississippi Democratic Party at the 1964 Democratic National Convention (see page). Ms. Hamer weighed well over 180 pounds, stood barely 5 feet tall, had a gold front tooth that sparkled among the gleam of her other evenly shaped white teeth, a round dark brown face that always seemed to be peppered with tiny beads of perspiration. When she spoke, she did so with a great deal of emotion and eloquence that immediately captured my undivided attention. She began her talk by invoking the name of God and thanking Him for bringing her this far. She followed with profound and unforgettable words of encouragement, spoken with authentic, fiery emotion through a commanding baritone voice that brought me to the edge of my seat. Some of those words remain, even today, permanently etched in my mind: *The road to freedom ain't easy, y'all. It takes a lot of hard work and a lot of sacrifices. Sometimes you gets tired and you just want to give up. You gets sick and tired of marching, sick and tired of getting beat up, sick and tired of going to jail and just sick and tired of being sick and tired! But I'm reminded of the old lady who said, my feets is tired, but my soul is rested. So, I ain't worried 'bout resting. I'll get my rest when I cross the Jordan. I just want you to know Hattiesburg that Fannie Lou Hamer is with you and you already know that the Lord is with you too. And if the Lord is with you, you k now, it don't matter who's against you.* Before she could say, *God bless you, Hattiesburg!* the congregation erupted in a thunderous ovation. No one was sitting and nearly everyone was shouting, "Amen!" As I watched her wipe her sweaty brow and slowly take her seat, I knew I had just seen and listened to an extraordinary woman with a marvelous gift for moving people beyond their other- and self-imposed limitations and ensuring them that despite the uncertainty of the moment, everything's going to be okay. In 1988, when I was asked during an interview for the Kellogg National Fellowship Program to name three people who I would most like to be. The first person I named was Ms. Fannie Lou Hamer.

As the mass meeting continued, there was sure to be lots of talking, from the pulpit and from the pews. And the talking was usually productive, but not always harmonious. There would be calls for unity and solidarity; calls for less talk and more action; calls for more talk and less action; and invariably, disagreements over tactics. But at the end of the day, there was consensus, if not unanimity, relative to purpose, strategies and tactics. And always there were reminders that God was on our side; therefore whatever we did, He would certainly guide our thoughts and our actions.

The appeal for unity and solidarity was constant throughout every mass meeting. We knew, however, that not all black people supported the civil rights movement in Hattiesburg, for reasons ranging from personal fear to being sell-outs and Uncle Toms. Black people in the latter group were especially dangerous because they not only refused to actively participate and support the movement, they actively worked to undermine it. They would attend mass meetings and strategy sessions and report information back to hostile white groups, e.g., law enforcement (local, state and federal), city officials, and the notorious Mississippi Sovereignty Commission. Often Uncle Toms were either paid or threatened as an inducement to sell out the movement and to commit shameful acts of betrayal. Uncle Toms and sell-outs were not unique to our era and were not anomalous. We understood that such people had been around since slavery, engaging in egregious and despicable acts of betrayal. They are still active today and unfortunately will always have a presence. (For additional information regarding black and white opponents of the civil rights movement, go to the Mississippi Sovereignty Commission Archives mdah. state.ms.us/arrec/digital_archives/sovcom/scagencycasehistory.php.)

To effectively deter and respond to Uncle Tom-ish behavior in Hattiesburg and to fortify solidarity and unity within the movement, an entity known as the "Spirit" was created. I never knew for sure, and I never asked, whether the "Spirit" actually existed, but I knew it was effective. The "Spirit," *allegedly*, would visit someone known or thought to be an Uncle Tom or sell-out. During those visits, "discussions" were held and following the "discussions," the person would understand that he/she should fear the "Spirit" more than the hostile white groups to whom he/she was supplying information about the movement. Also, in instances in which an individual broke ranks with the movement and chose to shop at a grocery store that was being boycotted, the "Spirit" would relieve that individual of his/her groceries, ensure that the groceries would go to someone needy, and finally impress upon that individual that he/she would be wise to never do that again.

I remember during several mass meetings the Reverend J. C. Killingsworth, President of the Forrest County Action Committee, sponsor of the boycotts, would announce that he had in his briefcase the names of every Uncle Tom in Hattiesburg and the names of everyone who was known to have violated the boycott. He also announced that he was turning over those names to the "Spirit." He even said some of the Uncle Toms and boycott violators were present at the meeting and that he knew who they were. He threatened to expose them on the spot if they did not get up and leave immediately, which of course, never happened. Whenever Reverend Killingsworth spoke everyone listened. He had a very demonstrable, emotional, and fiery brand of preaching and speech making. His raspy, baritone voice was compelling, and boomed out above the crowd, sans microphone. Standing well over 6 feet tall, bald, with a perpetual look of defiance on his dark brown face, he was very convincing about turning over the names of Uncle Toms to the "Spirit," whether he was bluffing or not.

When he raised the brief case, we all stood, cheered and called for him to tell us who the Toms were. To heighten the excitement for most of us and to heighten the anxiety and fear for any Uncle Toms present, he said that instead it would be best if he just gave the names to the "Spirit." Most of us believed that "Killer," as we affectionately called him, , knew more about the "Spirit" than anyone else. In fact, most of us had some idea of who constituted the "Spirit," although no one ever openly asked or talked about it. We only knew that the "Spirit" was to be both feared and respected. In fact, there was this one black woman who intentionally chose to ignore a boycott of one of the targeted grocery stores after she was warned not to shop there. She proudly and defiantly announced to everyone on the picket line that she would shop and spend her money wherever she "damn well pleased and ain't nobody gon' tell me where I can go and come!" From her body language and her very courageous and blunt words, she clearly believed that those words had put an end to any further discussion or action on the matter. Well the "Spirit" believed otherwise and did not take too kindly to such defiant and uncooperative words and attitude. Well, I was told by someone who was familiar with the "Spirit" that she did indeed make it home okay, but that the "Spirit" saw to it that she did so without any of her bags of groceries. The "Spirit" gave the groceries to members of a needy family that was enduring the inconveniences and suffering caused by their support of the boycott. The defiant grocery shopper never returned to that store for the duration of the boycott.

Mass meetings always ended with a prayer. A pastor would thank God for bringing us this far. He would give thanks for our leaders, and ask that they be blessed with the strength and wisdom to lead. Keep us safe. Keep us strong. Keep us in your everlasting arms. At the close of the prayer, my brother, my friends and I reprised our role as song leaders. We took our places in front of the congregation, crossed our arms, and joined hands. We began moving and swaying from side to side. Everyone else did likewise. Soon a discernible rhythm emerged that matched the movements of the sways. In unison, we sang, *We Shall Overcome,* that revered and venerable song of praise and joy that ended every meeting. As we closed one round of singing, several phrases were substituted for the opening phrase, We Shall Overcome. Depending on the mood of the meeting, we might sing one additional phrase or as many as five before the song ended. A couple of the favorite phrases were: *Black and White Together* and *God Is on Our Side,* which were substituted for the phrase, *We Shall Overcome.* Sensing that it was time to end the singing, my cohorts and I at the front of the congregation would release our hands from their grips and unfold our arms. Everyone else followed our lead. Another meeting and another milestone in our fight for freedom had ended. It was time to go home and prepare ourselves for another day of struggle.

Deacons for Defense

Organizations like the Deacons for Defense were instrumental in instilling a sense of pride and self-sufficiency in the movement. It also engendered fear and resentment by some in the movement who thought that any effort to respond to violence with physical rather than soul force ran counter to the principles of nonviolence and civil disobedience.

The Deacons for Defense were organized to defend the black community from attacks by the Ku Klux Klan in Bogalusa and in other black communities that could not depend on the police for protection from Klan violence. Their goal was not confrontation. Instead, they emphasized self-protection within the framework of the law. Despite their philosophy of following legal guidelines, the FBI regarded them as a hate group that needed to be neutralized. In a memorandum to agents in 1967, the FBI encouraged agents to essentially do whatever they needed to do in order to destroy the Deacons for Defense and any other organizations the FBI regarded as subversive. The contents of the following memorandum illustrate the extent to which the government would go to undermine the civil rights movement and the individuals and organizations that supported it.

SAC, Albany   August 25, 1967
PERSONAL ATTENTION TO ALL OFFICES
Director, FBI
   1 - Mr. C. D. Brennan
COUNTERINTELLIGENCE PROGRAM 1 - Mr. Bland
BLACK NATIONALIST - HATE GROUPS 1 - Mr. Trainor
INTERNAL SECURITY   1 - Mr. B. A. Wells
   1 - Mr. C. W. Thompson
   1 - Mr. Ryan

Offices receiving copies of this letter are instructed to immediately establish a control file captioned as above, and to assign responsibility for following and coordinating this new counterintelligence program to an experienced and imaginative Special Agent well versed in investigations relating to black nationalist, hate-type organizations. The field office control file used under this program may be maintained in a pending inactive status until such time as a specific operation or technique is placed under consideration for implementation. The purpose of this new counterintelligence endeavor is to expose, disrupt, misdirect, discredit, or otherwise neutralize the activites (sic) of black nationalist, hate-type organizations and groupings, their leadership, spokesmen, membership, and supporters, and to counter their propensity for violence and civil disorder. The activities of all such groups of intelligence interest to this Bureau must be followed on a continuous basis so we will be in a position to promptly take advantage of all opportunities for counterintelligence and to inspire action in instances where circumstances warrant. The pernicious background of such groups, their duplicity, and devious maneuvers must be exposed to public scrutiny where such publicity will have a neutralizing effect. Efforts of various groups 2 - Atlanta   2 – Philadelphia 2 - Baltimore 2 – Phoenix 2 - Boston

   2 – Pittsburgh 2 - Buffalo   2 – Richmond 2 - Charlotte   2 - St. Louis 2 - Chicago   2 - San Francisco 2 - Cincinnati   2 - Washington Field Office 2 – Cleveland 2 - Detroit

   2 – Jackson 2 - Los Angeles 2 – Memphis 2 – Newark 2 - New Orleans 2 - New York

- END PAGE 1 of 3 -

Letter to SAC, Albany
RE: COUNTERINTELLIGENCE PROGRAM
BLACK NATIONALIST - HATE GROUPS

to consolidate their forces or to recruit new or youthful adherents must be frustrated. No opportunity should be missed to exploit through counterintelligence techniques the organizational and personal conflicts of the leaderships of the groups and where possible an effort should be made to capitalize upon existing conflicts between competing black nationalist organizations. When an opportunity is apparent to disrupt or neutralize black nationalist, hate-type organizations through the cooperation of established local news media contacts or through such contact with sources available to the Seat of Government, in every instance careful attention must be given to the proposal to insure the targeted group is disrupted and not merely publicized. Consideration should be given to techniques to preclude violence-prone or rabble-rouser leaders of hate groups from spreading their philosophy publicly or through various mass communication media.

Many individuals currently active in black nationalist organizations have backgrounds of immorality, subversive activity, and criminal records. Through your investigation of key agitators, you should endeavor to establish their unsavory backgrounds. Be alert to determine evidence of misappropriation of funds or other types of personal misconduct on the part of militant nationalist leaders so any practical or warranted counter- intelligenc (sic) may be instituted. Intensified attention under this program should be afforded to the activities of such groups as the Student Nonviolent Coordinating Committee, the Southern Christian Leadership Conference, Revolutionary Action Movement, the Deacons for Defense and Justice, Congress of Racial Equality, and the Nation of Islam. Particular emphasis should be given to extremists who direct the activities and policies of revolutionary or militant groups such as Stokely Carmichael, H. "Rap" Brown, Elijah Muhammad, and Maxwell Stanford. At this time the Bureau is setting up no requirement for status letters to be periodically submitted under this program. It will be incumbant (sic) upon you to insure the program is being afforded necessary and continuing attention and that no opportunities will be overlooked for counterlligence (sic) action.

This program should not be confused with the program entitled "Communist Party, USA, Counterintelligence Program, Internal Security - C," (Bufile 100-3-104), which is directed   *- END PAGE 2 of 3 -*

Letter to SAC, Albany
RE: COUNTERINTELLIGENCE PROGRAM
BLACK NATIONALIST - HATE GROUPS
against the Communist Party and related organizations, or the program entitled Counterintelligence Program, Internal Security, Disruption of Hate Groups," (Bufile 157-9), which is directed against Klan and hate-type groups primarily consisting of white memberships. All Special Agent personnel responsible for the investigation of black nationalist, hate-type organizations and their memberships should be altered to our counterintelligence interest and each investigative Agent has a responsibility to call to the attention of the counterlligence{sic} coordianator{sic} suggestions and possibilities for implementing the program. You are also cautioned that the nature of this new endeavor is such that under no circumstances should the existence of the program be made known outside the Bureau and appropriate within-office security should be afforded to sensitive operations and techniques considered under the program.

No counterintelligence action under this program may be initiated by the field without prior Bureau authorization. You are urged to take an enthusiastic and imaginative approach to this new counterintelligence endeavor and the Bureau will be pleased to entertain any suggestions or techniques you may recommend.

Clearly, the concern within the civil rights movement was not only for the actions of the Ku Klux Klan, but also given the hostility of the FBI and other law enforcement agencies, concern also had to be given to those who were sworn to uphold the law. This type of hostility directed at the civil rights movement and against law-abiding citizens by law enforcement organizations is what makes movies like *Mississippi Burning* so misleading as to the role of the FBI during the civil rights movement. That movie portrayed the FBI and its field agents as vigilant protectors of civil rights workers in Mississippi, as sincere in their efforts to find the murderers of James Chaney, Michael Schwerner, and Andrew Goodman in Philadelphia, Mississippi, in 1964, and as not in cahoots with local law enforcement to destabilize the civil rights movement. As evidenced in the aforementioned document, and known to most black people all along, many associated with the FBI, including Director of the FBI, J.Edgar Hoover, were fiercely opposed to the civil rights movement and did all they could to undermine it and its leaders.

Chapter 10

Mack Charles Parker and Clyde Kennard

No story about the legacy of segregation and racism in Hattiesburg and in southern Mississippi is complete without mention of Mr. Clyde Kennard and Mr. Mack Charles Parker. Although these two men had completely dissimilar roles in the civil rights movement in Hattiesburg and in southern Mississippi, both suffered the needless loss of their personal freedom and ultimately the needless loss of their lives.

In 1959, Mr. Parker was a 23-year-old military veteran (2 years in the army) who worked as a truck driver and lived in Lumberton, about 20 miles from Hattiesburg, with his mother, brother, sister, and nephew. He was arrested for the alleged rape of a white woman, Mrs. June Walters. The arresting officer, a Mississippi State trooper, offered his service revolver to Mrs. Walters' husband, Mr. Jimmy Walters and urged him to shoot Mr. Parker on the spot. Mr. Walters refused, saying his wife was uncertain about the rapist's identity. Three days before Mr. Parker was to stand trial, he was removed from his jail cell in Poplarville by a group of white vigilantes with the cooperation of the local police. A cruel irony of this case is that Poplarville was the summer home of former Mississippi United States Senator Theodore Bilbo. Senator Bilbo's claim to fame was his zeal in filibustering federal anti-lynching legislation and numerous bills to repatriate black citizens to Africa.

Driven by an insatiable lust for revenge, steeped in raw hatred, these self-appointed executioners dragged a screaming and pleading Mr. Parker by his feet down a long flight of concrete stairs as his head bounced like a basketball on each step. Ten days later, on April 25, 1959, his badly beaten body with a bullet hole in the heart was pulled from the Pearl River. The County Attorney condoned the lynching and vowed he would never prosecute anyone for what he regarded as a justifiable act of revenge. Reacting to the negative publicity resulting from the lynching, and not being content or even remorseful over the death of one black person, racist whites in Poplarville threatened to kill Mr. Parker's mother, Mrs. Liza Parker. She was forced to flee to California in fear for her life. En route to California she learned that her son's body had been found.

Curiously, according to my parents, a local white country western singer who had a weekly musical show on the local television station made an interesting remark on his show that proved to be eerily prophetic. Before Mr. Parker's body was pulled from the Pearl River, the balding, diminutive, aspiring country western singer, with a smile and a wink at the camera, warned his fishing buddies to avoid fishing in the Pearl River for a while because they might find more than fish. Naturally, no one ever confessed to and no one was ever charged with Mr. Parker's murder.

Mr. Clyde Kennard's place in Hattiesburg civil rights history is truly remarkable and points out the staggering Catch-22 situation a black person had in gaining college admission at a predominately white college in the south. Mr. Kennard attempted to enroll at Mississippi Southern College (now University of Southern Mississippi) several times from 1955 to 1959. Each time he attempted to enroll, his application was denied, technically because he could not produce the required letters of support from five Mississippi Southern alumni. Each letter, according to Dr. W. D. McCain, then President of Mississippi Southern College, should be from alumni who have known the applicant for at least two years and could vouch for his good moral character and fitness for candidacy for admission. Since no black Mississippi Southern alumni existed and it was highly improbable that any white alumni would write such a letter, Mr. Kennard was never allowed to enroll and remained stuck in an unending pattern of submitting his application only to be told that he was not qualified to enroll at Mississippi Southern. Throughout Mr. Kennard's many ordeals and efforts to enroll at Southern Miss, operatives of the Mississippi Sovereignty Commission were very active in creating strategies that would keep him from applying for admission. Zack J. Van Landingham was the Sovereignty Commission's agent in charge of investigating Mr. Kennard for being an "integration agitator." In a report sent to his superiors, Mr. Landingham stated the following (Source: Mississippi Sovereignty Commission Archives): ..."A negro committee composed of a negro preacher and several negro educators have agreed to contact Kennard for the purpose of getting him to withdraw his application and desist in his efforts to enter Mississippi Southern College..." Governor J. P. Coleman along with members of the Board of Trustees and members of the Sovereignty Commission conspired with local and state black educators and pastors to discourage Mr. Kennard in attempting to gain admission to the college. According to Commission records, several of the black educators were wary about cooperating with the Commission for fear of being labeled Uncle Toms by the black community. The local black educators were considered by the Commission to be primarily interested in negotiating a black junior college in exchange for their cooperation. Their position was, build us a college, and you never have to worry about black students wanting to attend a white college. Unbeknownst to those black educators, however, state education and political leaders were not the least bit interested in establishing such an institution.

After these tactics failed to dissuade Mr. Kennard, the Sovereignty Commission, it is believed, conspired with law enforcement and members of the business community in Forrest County to make an example of Mr. Kennard, once and for all. After returning to his car from one of his visits to the Admissions Office, on September 15, 1959, Mr. Kennard was arrested and charged with reckless driving and possession of illegal whiskey (stoop or stump liquor), although Mr. Kennard did not drink. Mississippi Sovereignty Commission documents released in 1998 would reveal what most black people believed all along – operatives of the Mississippi Sovereignty Commission actually planted the whiskey in Mr. Kennard's car. In any event, he was later released from jail. While returning to his home, he stopped at the local Farmers Co-op to purchase chicken feed. The Co-op clerk told him that his account had been closed; and therefore, he could not purchase the feed on credit. Not having sufficient cash to pay for the feed, Mr. Kennard returned to his home empty-handed. Later that night, while at home with his mother, Mr. Kennard heard noises outside his home and went to investigate. He saw several men tossing bags of chicken feed into his yard. Almost immediately and without warning, county deputies appeared on the scene, handcuffed him, placed him under arrest, and charged him with possession of five bags of stolen chicken feed. For this "crime," Mr. Kennard was convicted and sentenced to seven years at the State Penitentiary at Parchman. Mr. Medgar Evers, the State Field Secretary for the Mississippi NAACP reacted with outrage at the verdict and sentence. In an interview with the *Jackson Daily News*, he called the trial a mockery of justice because there was no evidence that Mr. Kennard committed a crime and that a sentence of seven years in prison was excessive. He further asserted that the harsh sentence was retaliation for Mr. Kennard's effort to enroll at Mississippi Southern College. For those comments, Judge Stanton Hall charged Mr. Evers with obstruction of justice and fined him $100 and 30 days in prison. With the aid of Attorney Jack Young, a black civil rights attorney in Jackson, Mr. Evers appealed his case to the Mississippi Supreme Court, which threw out the conviction, but labeled Mr. Evers' comments as false and ignorant. While in prison, Mr. Kennard was diagnosed with cancer and despite his grave condition, was required to perform hard labor, denied proper medical treatment, and denied visits from family members.

Upon hearing about the conditions under which Mr. Kennard was forced to live, Attorney Jack Young managed to get Mr. Kennard transferred to Baptist Hospital in Jackson for proper treatment for his cancer. In an unusual display of humanity and justice, state officials granted Mr. Kennard a full pardon while he was hospitalized. Actually, the sudden and unexpected display of humanity and justice would not have occurred at all had it not been for the courageous and timely efforts of Attorney Young and social activist and comedian, Mr. Dick Gregory, who had made Mr. Kennard' case a highly visible public crusade. In addition, the national black news media, particularly the *Pittsburgh Courier*, created enough negative publicity for the state of Mississippi through its coverage of Mr. Kennard's case that state officials had to do something. The truth of the matter was that state officials were more interested in public relations and avoiding another stinging rebuke from the rest of the nation than in freeing a wrongfully incarcerated black man. So, the pardon was as much an effort to preserve what was left of the State's sullied image as it was to perform an over-due humanitarian act.

Meantime, in Hattiesburg, the Reverend Johnny Cameron, a local civil rights leader, asked my father to accompany him to the State Mental Hospital at Whitfield to check on a patient and then to Baptist Hospital in Jackson to check on Mr. Kennard. As they arrived at Baptist Hospital, Mr. Medgar Evers, who would be slain a few months later, was there to drive Mr. Kennard to Hattiesburg. Reverend Cameron asked if he and my father could have the honor of driving him home, since they were returning to Hattiesburg. Mr. Kennard and Mr. Evers agreed. The three of them, with a full police escort, drove the 90 miles back to Hattiesburg. News reports indicated that two "Negro" ministers were bringing Mr. Kennard back; however, only one of the "Negroes" was actually a minister. Later, Mr. Kennard was taken to the University Hospital in Chicago and died July 4, 1963 at the age of 38. In 1990, the Mississippi Supreme Court cleared Mr. Kennard of all charges.

Mr. Kennard's intellectual astuteness and his ability to eloquently state his case for equality is contained in a letter to the editor of the *Hattiesburg American* that he wrote December 6, 1958, following repeated attempts to enroll at Mississippi Southern College. Excerpts from that letter are as follows: *As the public schools are the essential organs for general intellectual discipline, and the preparation for private life and public service, let us superimpose the plan of separate but equal on the public school system. It is my understanding that separate but equal means that in matters where public funds are involved every time a dollar is spent for the development of Negro students, a dollar will be spent for the development of White students, and vice versa.*

This plan is to be followed through Junior college, Senior college, medical schools, law schools, divinity schools, graduate schools and all supported by public funds. After our paralleled graduate schools, where do our parallels of separate but equal go? Are we to assume that paralleled hospitals are to be built for the two groups of doctors? Are we to build two bridges across the same stream in order to give equal opportunities to both groups of engineers? Are we to have two courts of law so as to give both groups of lawyers the same chance to demonstrate their skills; two legislatures for our politically inclined, and of course two governors?

The folly of such a conclusion is perfectly obvious. Yet, the question remains, what is to become of the doctors who are not allowed to treat their patients in public hospitals? What will the engineers do when there are no roads or bridges for them to build? How must the lawyers occupy their time when the state courts restrict their opportunities to practice? How shall young statesmen, who can't even get their names on the ballot, ever hope to be elected to the legislature?

We say that if a man is a good doctor though his face be white as light or black as darkness let him practice his art. We believe that the best engineer should build the bridge or run the train. We believe that the most efficient should get the best paying job and the greatest scholar the professorship. We believe in the dignity and brotherhood of man and the divinity and fatherhood of God, and as such, men should work for the upbuilding of each other, in mutual love and respect. We believe when merit replaces race as a factor in character evaluation, the most heckling social problem of modern times will have been solved.

Thus we believe in integration on all levels from kindergarten to graduate schools; in every area of education; in government, federal, state, local; in industry from the floor sweeper to the superintendent's office; in science from the laboratory to the testing ground.

This, I believe, is our creed. And though it is not perfect, still I had rather meet my God with this creed than with any other yet devised by human society.

Respectfully submitted, Clyde Kennard, RFD1, City

Although Mr. Kennard never succeeded in enrolling at the University of Southern Mississippi, his martyrdom would eventually play a major role in the matriculation of thousands of black students at USM, and he will be forever noted in the annals of USM's history. An administration building on the campus now bears his name, along with the name of Dr. Walter Washington, former President of Alcorn State University, and the first black person to receive a Ph.D. degree from USM.

Chapter 11

Public School Segregation and Desegregation

One of the South's most enduring legacies and its most notorious testament to how segregation became so institutionalized was the legalized system of racially segregated public schools. Despite its blatant immorality, racial segregation was based, legally, on the *Dred Scott Decision*, in 1857 in which the U.S. Supreme Court ruled 7-2 that a black person, whether free or slave, had no rights as a citizen, and therefore could not sue for his freedom as Mr. Scott had attempted to do. The Court "reasoned" that slaves were like cattle, with no civil or human rights and were the possession of their owner. Also, in *Plessey v. Ferguson*, the U.S. Supreme Court ruled in 1896 that operating separate facilities for blacks and whites was legal as long as the facilities were equal. Based on such inane rulings as those in *Plessey v. Ferguson* and *Dred Scott*, Southern states were able to codify their belief in white supremacy and to reinforce their long-established practice of racial segregation by enacting racist, but at the time, legal, state and local ordinances and statutes. Even with such an unjust ruling, most public facilities in the south were, in fact, separate and unequal.

In 1954, the *Brown v. Topeka Board of Education* decision nullified the *Plessey* ruling, and required public entities to abandon the separate but equal doctrine and to do so with all deliberate speed. Given the practices of delay, interposition, resistance, and defiance of the law of the land, it seemed that all deliberate speed in the south meant slow speed or no speed. Although the *Brown* decision applied to all public entities, public schools were most affected by the U.S. Supreme Court's dramatic decision that began to theoretically dismantle legally sanctioned racial segregation.

Following the *Brown* decision, many areas of the south simply chose to ignore the Supreme Court's ruling, as though it never happened. In fact, many school systems in the south went so far as to repeal their compulsory school attendance laws. The clear message in repealing such laws was that school officials would rather children not go to school at all than have them go to a racially mixed school. Hattiesburg was no exception.

The City of Hattiesburg, for 12 years following the Brown decision, maintained a dual and unequal school system, one for white students and one for black students. To make matters worse, Hattiesburg school administrators and members of the school board not only illegally maintained separate schools for black students and white students, they consciously and intentionally attempted to ensure that the quality of the white schools was superior to that of black schools. It was common practice, for example, for black students to be issued used, worn-out, and outdated textbooks that were handed down from white students after they received brand new textbooks. The same was true for science laboratory equipment, desks, chairs, tables, band instruments, football equipment and office equipment. Separate? Yes. Equal? No.

In the tradition of establishing and preserving racially segregated schools, Hattiesburg maintained 6 all-black schools – Rowan High, Lillie Burney Junior High, W. H. Jones Elementary and Junior High, Eureka Elementary, Mary Bethune Elementary, and Grace Love Elementary. I attended Mary Bethune for my elementary grades and spent my first year of junior high (7th grade) at Lillie Burney Junior High School. There were eight all-white schools: Thames Elementary and Junior High, Woodley Elementary, Jeff Davis Elementary, Camp Elementary, Grace Christian Elementary, Eaton Elementary, Hawkins Junior High, and Hattiesburg High.

Not only were all 14 public schools racially segregated; the black schools were intentionally and systematically neglected by the school district administration for decades. Neglect typically came in the form of inequitable allocation of resources, whereby the white schools received their usual lion's share of local and state resources and black schools, of course, had to pick up the scraps. It was quite common for black students to have obviously used and worn textbooks that had the name of one of the white schools stamped on the inside cover.

Despite such neglect, the black community of Hattiesburg was extremely proud of its schools. In fact, black schools were not just brick and mortar. Instead, they, along with the Church, formed the spiritual, intellectual and cultural epicenter of the community, producing numerous outstanding leaders and professionals in the fields of law, medicine, ministry, music, education, and athletics. These two institutions also gave birth to and nurtured long-standing traditions that fortified community bonds and enriched the quality of life. These traditions were as important to the spirit and solidarity of the community as Easter Egg Hunts, 4th of July picnics and high school commencements.

One of my favorite traditions was the weekly Friday night football game between the Tigers of Rowan High School and one of the other highly talented teams from the Negro Big Eight Conference. Teams from such towns as Greenville, Greenwood, Jackson, Brookhaven, McComb, Natchez, and Laurel would provide football fans – black and white – enormous excitement and entertainment that would be talked about for days. Players such as Harold Jackson, Marvin Woodson, Don Williams, Bobby Ray Thompson, Taft Reed, Eugene Barnes, Eddie Pope, Tank Walker, Wayne Thames, Alfred Hall, Excell Moore, and Willie Townes were some of the most well-known and talented football players of that era. Arguably, Bobby Ray Thompson was the best football player to ever play football in Hattiesburg.

There were several very intense football rivalries that always generated extra excitement, regardless of won-loss record; and more often than not, the game was for bragging rights or for outright ownership of the Negro Big Eight State Championship. Chief among those rivalries was the annual clash between Rowan High of Hattiesburg and Oak Park High of Laurel, located 30 miles north of Hattiesburg. Because of the proximity of the two cities, the game took on extra meaning and the hype surrounding the game always made it the hottest topic of conversation weeks before and after the game. The battle between Rowan and Oak Park was always more than a contest between two excellent football teams competing for the state championship or for bragging rights. It was also as much a contest between residents of two cities who did not have any special fondness for each other. Deep animosity existed between Laurel and Hattiesburg from decades of heated rivalries in track, football and basketball. This animosity and the intensity of the rivalry between the schools and the towns invariably produced not only unforgettable action on the field during the game, but also there was just as much unforgettable action off the field, during and after the game. Regardless of whether the game was played in Laurel or in Hattiesburg, there would always be a fight, involving fans and players from each school. In contrast to the all too often violent and deadly encounters in schools today, the clashes during that time involved nothing more than heated words and a few fisticuffs. Fans of the losing team felt honor-bound to exact some revenge by throwing eggs at players from the winning school and rocks at the winning school's band bus.

There was also less violent mischief that always took place just before and just after the beginning of the game. Although admission to a football game was no more than $.50, it just seemed to be an irresistible challenge for some of us youngsters to try to get into the stadium without paying. In fact, it was considered a distinct honor to come up with the most creative means of avoiding detection by vigilant school officials and security officers. One of the more creative means of avoiding detection was to march undetected into the stadium with the marching band, cleverly tucked between the tubas and the bass drums. The most frequently used means of "sneaking" into a game, however, was to crawl underneath a cyclone fence at the north end of the football stadium. To do so, however, one needed the assistance of at least two accomplices – one to serve as a lookout and the other one to hold up the bottom section of the fence high enough to make it easy to slide belly down or belly up underneath the fence. Once the person made it inside the stadium, he stealthily ran along the perimeter of the fence, avoiding direct light, and finally eased himself into the flow of the crowd that was milling around or standing in line at the concession stand. It was always easy to tell who sneaked into the stadium. If there were a wide streak of dirt on the front or backside of someone who was otherwise wearing clean clothes, it was safe to assume that he did not pay to get into the stadium. After some strong urging from my cousin Billy Earl before the start of a game one night, I ended up with a streak of dirt on the front of my clothes. I never attempted it again. I was too afraid of getting caught and getting my behind whipped by my dad.

Another of my favorite pre-desegregation traditions was the annual Thanksgiving Day parade. Few events in black Hattiesburg could generate as much excitement, anticipation, and cooperation as preparing for, participating in, and watching the Turkey Day parade. The parade would consist of numerous beautifully decorated floats and cars, along with several high-stepping marching bands from area black high schools, black colleges, and the local black elementary schools. There was also the added excitement of seeing Miss Rowan High School, riding in a car elaborately decorated with glitter, crepe paper, and colorful, shiny, streaming ribbons strewn the length of the car. At the parade in 1960, I was especially proud of the titleholder who sat so majestically atop the back seat of a shiny red Ford convertible, waving in typical queenly fashion to the throngs of admirers, friends, and family, who enthusiastically and eagerly returned her royal wave and hand-thrown kisses. This talented beauty queen who gave me so much pride was my cousin, Barbara King, crowned Miss Rowan High after some tough competition in the annual high school pageant. The term queen was so fitting for her. She was smart, well liked, friendly, talented, and drop-dead gorgeous. She epitomized grace, elegance, and humbleness. In fact, all those qualities still apply today!

While keeping a prideful eye on the attention Barb was commanding, I had another weighty detail to which I had to give the remainder of my attention. I had the distinct honor of being one of two banner carriers for Mary Bethune Elementary School's drill team and rhythm band. Being a banner carrier was a really big deal. We were selected by a group of teachers who thought we best represented the school, supposedly through our exemplary behavior and good grades. However, given the times we lived in when the whole colorism thing was in vogue, I now suspect that our selection as banner carriers had more to do with our light skin tone than with good grades or laudable comportment. Nevertheless, it was fun but very exhausting walking the several miles from one side of town to the other.

My fellow banner carrier and I were always told how cute we looked in our bright red pants, freshly starched long-sleeve white button-down collar shirts, and freshly polished white sneakers. We were like proud sentinels leading a conquering band of soldiers through narrow, crowded streets, proudly clutching the rectangular-shaped white silk banner that announced the name of the school and band in bright red block-shaped letters.

The parade would begin at Eureka Elementary School, snake its way through downtown and finally end at Rowan High School, followed by a competitive and entertaining daytime football game. The Thanksgiving Day Parade was the highlight of the fall season and a source of immense community pride for parade participants and spectators. Regrettably, with the beginning of desegregated schools, this hallowed annual tradition came to a screeching halt in Hattiesburg.

School Desegregation

Not so regrettable, however, was the impending demise of legalized school segregation in Hattiesburg. Jim Crow's grip on the Hattiesburg Separate School System officially began in the Fall of 1966, the first year for the implementation of the desegregation plan known as Freedom of Choice, which ostensibly, was created to achieve racial balance in the schools on a voluntary basis. Five young teenage children -- James Hicks, Aljorie Clark, Velisa Clark, Benton Dwight, and Anthony Harris enrolled at W. I. Thames Junior High School and became the first black students in the history of the Hattiesburg Separate School System to attend a racially desegregated public school. For James, Benton, and me, the decision to enroll at Thames Junior High School and to become trailblazers for school desegregation came about in similar ways and for similar reasons. One day in May 1966 near the end of the 7th-grade year at Lillie Burney Junior High, each junior high student, except 9th graders, was given a Freedom of Choice Form on which we were to indicate our school preference for the next year. The choices were W. H. Jones Junior High, Lillie Burney Junior High, W. I. Thames Junior High, and Hawkins Junior High. The latter two were predominantly white schools. James,

Benton, and I talked the same day about which school we wanted to attend for the eighth grade. The three of us were close friends and we wanted to be together in the same school. Moreover, we were actively involved in the movement through several years of active participation in marches, boycotts, Freedom School, voter registration drives and leading freedom songs at mass meetings and passing out leaflets advertising mass meetings.

It seemed only natural, then, that the next step in that struggle would be for the three of us to step up to the plate and knock down one of the last vestiges of legalized racial segregation in Hattiesburg. We just hoped that our parents would give their consent. I took the form home to my mother and told her that I wanted to attend W. I. Thames next year and that James and Benton also were planning to do the same. Being the civil rights warrior that she was, she immediately signed the form as did Benton's and James' parents. Mr. and Mrs. Clark, who both taught in Hattiesburg, pretty much decided for Aljorie and Velisa that they would attend W. I. Thames Junior High. Actually, Velisa went to W. I. Thames Junior High primarily because her parents did not want her sister Aljorie to go alone. Mr. and Mrs. Clark were especially courageous in enrolling Velisa and Aljorie in W. I. Thames Junior High, because school district administrators highly discouraged and even threatened with termination any school employee who participated in the civil rights movement. Stepping out on the shaky limb of school desegregation and enrolling their daughters in an all-white school could have very easily caused Mr. and Mrs. Clark to be fired from their jobs. However, being the owners of a successful funeral home business, Mr. and Mrs. Clark were able to take risks that most of their colleagues could not. Plus, I do not think that Mr. Clark was easily intimidated by anyone. I was a student in his 7th-grade English class at Lillie Burney Junior High School; and he is the one who did the intimidating.

Benton, Aljorie, and I entered the 8th grade and Velisa, the 9th grade. Among the five of us, Velisa was the most isolated and, by necessity, the most courageous. Because her classes were in a different section of the school and because of the extreme ostracism she experienced, Velisa did not have the opportunity to interact with any of the rest of us or with any friendly white classmates during school hours. In contrast, the four of us eighth graders were able to occasionally see and talk to each other and experience welcomed, albeit, intermittent episodes of comfort and reassurance. The level of ostracism, isolation, and neglect that Velisa experienced was far greater than what we eighth graders experienced, although she never suffered any physical violence. Such treatment by her white classmates required her to be exceptionally strong and courageous in order to persevere; and she did a remarkable job of persevering throughout high school, college, and graduate school, eventually becoming a college professor. On April 23, 1992, an intruder murdered Aljorie, who had become a U.S. Postal worker in Paulina, Louisiana. After high school, James moved to Atlanta, Georgia, and worked for a major airline carrier. Benton eventually became a pharmacist.

During the two years I spent at W. I. Thames Junior High School, I was routinely subjected to racially motivated acts of hostility – some unbearable and some less so. Being called a nigger was an everyday occurrence. In fact, one white classmate, in trying to explain to one of his friends the difference in my skin color and Benton's, once referred to my light skin color as Anthony-nigger black, and to Benton's dark skin as Benton-nigger black.

Two memorable events occurred which, in many ways, perfectly captured the cold-hearted resistance to the *Brown* Decision by those who were unwilling to accept the impending demise of school segregation and white supremacy. One event occurred while I was walking alone to class on what started out as a rather routine day. Being alone and isolated was the norm for the five of us, except for those rare instances when some of us would have lunch or a class together. As I was strolling in my typically slow fashion to my class, one of my bigoted white classmates decided he would very crudely and publicly show his contempt for my presence in his school. With other white students looking on, he just hauled off and spat on me as I passed him in the corridor. This big nasty glob of spit landed square on the upper part of my pant leg, even though he was aiming much higher. Although I knew to expect almost any type of brutal treatment from hostile white students, being spat on was totally unexpected and downright disgusting. The spitter and the other white students paused and, while continuing to taunt, jeer and laugh, watched to see what my reaction would be. To their surprise and probably disappointment as well, I chose not to retaliate with violence or with spitting, although I was plenty angry. I was feeling extremely humiliated and vulnerable after having gone through such an embarrassing and threatening experience. No one was there to intervene. No one was there to tell them to stop. Instead I was alone and outnumbered. I was not sure what I should do next. Follow my heart or my head. Stay and fight back or walk away. Because of the humiliation I was experiencing I just wanted to get out of there and find some safe haven that did not exist. I did not consider going to the principal's office because I knew that would do no good.

Although I felt hurt, embarrassed and angry, my reaction was not at all what the unfeeling perpetrators of this ugliness expected at all. Instead of hitting or spitting, I proceeded to the nearest restroom, took a paper towel, wiped what remained of the spit from my pant leg, and went on to my next class. However, with every step I took toward that class and away from those jerks, I kept reminding myself to be strong, to not show any signs of intimidation, and for God's sake, to not give in to the temptation to go back and knock one of them upside the head.

Even with the justified anger and the desire to escape the humiliation of the moment, the choice not to retaliate with violence was actually an easy one. All five black students at Thames Junior High and our parents believed very strongly that it was important for us to prove to everyone, especially the bigots in Hattiesburg that black and white kids could indeed go to school together. If any of the five of us had responded to violence and insults with our own insults and acts of violence, the bigots would have been proven right in their irrational and wrongheaded thinking that blacks and whites cannot coexist and that black and white students should not attend school together. We knew that if hostile whites wanted the five of us removed from Thames Junior High, provoking violent reactions from us would be the perfect strategy. If each of us could be coaxed into reacting violently to their racial insults and attacks, chances were good that one-by-one we would have been expelled or transferred to all-black Lillie Burney Junior High School. Nevertheless, we were able to resist the temptation to strike back when faced with words and actions spurred on by racial hatred from some of our white classmates. To our credit, we all chose to adhere to the principles of nonviolence, which unequivocally and unconditionally require one to avoid the temptation to respond to violence with violence. My own ability to keep my eyes on the prize and to remain faithful to the principles of nonviolence came (and continues today) in daily reminders of a sobering message by Dr. King: *If, as a nation, we continue to follow the retaliatory notion of an eye for an eye; tooth for a tooth, we will end up being a blind, toothless society.*

I often ask young black children today what they would have done had it been they who were spat on. Almost always, the unanimous answers are, "Hit him" or "Spit back," or worse. Regrettably, I find it increasingly difficult to persuade young people to accept the principle of nonviolence and to choose more constructive means of resolving conflict, whether the conflict is interracial or intraracial. My sense of regret is not only for the emotional and physical hurt caused by wanton violence, but also for the total disregard of the teachings of Dr. King, especially by those who claim to honor his memory.

The second event at Thames Junior High that typified white hostility and hatred toward black students was my having to listen to the cheers and celebration from my classmates, on Friday April 5, 1968, the day after Dr. King was assassinated. I was the only black student in a class of maybe forty white students. Except for the spitting incident, until that moment, I had never felt as tormented, as alone, and as friendless. I sat stoically in my seat, facing the teacher's empty desk, and intentionally avoided eye contact with my callous classmates. The teacher was out of the room at the time, which undoubtedly added to my classmates' sense of freedom to behave so insensitively. I was immersed in my sorrow and did not want to be bothered. I tried to block out the sickening sounds of celebration coming from all directions in the classroom, piercing my brain and my heart. I did not want to speak to anybody and I did not want anybody to speak to me. All I could think was, how ironic -- a great man, a man of peace who faithfully followed the teachings of Christ -- *love your enemies, pray for those who misuse you, and when a man strikes you on one cheek, turn and give him the other to strike* -- had been killed in such a violent and cowardly fashion. What is America coming to? Why do we slay our leaders? I thought. These thoughts led me to recall the night Dr. King came to Hattiesburg and how happy I was that I had the opportunity to see him and to listen to his magnificent oratory. The contrast in that feeling of happiness and the present feelings of overwhelming sadness, pain, and emptiness brought tears to my eyes, tears that I tried so desperately, albeit, unsuccessfully to conceal from my classmates.

The solemnity of my thoughts about Dr. King and my ability to block out the celebratory sounds of my classmates were suddenly interrupted when one classmate from the other side of the room yelled to one of his friends, "Hey, Tom. Nice aim. Good shot. How did you get from Memphis so quickly?" Then another one chimed in, "Hey, Billy. The King is dead. Yeah!" Those and other equally hurtful remarks were repeated over and over for what seemed like an eternity. The remarks were intentionally directed toward me and at a decibel level that ensured that I heard each ugly word. I felt helpless to stop them. They were forty and I was only one. How can anybody be so joyful at a time like this? What kind of sick, demented minds could find reasons to celebrate the death of another human being, let alone the death of Dr. King? To pass their insensitive behavior off as typical, junior-high callousness and rudeness was dreadfully wrong. No! Their remarks went deeper and further than childish, pubescent immaturity. Their words were full of hatred that had been handed down to them from generations past. They were parroting and mirroring the same, cold, calculating racist remarks and feelings they learned from their parents! Bottom line, they were glad that Dr. King was dead, and I was sad about it. The gulf between our worldviews, cultures and races seemed even greater than ever. One tragic event, and two distinct responses – gladness and sadness. After what seemed like hours of listening to an unending torrent of insulting and hurtful remarks, I felt some relief when the teacher, Mrs. Wisler finally walked into the classroom. They did seem to get noticeably quieter when she walked in, but the snickering and laughter continued anyway. Apparently, she had heard some of the remarks as she walked in, and in a tone of voice that evidenced incongruence with her words, told them to hold down the noise and to not be so insensitive. Her words did not provide the solace I was so desperately hoping for, but they did bring a halt to the insults. I did not believe for one moment, however, that her words would make one bit of difference in how she or any of the other whites in that classroom or in the entire school felt about Dr. King. I felt that they hated him and were relieved that he was dead. As I sat there stewing in my anger and hurt, my mind easily flowed back to that contrastingly wonderful night, less than a month earlier, when I had the unforgettable privilege of seeing Dr. King in person at Mt. Zion Missionary Baptist Church. His life, his voice, his physical being were seared into my brain, as I struggled to find a place in my head and heart that made sense of all this madness. I found a bit of solace, not from my teachers and certainly not from my classmates. I found that elusive solace by actually concentrating on Dr. King's life, not on his death. It also helped, at least for the moment, to concentrate on March 19, 1968 - , and not of April 4, 1968. My thoughts went along this path: Dr. King's life and death affected most Americans in very profound ways. A man with a unique gift of selfless commitment to human rights, he was a godsend. Without his amazing ability to inspire, to motivate, and to lead, the civil rights movement would not have achieved the successes it did. Looking back, one of the things I admire most about Dr. King is that he spoke with a consistent voice on the issue of violence. Not only did he oppose violence in the south and in the ghettos of the north, but also he was one of the first national leaders to oppose the United States' involvement in the Vietnam War. In taking such a bold and controversial stand on the war, he was severely rebuked and roundly criticized by many of the same political leaders who supported his civil rights efforts, but thought he had inappropriately crossed over into an area in which he had no business. Amazingly, as time passed, many of the same critics came to see just how right Dr. King was in opposing the Vietnam War. His moral compass was always pointed in the direction of sustaining humanity, not in destroying it.

Dr. King expressed his views on war and violence in a speech titled *Beyond Vietnam: A Time to Break Silence* that he delivered at the Riverside Church in New York, April 4, 1967, exactly one year before his death. In that speech, Dr. King was typically eloquent in his oratory, and near the end of that speech he issued a very eerie and prophetic warning: *We still have a choice today; nonviolent coexistence or violent co-annihilation.*

For those of us who had the opportunity to actually see Dr. King and to listen to his great oratory, his death was as painful as his life was inspiring. Months before his death, many of us in Hattiesburg received a wonderful blessing by actually seeing this great leader and hearing his magnificent words. On March 19, 1968, through word of mouth on the streets and on telephones, information quickly circulated around Hattiesburg that Dr. King would be making an appearance at the Mt. Zion Baptist Church. Mr. Benton Dwight, Sr. was the individual who was most responsible for arranging for Dr. King's visit to Hattiesburg. Dr. King was scheduled to arrive at 6:30 p.m. and the church had been completely filled hours before. As the time came for his arrival, he was not there. Several hours passed, and he was still missing. Because of the many threats on his life and given the reputation of Mississippi Klansmen, I began to fear that something had happened to him. To my relief, he finally arrived around midnight accompanied by Dr. Ralph David Abernathy; and the church was just as crowded at midnight as it was at 6:30.

I was completely mesmerized by Dr. King's physical presence as I seared into my mind everything about this moment and this man. Like a sharply focused laser beam, my attention was zeroed in on his relatively small stature, his well-fitted, green, two-piece suit, and his white French-cuff shirt perfectly accessorized with a green necktie. More memorable than what he was wearing or his physical stature was the charisma and energy he seemed to so effortlessly exude. There he was, not more than twenty feet from me. Dr. Martin Luther King, Jr. The great orator, the courageous leader of the civil rights movement, and winner of the Nobel Peace Prize was standing at the mustard-colored pulpit before a massive sea of black humanity, sharing the humidity, the heat, and the hallelujahs. He spoke to the assembled denizens for perhaps thirty minutes, but no one was timing his speech. As far I was concerned, his speech lasted hours. While I have little recollection of his exact words, I am confident that he posited words of encouragement. I am certain that he encouraged us to keep the dream alive, to keep the faith, and to keep our eyes on the prize. What I do remember is that he delivered his message in a deeply moving manner. His intonation, his vocal variety, his energy, and his rhythm and pace all melded to produce a classic MLK speech. The standing ovations and the hearty shouts of *Amen* punctuated his speech from beginning to end. And when the end finally came, no one wanted to leave. I had gotten what I had wanted and needed from this historical moment, so I was ready to leave. I came for inspiration, motivation, and affirmation that the struggle for equality and justice had been worth it. The fact that the next day was a school day and that I was up way past my bedtime made no difference to me. I left Mt. Zion Missionary Baptist Church in the wee hours of the morning in possession of a precious gift – a gift of moments – moments that would inspire and motivate me for the rest of my life.

Blair High School

The two years I had spent at W. I. Thames Junior High School were emotionally very troubling, although academically I was pleased with my efforts, if not always with the outcome. Following the end of the school year in 1968, I gave serious consideration to retreating from the racist assaults and insults that I had endured the previous two years and immersing myself in total blackness by opting to attend Rowan High School. In a span of two short years, I had been spat on, routinely threatened, laughed at, insulted, ignored, shunned, and regarded by some white teachers as undeserving of any grade higher than a C, all because of my race. I was an oddity to them. I was not from their side of town. I did not attend their churches. I was not a member of their scout troops. I was not in their cliques. I was not in their social or economic class. On the other hand, I spoke their language, had similar physical features, wore matching store-bought shoes and socks, and wore clean pressed clothes. I took a bath every day, wore deodorant, and kept my hair neat. Yet, in their eyes, I was their intellectual and social inferior. They failed to see our common characteristics, our common humanness. Instead, they were able to see only my skin color, and concluded that the amount of melanin in my skin would be the one and only determinant of my worth, dignity, and intellectual abilities. In fact, to some of my white classmates and teachers, I might as well have been from another planet, someone who did not belong in their schools or in their presence. In their twisted way of thinking, I was someone who easily albeit erroneously reinforced their sense of superiority. So, I was fed up. I was fed up with the insults. I was fed up with being considered less intelligent because of my race. I was fed up with white teachers who had low expectations of me, only because of my race. Regretfully, I was growing tired of the struggle – the struggle for respect, the struggle for fairness, and the struggle for acceptance. So, I wanted desperately to retreat to some place where I would not have to daily calculate where to walk, where to sit, where to eat, or when to avoid going to the bathroom. I just wanted to get out of that hell hole and try to reclaim some peace of mind that had eluded me for two years. I knew that if I attended Rowan High School, I would avoid racist and nasty treatment by black classmates and black teachers. I would have been able to hang out with my neighborhood friends and would have had the distinct pleasure of learning from those wonderful black high school teachers who approached teaching with the same loving attitude and feelings shown by those great black women who taught me in elementary school. However, I also knew that if I had selected the path of least resistance and enrolled at Rowan High School, I would have betrayed the cause of ridding Hattiesburg of one of the few remaining vestiges of racial segregation. Although serious, such thoughts and feelings about attending Rowan High School turned out to be only temporary responses to the emotional drain of having to deal with racists and racism on a daily basis while attending Thames Junior High School. It was not easy, intellectually or emotionally, to choose to return to the lion's den and quite likely subject myself to additional racially motivated assaults and insults from racist classmates and teachers. Ultimately, however, I did make the decision to attend

Blair High School; and I made it completely independent of any discussion and consultation with parents or friends, none of whom had any idea of my ambivalence about where to attend high school.

As I had done at Thames Junior High, I participated in band at Blair High, playing the baritone saxophone. There were only three other black band members – my long-time friend Benton Dwight played percussions, Helen Faye Hollimon played French Horn, and Cedric Brown played tuba. One of my most memorable and embarrassing moments as a member of the Tiger Band was during a half time show at a home football game. As I was marching in a straight line with the other saxophones, the drill we were performing called for the saxophone section to march to a specific yard line, touch that line with our right foot and turn 180 degrees and go in the opposite direction. Well, a few seconds after my right foot touched the yard line that marked the turning point, I looked to my right and then to my left and quickly developed a sinking feeling when I did not see any of my fellow saxophonists. I kept right on marching for another 10 seconds or so, thinking to myself: Where did they go? Why aren't they marching next to me? Uh Oh! I think I just messed up. I was out in no-man's land, feeling naked to the world, and marching solo down the field for another 5 yards. In a near panic, I turned around and hurriedly caught up with the others in my line and took my place next to Roger Moore, a tenor saxophone player, who tried his best to calm me down by saying, "Just relax, Anthony. You'll be okay!" What was ironic about this faux pas was that I intentionally did play my saxophone during the entire show so that I could concentrate on my steps and turns. Uncharacteristically, yet to my delight, the band director chose not to chew me out after the show. I think he realized that there was nothing he could say to make me feel any worse than I was already feeling.

Our band director, Mr. Tommy O'Neal, was a short, well-tanned white man with an aggressively receding hairline who maintained, and also insisted that the entire band maintain extremely high standards of musical excellence. In addition to motivating me to achieve musical excellence, he reinforced in me the importance of self-discipline and taking care of one's details. One of his more interesting and dreaded techniques to help instill self-discipline took place during summer band camp when he would line up the entire band on the goal line. He told us that we were to stand at attention for 20 minutes while holding our instruments, and for each flinch, body twitch, or sound emitted other than normal breathing, another minute would be added to the original 20. Ten minutes into the routine, people started dropping like flies from locking their knees, cutting off blood circulation to the brain, despite the warning not to lock our knees. Swarms of giant and hungry mosquitoes feasted on every exposed part of our bodies. Camp counselors whispered jokes in our ears daring us to laugh. Yet, we were to stand completely motionless and speechless like palace guards. We stood on that goal line for over 25 minutes, even though we surely deserved to stand much longer. At the time, such an exercise seemed cruel, stupid and pointless. But the lessons learned from that, as well as from other character-building techniques, ultimately became another source of strength for me, helped me to develop more self-control and self-discipline, and improved my ability to cope with racial insults and attacks.

I developed a deep appreciation for Mr. O'Neal. Not just for his efforts to help instill self-control and self-discipline, but also because he was not afraid to stand up for his beliefs. The only men I had ever personally known with the courage to take risks to preserve their principles were black men like Mr. James Nix, Mr. J. C. Fairley and the Reverend J.C. Killingsworth, leaders of the local civil rights movement. Mr. O'Neal's uncommon courage was best exampled when the band traveled to Jackson to compete in the annual state band contest, which consisted of inspection, a marching routine, playing a concert tune and sight-reading. Although I was no longer a student at Blair High School, Mr. O'Neal allowed me to travel with the band to Jackson to watch the contest. To Mr. O'Neal's chagrin, state band contest officials required bands to compete in both the marching and concert portions of the contest during the spring, which was traditionally concert band season. He unequivocally clung to his conviction that the marching competition should take place during the fall when bands performed their halftime marching routines, and that concert competition should take place during concert season when bands typically worked on concert tunes. So, in order to drive home his point to state officials, he did something that had never ever been done in the history of state band contests and has never been attempted since. He lined up the band in a single line on the goal line and ordered it to march from one end of the field to the other, with only the steady cadence of a lone snare drummer's beat. No music and no precision drills. Just the steady beat of a snare drum. I loved it. A southern white man challenging the system. While not referring to the incident as an act of protest, Mr. O'Neal believes that he made his point very emphatically and dramatically, and that everyone present at Jackson's Memorial Stadium, including state officials, got it. Despite his sternness and no-nonsense approach to being a band director, Thomas O'Neal e also appreciated moments of levity. One such moment came during an after-school rehearsal in the band hall. He deviated from the normal flow of the rehearsal and decided to lecture the band on the importance of proper breathing. He stressed that in order to get a full sound from our brass and woodwind instruments, we had to properly use our lungs in order to achieve maximum efficiency. He illustrated the link between blood flow and breathing as a way of making his point. He asked everyone, including the percussion section, to press a spot on our forearm with an index finger and hold it for a few seconds. He then told us to look at the change in color on your arm from white to red, which was a phenomenon caused by the natural and intentional regulation of blood flow. In other words, by breathing properly, we could regulate the flow of blood throughout our bodies, which in turn helped the breathing process. The white students had clear, indisputable evidence that Mr. O'Neal was absolutely correct. The coloration of their forearms indeed changed from white to red and back to white. Because of my light complexion, I was able to see the colors in my arm change. My friend Benton, however, continued to press his finger to his arm as instructed by Mr. O'Neal. I glanced over at Benton to find out how he was handling this activity. What I saw on his face was a look of exasperation bordering on panic. His attention and gaze quickly went back and forth between his arm and Mr. O'Neal. He looked around at other band members, and it was clear from the look on his face that this impromptu lesson on proper breathing was not working for Benton. He finally raised his hand to get Mr. O'Neal's attention. After getting it, he pointed out the obvious. "Mr. O'Neal, sir. My skin color is not changing. Is there something wrong with me or am I just not doing it right?" Immediately, we all reacted in the same manner to Benton's predicament. Everyone, including Mr. O'Neal cracked up. Given that Benton, who had very dark skin, was trying so hard to make his skin turn red was so ironic that it became spontaneously funny. The futility of his non-stop efforts triggered hearty laughter, which easily turned into comic relief among all, including Benton. No one was laughing at Benton or making fun of him. It was just the irony of the situation and the futility of his ever being able to make his skin color go from white to red and back. It was also a reminder, albeit somewhat subtlely, that teaching techniques have to be taught sometimes, within a cultural context.

While I was a student at Blair High School, my musical talents with the baritone saxophone landed me a stint as a musician in a local soul band, called the *Soul Fanatics*. It was not something I sought out, but I was elated when the members of the band asked me to join. I had heard of the band and knew all the members – Terry Leggett, Jr. - tenor sax, Melvin Miller - trombone, Tony Fluker- keyboard, Greg Walker- Trumpet, Maurice Pope - Bass, and James Nix – vocalist and manager. When playing our gigs, typically at local nightclubs and at frat parties at USM, we were uniformly attired in green dashikis, white bell bottom pants and white patent leather shoes with two-inch stack heels. We performed all of the latest R & B hits; and patrons at the nightclubs and at the frat parties really enjoyed our sound. We were even good enough to take requests.

The most unforgettable gig, however, was at the Elks Club in Palmers Crossing not long after I joined the band. The band had been contacted by an agent to provide the instrumental music for a group of black female singers and entertainers from Detroit, Michigan, who were going to perform at the end of the week in a musical variety show. James Nix, our manager agreed to the terms; and when the singers and entertainers arrived from Detroit, we rehearsed with them nightly for nearly a week. From the first moment we started working together, I was very impressed with them, although I never talked to any of them. I mostly just looked and listened whenever I was around them mainly because I did know what to say. They sang and danced very well and were easy to work with; and I thought they looked great. Even in rehearsals, they wore performance makeup, elegant dresses and high hill shoes and were accessorized with impressive jewelry. I knew that the show would be a huge hit, unlike anything Hattiesburg had ever seen before. And I was glad that the *Soul Fanatics* were going to be a part of this dazzling production. As the band was warming up and preparing for the show to begin, Greg strolled over to me with his trumpet in tow, with his sunglasses pulled down on his nose, revealing his one good eye, and with a sly grin plastered on his face. I could see that the other guys in the band were looking at me with their own sly grins that quickly turned to laughter after they saw Greg whispering in my hear. "Brother Ant. I need to tell you something, man I don't think you know." "Okay, Greg, what it is?" He started laughing, and said, "Man you know these ain't no women. They men dressed up like women. They female impersonators, man!" I must have turned three shades of red when I heard him say that. All I could do was stand there with my mouth wide open as I took a long look at one of the "women", trying to visually detect evidence that would either confirm or contradict what Greg had just told me. I could find nothing to contradict this unexpected and surprising bit of news as I sadly realized that for a whole week I was the only one in the band who was either too naive or too gullible to distinguish real women from men who looked, talked, walked, dressed, and sang like women. After I got over my shock, the show proceeded and as predicted, was a huge success. But from that moment on, I never assumed a woman was actually a woman unless I was certain that she did not have an Adam's apple or that there was some other compelling evidence that made it indisputable.

Socially, life at Blair High School was not very exciting. In fact, for the handful of black students, a social life was downright nonexistent. Adding to the challenge of trying to have any type of social life, particularly dating, black students knew that if we did not conform to conventional Jim Crow rules, serious trouble would follow.

The unwritten Jim Crow prohibition against inter-racial dating was strictly enforced, although sometimes unevenly. During my sophomore year, a black male student at Blair High School developed a mutual infatuation with a white female student, and for a couple of weeks, the two of them passed love notes to one another. One day, someone in the administration intercepted one of the notes and reacted in a typical one-sided, Jim Crow fashion. The black student was summoned to the principal's office and was immediately transferred to all-black Rowan High School. The reaction by the administration was calculated and sent a clear message to all students – interracial dating would not be permitted at Blair High School. Although there were not written rules in the Student Code of Conduct against such dating relationships, the prevailing Jim Crow prohibition and accompanying forms of punishment were sufficient to squelch any budding inter-racial romances and to serve as deterrence to others. At the same time, the administration's reaction to a black male student writing a love note to a white female student lent credence to the popular belief among many blacks that resistance to racial desegregation by bigots was based on a deeply felt and long suffering fear that has been at the root of racial segregation since the presence of the first slaves – interracial romances producing interracial marriages and biracial children.

On another occasion, during my junior year at Blair High School, I was sent to the assistant principal's office under, what seemed to me, very secretive and mysterious circumstances. After turning in my test paper, my chemistry teacher handed me a folded slip of paper and told me to take it immediately to the Assistant Principal's office. *Was I running an errand for her, or was I in trouble for some unknown transgression?*, I thought to myself. For the love of God, I could not fathom what I could have possibly done so wrong to warrant being sent to the Assistant Principal's office. *It has to be. I'm just running an errand for her*, I decided. If one were not running as errand for a teacher, going to the Assistant Principal's office meant that one had really messed up. I knew with absolute certainty that I had not cheated on the exam, and that I had not created any sort of disruption in class. So, I proceeded to his office and waited in the outer office with other apparent wayward students for my turn to see the Grim Reaper. His secretary read the note and from the frown that quickly shown on her face, I sadly concluded that I was not running an errand at all. She handed the note back to me and slowly shook her silver, bee-bonnet-hair-topped head from side to side, tightened her lips, and let out a loud sigh and a sarcastic, *hmmm!* I just held the slip of paper tightly between my fingers, too nervous and afraid to sneak a peek at the note, for fear that it would confirm my suspicion that, indeed, I was in deep trouble. The butterflies and sweaty palms that were controlling my body were only a prelude to what I would feel in the next few moments. After sitting in the infamous death chamber, stewing in my rapidly increasing fear and constantly drying my wet palms on my pant leg, counting minutes on the office wall clock, which seemed like hours rather than minutes, my turn finally came to meet Blair High School's judge, jury, and executioner. In his own inimitable booming gruff voice, the Assistant Principal snapped, "Harris, what you doing here?" Still too confused, afraid, and nervous to speak, I simply handed him the folded up piece of paper that Mrs. Hatten had given to me. As he read it, he shook his head from side to side just as his secretary had already done, made the same *hmmm* sound that she had made, and his huge, square, bespectacled face began to take on that same look of disgust that the secretary had already shown me. He then looked me over from head to toe, started sucking on his teeth, and said, "Boy, get in here to my office, on the double!" Obligingly, I got up from my seat, faced his office door, put one foot in front the other and quickly found myself moving in the direction of his office, then slowing a bit before entering to ponder once again, *what in the world could I have done to find myself doing this dead-man-walking routine?* With that look of disgust still plastered across his face, he closed the door with such a bang that I froze momentarily, waiting for the stain glass in his door to shatter into a million pieces. But it didn't, no doubt because he slammed his door so much, he must have had the type of glass that did not shatter. "Boy, sit your behind down!" I moved over to an armless metal chair directly across from his desk and lowered my bottom until it made contact with the cold metal. *This must be what Judgment Day will be like*, I imagined. Sitting there before the Almighty, accounting for all of my transgressions, waiting to learn if I would be going to heaven or hell. By then, my hands were wringing wet, as if all of the pores in the palm of both hands had suddenly opened like flood gates and unleashed an out-of-control torrent of pinned up water. They were clammy and sticky from the buildup of sweat. Butterflies were flying out of control and adrenaline was gushing like a geyser. Unrelentingly, I kept searching my mental databank trying to discover some clue as to what I had done to find myself in this unfortunate predicament. I could come up with nothing. Then he finally ended the suspense. "Boy, that shirt you wearing! Can't allow you to wear something like that to school."

"Sir, you mean this dashiki?", I asked with some new found vigor, now that I realized what this was all about.

"That's what you call it?" he replied.

"Yes, sir. It's a traditional African shirt. For me, it represents pride in my heritage."

"Well, that's more reason we can't have you wearing something like that. This ain't Africa, and it ain't no hardship that you gotta wear it. So, you gonna have to take it off. Let you wear it, every colored in the school will want to wear one of 'em. Before you know it, we gonna have a race war. And I can't allow that. See, Harris, when you come to *this* school you got to abide by our way of doing thangs. Over at Rowan, they'll let you wear your, what you call it, dashiki, cause Rowan is all colored. But here at Blair, this is a white school, and you can't do such a thang, cause it aint't gonna do nothing but cause trouble. And now, anytime you want to transfer to Rowan so you can wear your dashiki and be with your own kind, I'll be more than happy to arrange for you to transfer."

So, this was what it was all about – a dashiki. Sending me to the Assistant Principal's office and going through all of the rigmarole, worrying about whether I had done something wrong, was all about my wearing a dashiki. Nevertheless, I had to remove my green dashiki, the very same one I wore when I performed with the *Soul Fanatics*. Although nothing in the student handbook specifically prohibited the wearing of a dashiki, the Assistant Principal and my chemistry teacher, obviously, objected to it, fearing that I would incite a riot or something. Noting that I was wearing a black turtleneck shirt underneath the dashiki, Mr. Snell told me to remove the dashiki, take it to my locker, and warned me to never wear it to school again. Considering what had happened to the black student, who was transferred to another school because of his infatuation with a white girl, I suppose I felt slightly lucky to have gotten off with only having to remove my favorite dashiki. A simple and clean article of clothing that I wore to express pride in my heritage had become, in the minds of at least two people, a dangerous symbol of subversion and radical Black Nationalism that was going to cause a race war at Blair High School. Such were the times at public schools during desegregation in Hattiesburg!

Dealing with insensitive and mean-spirited classmates was a constant struggle that every black student at Blair High School faced. However, dealing with insensitive and mean-spirited teachers was a different struggle, and for me, far more frustrating. As if the dashiki incident were not frustrating enough, I soon experienced that same frustration again with another insensitive and bigoted teacher. I sat in my history class one morning trying to maintain some interest in what the teacher was trying to teach. Actually, he was not teaching at all. He was reading to the class word-for-word from the textbook as he always did; and his reading skills betrayed the fact that he was a certified school teacher with a college degree. As was his daily custom, he taught/read while leaning back in his seat with his legs resting on top of his desk, dressed in his purple and gold coach's wind suit. This particular morning, he was reading a passage about the harshness and cruelty of slavery, and then uncharacteristically, he abruptly stopped reading in mid-sentence and slammed the book face down on the desk. His face turned as red as a beet and he plunged head first into a diatribe, challenging the author's assertion that slavery was a hardship on slaves and an example of the South's economic exploitation of slaves. He took strong exception to that claim and stated very matter-of-factly that slavery was not a hardship on slaves. After all, he insisted, slavery actually rescued African slaves from a savage land and provided them a much better home, better food, and most importantly, introduced them to Christianity.

He continued, saying that slaves did not have the intellectual skills to do anything else but to work on the plantation. Everyone, he said, had their place in southern society and that slaves were best suited for work on a plantation, such as picking cotton and other jobs that didn't require a lot of intelligence. He went on to say that the plantation owner needed to make money and that slaves needed a place to live, so as far as he was concerned, it was a perfect arrangement. I could not believe what I was hearing. *This racist pig!*, I thought to myself. I began to feel something inside of me that went beyond anger. It went to that place in all of us where we just want to explode and totally go off on someone. What I was feeling was rage, quickly approaching the point of explosion. Accompanying the rage was an equal amount of anxiety, as I could feel my stomach twisting itself into knots. My face was probably turning red as I shifted in my seat and shook my head from side to side. Not wanting to let him get away with such stupidity, I just blurted out, "*You* are wrong; and slavery *was* wrong!" I remember looking behind me for some support from the only other black student in class. To my disappointment and surprise, however, she just dropped her head. Either she did not know what to say or was too afraid. I felt like I had thrown myself into the lion's den and was there all by myself with no one to back me up or to assist me. That all too-familiar and painful feeling that comes from being the target of a racist insult revisited me and hit me right square in the gut. Once again I was out on a limb all by myself fighting against another of the many forces of ignorance and bigotry. Just before the bell rang, he told me that I did not know what I was talking about and that I had better not ever contradict him again. I closed my book, gathered my belongings, and left the class feeling abandoned by my lone black classmate, ignored or sneered at by my white classmates, and insulted by my white teacher. But I was determined that this was not going to deter me from speaking my mind, no matter how alone or insulted I felt. I found myself humming, *Ain't Gonna Let Nobody 'Turn Me 'Round*. After all, I hadn't let the daunting and well-entrenched forces of Jim Crow in Hattiesburg turn me around, and I certainly was not about to let this racist teacher even come close to doing so.

Except for these glaring exceptions, by the time I had reached my junior year, my exposure to blatant racist activity at school had diminished slightly. That may have been because there were more black students at Blair than there were at Thames, although the numbers were still small; also because white students were becoming more accustomed to being around black students and the novelty of desegregation had worn thin for many of them.

Rowan High School

The four years I spent at Thames Junior High School and Blair High School contributed to some awkwardness in my social development, especially in the area of dating. While attending predominantly white schools, I was subjected to a time-honored Jim Crow law, which forbade interracial dating, especially between a black male and a white female. During my four years at Thames and Blair, I never violated that law, although there was a definite conflict between my desire to date and the opportunity to do so.

A latent period of social awkwardness and ineptness dominated my life when I initially enrolled at predominately black Rowan High School my senior year in the Fall of 1970 (The new desegregation plan, following the failure of Freedom of Choice, assigned students to a school on either side of an arbitrarily drawn boundary line. I was on the Rowan side of the line.) With virtually no experience and skills in dating, which is vitally important for a high school senior, I struggled for at least half a year to learn how I was to conduct myself in dating relationships. I remember being interested in several young ladies, but Sandra and Jean stand out above the others. The first time Sandra and I saw each other, we both did a quick and lingering double-take at each other as she and I were both entering the band hall for our first band class of the new school year. I was very impressed with her dazzling eyes and warm smile. I was also impressed with the fact that, like me, she had a rather full and well-coifed Afro. Upon seeing her for the first time since the seventh grade, I was both pleased and nervous. I found myself in such an emotional tug-of-war because, although we both seemed to be impressed with each other,

I knew that my shyness and inexperience would never allow me to do more than just look at her. Besides, I thought, she was beautiful, popular, smart, and way out of my league. And to my regret and maybe to hers as well, I never felt confident enough to act on my feelings for her. I never even attempted to call her on the phone or offer to walk her home after school. I just felt a lump in my throat anytime she would say something to me or come near me. The more this happened the more I knew that I would never have the nerves to do more than look and dream. I believed that I could have been the inspiration for the Temptations hit song, *Just My Imagination*. But as time passed Sandra and I did become speaking friends, played in the band together; and were voted by our peers as superlatives – Most Beautiful and Most Handsome, which for me was both embarrassing and flattering.

Jean and I also had a "crush" on each other, but I think she finally lost patience with me one evening after I had gotten up the nerves to visit her at her home. I walked instead of driving the nearly three miles to her house, mainly to calm myself and rehearse what I wanted to say once we were alone. During my rehearsals, I sounded pretty confident and convincing. But rehearsing what should be spontaneous did not do much to calm my nerves. With each step toward her house in East Jerusalem Quarters, I somehow managed to resist the powerful urge to turn around and walk all the way back to my house. My nerves were getting the best of me as I played out in my head a million times what I was supposed to do once I got to her house and started courting her. Was I to hold her hand? Kiss her? Put my arms around her as we sat on the couch? I was absolutely clueless. I thought that I wanted to do all three, but was not at all confident in my skills to do any of them without making a fool of myself. So, not to my surprise but much to my disappointment, I stayed at her house for over an hour and never once attempted to kiss her, put my arm around her, or hold her hand. Instead, I could only nervously engage in silly, mindless banter about school until I finally sensed that I had overstayed my welcome. Jean was nice to me, but I knew the evening had been a disaster. So, I walked the three miles back to my house, feeling like a defeated warrior who had gone into battle ill-prepared and ill-equipped. But my resolve to eventually get it right never waned, although I knew that I would not be going back to see Jean again. Actually, my rationalization for being such an unskilled suitor was both humorous and serious, as I often jokingly remarked to my friends that my lack of dating skills was simply due to my going to white schools for so long and being a victim of Jim Crowism, although there was a measure of truth to that statement.

One young lady at Rowan High made it clear to me that she wanted to go with me. She just walked right up to me one day and said, "Anthony Harris, you talking to anybody? If you're not, how about giving me a chance?" I tried to say that I was not interested, but the words got stuck in my throat. So, instincts and habits kicked in, and I let my silence and brusque exit let her know that I was not interested. Of course, she did not know what I knew all too well – my apparent lack of interest in her stemmed directly from my long-suffering shyness and a nagging, frustrating feeling of being socially clumsy when it came to talking to and dating girls. Adding to my reticence was the fact that this particular young lady, Helen Jean, was very popular; and I had convinced myself that if I went with her, I would be like a fish out of water and people would make fun of me when I would inevitably trip over myself because of my lack of skills. However, I never told her directly that I did not want to go with her nor did I ever tell her why. But it all came to a head later that same day when one of her friends came to me in the cafeteria and asked me if I liked Helen Jean and if I wanted to go with her. With no hesitation, I said no. Well, when Helen Jean learned of my response, it went over like a pregnant pole vaulter with her; she did not like my answer one bit. Later that day, as I was going to one of my classes, I could see her at the other end of the hallway walking in my direction at an unusually brisk pace with her eyes locked on to me like a laser beam; and she looked angry enough to spit. There was absolutely no way I could avoid her since we were both going to the same class. My heart was pumping like a steam engine. My face was turning several shades of red. My breathing became so shallow I thought I was going to hyperventilate. Then the inevitable happened. She abruptly stepped in front of me just I was about to turn right and go into the classroom. And with an intimidating and menacing scowl, she said, "I know why you don't like me! You're color-struck. That's your problem. You don't like me because I'm black." I knew what she was getting at. In that context, black referred to her dark complexion, not her race. I said nothing to her; but I was aware that my now very familiar awkwardness and embarrassment were bolstered by a disturbing little factoid known only to me: *I was actually too shy to tell her that I was too shy to go with her!!* I just walked away and looked for a hole to crawl into but could only find my conspicuous desk at the front of the class, which offered no cover at all. As I sat there thumbing through my textbook, appearing to not be bothered by that disturbing, one-sided discussion with Helen Jean, I really felt hurt that she would think that I did not like her because she was black. That was not true at all. I was not color-struck. I did not find dark skin a turn-off. As a matter of fact, in so many of my own private moments I longed to have skin that was at least three shades darker. There was no living person on the face of the planet more proud to be black than I; but I would have felt even prouder if I just had darker skin, so that no one would ever have to ask me my race. I wanted everyone I met to know that I was black and proud of it. I eventually came to believe unequivocally that blackness is an attitude and not just a skin color. And by that point in my life, I had the attitude part down pat! The truth of the matter is that I would have said the same thing if Helen Jean had been high yellow! Nevertheless, I still liked Helen Jean and we eventually became friends. I was very proud of her when she became Miss Black America in 1976.

During my high school senior year (1970-1971), a tragic event occurred in Hattiesburg that shocked and outraged black students at Rowan High and Blair High, and prompted most of us students to publicly express our shock and outrage. Mr. John Albert White, a black man in his mid-30s, who lived in a black section of town called the Brick Yard, was fatally shot by white police officers in front of his home. The official version of the incident was that Mr. White was a drug dealer who, after being ordered by the officers to come outside with his hands over his hands, appeared to have a weapon in his hands. Shortly after stepping out into the street in front of his home, he was shot and killed by the officers. The part of the story that most black people, including we students, did not believe was that he had a weapon in his hands. That belief was based on statements by eyewitnesses that Mr. White had only a transistor radio in his hand, not a gun. The police department, of course, conducted the obligatory "official" investigation and as expected, cleared the officers of any misconduct. To protest what we regarded as an execution of Mr. White and to register our collective outraged at what we regarded as yet another example of how little some whites regarded the life of a black man, the majority of black students at both high schools – Rowan and Blair – walked out of school the day following the shooting and marched downtown, at least 300 strong, to the school administration building on Main Street. The march was completely spontaneous; so, there was no time for school or city officials to tell us that we could not march. I was proud of my classmates at both schools. For me, this was like the good old days when I participated in scores of marches during the heyday of the civil rights movement in Hattiesburg. We chanted freedom songs, carried signs that read, "No Peace, No Justice" ; and in each of us, there was an enormous amount of pride coupled with an overwhelming sense of group empowerment – that feeling that comes from knowing that we did the right thing and that our collective voices has been heard. As in the Vernon Dahmer march on January 15, 1966, we were using our feet and our sheer numbers to let everyone in Hattiesburg know that we were not going to forget Mr. White and that we strongly believed that his death was senseless and totally unnecessary. To my knowledge, no group of students in the history of the Hattiesburg Public School System had ever actually walked out of school en masse for any reason and not gotten expelled. As a matter of fact, I personally never even considered the possibility of expulsion, mainly because I believed so strongly that what we were doing was absolutely the right thing to do and besides, they could not expelled all 300 of us.

Band students at Rowan High School proved to be just as rebellious as the regular student body. One afternoon at band practice, Mr. Winters, the band director, walked out of his office to begin a routine rehearsal that turned out to be anything but routine. What made this rehearsal unusual was that when he walked out of his office and took his normal spot on the podium to begin rehearsal, no one had instruments. All 40 of us just sat in our chairs as though we were there to listen to a speech rather than prepare for state band contest. We were, in fact, staging a silent protest over Mr. Winters' decision to not allow the band to perform at the upcoming Rowan vs. Jackson Jim Hill football game in Jackson. As Mr. Winters slowly shifted the weight of his 5-foot frame atop the square-shaped, 6-inch high podium, he had that astonished look of a deer caught in the headlights. He softly and dejectedly asked the group, "What's going on? Why don't you have your instruments out?" On cue, Ratio Jones, who was drum major and band president, stood up from his seat and asked Mr. Winters, "Are you going to change your mind and let us go to Jackson? Mr. Winters, did not hesitate as he responded with an uncharacteristically stern, "No!", indicating that his dejection had now turned to rage. Not giving an inch, Ratio responded, "If you are not going to let us go to Jackson, then the band is not going to practice and we will be walking out". With escalating rage, Mr. Winters responded again that he was not going to change his mind. He reminded everyone that the band could only take three out of town trips and that Jackson was not on the schedule. With those words, the line was drawn in the sand; and most of us slowly got up from our seats and walked out of the band hall, leaving Mr. Winters standing there with a look of both hurt and disbelief. I am sure that he was also embarrassed because he had invited several other band directors to attend our rehearsal so that they could critique our state competition routine. Nonetheless, we walked. At least most of us did. One student adamantly refused to join us; and for that decision was unfortunately physically attacked by Diane, one of our more zealous striking band members. Diane was generally in trouble with Principal Burger, so she figured one more incident would not make much difference to her, especially if it would ensure solidarity among students. The next day Principal Burger and Mr. Winters, predictably, suspended the entire band. They then announced that anyone who wanted to rejoin the band could do so; but each returning band member had to agree to follow all instructions and accept all decisions by Mr. Winters, including participating in all rehearsals and going only on football trips that he approved. Ninety-five percent of the band members returned, and I was among them. In fact, I was voted band president because Ratio refused to return.

As time drew near for graduation, I began to have mixed feelings about leaving Rowan. I was looking forward to graduating, but not necessarily to leaving Rowan. I was pleased that I had a number of unforgettable coming of age experiences and was thoroughly enjoying my senior year at L.J. Rowan High School. Despite the rough start in the fall of 1970, I managed to settle into a comfortable routine by the time spring 1971 rolled around. I was making all As in my classes. I really enjoyed being in the band. Most refreshingly, I did not have to deal with bigoted classmates, teachers, and administrators. After spending four years of putting up with racial insults from white classmates and low expectations from white teachers at Thames Junior High and Blair High, being amongst my black friends and black teachers at Rowan High was like a cool summer breeze in the midst of an oppressive heat wave.

In the spring of 1971, I received several academic and band awards at the Awards Assembly, which I remember not just for the awards themselves, but also for a funny and spontaneous moment created by a classmate. I was called to the stage at least six times to receive an award for various achievements. I was proud and embarrassed at the same time, with all of the attention focused on me each time my name was called. After Principal Burger, read the name Anthony Harris for the final award, Anthony Putman, a.k.a Putie Jug stood up front his seat and quickly walked to the stage. As I saw Putie Jug walking in my direction, I stopped in my tracks, not knowing what he was up to. He was always doing something screwy; and I thought I'd better let him make his move first before I take another step. When Putie Jug got to the stage he walked over to Mr. Burger and said, "You called my name. I'm here to get my award." The crowd, including Mr. Burger and the teachers, just fell out with laughter. Putie Jug was a great guy who had an amazing sense of humor, but he and everyone in the auditorium knew that academics were not his strong suit. In fact, Putie Jug should have graduated two years earlier. After playfully trying to accept the award, he walked over to me, shook my hand, and walked back to his seat. I think everybody appreciated his gesture, and at the same time felt relieved that he did not do something more outrageous.

Although, I had enormous respect for my teachers and for the school's administrators, I thought they did something one morning that was totally humiliating to some of my classmates. A week before graduation, the counselors called all seniors to the gymnasium. At the time, I was not sure why we were there, but since we were seniors I figured it must have something to do with our impending graduation. What happened that morning was downright embarrassing and humiliating and with the passage of time, reflection on the events of that morning causes me even more outrage. Before starting a roll call of each student sitting in the gymnasium stands, one of the two counselors announced, "I will call names alphabetically. When you hear your name, make your way to the gym floor. Do not come until you hear your name." As if they had rehearsed their parts, the counselors took turns calling names. Naturally, when they reached the letter "H" and called my name, I made my way to the gym floor. As was the case with everybody in the gym, except for the counselors, I had no idea why any of us were being asked to come to the gym floor. Yet, there we were – nearly 100 young people standing, fidgeting, and not making any sounds Like all of my classmates standing with me on the gym floor, I still had no clue about what was going on. After hearing the last name, I found my attention focused on the counselors, hoping for some clue as to what in the world this was all about. It did not take long for the mystery to be solved. One of the counselors announced, "If I *did not* call your name, I want you to stay seated. That means that you are not going to graduate with your classmates. You will need to see me after this meeting is over. " Regrettably several of my classmates remained in their seats, ashamed and humiliated in being so callously informed that they were not going to graduate. And I, too, felt ashamed and humiliated because what they did to these guys was so unnecessary. There was a better and less public way to let them know that for whatever reason they would not graduate.

Nevertheless, by the end of the school year, I had overcome much of my shyness around girls and started going out with Ira Nell Woullard, who lived in Palmers Crossing and was a senior at a high school in the nearby town of Petal. She and I were really crazy about each other and spent most of our free time at her home courting and hanging out with her family. I had my first real kiss with her. I learned a lot about girls and how to be a boyfriend during the year she and I spent as a couple. We both enrolled as brand new freshmen at USM. Before meeting me, she had actually planned to attend Jackson State University, which was a Woullard family tradition. Her older sisters and brothers had all graduated from Jackson State. However, out of a desire to be in a relationship with me, she turned down a scholarship at Jackson State and decided to enroll at USM. A few months after the fall 1971 semester began, I turned into a jerk and abruptly ended the relationship one night after a rather routine date with her. My reason for breaking up with her was because I foolishly and incorrectly thought that the grass was greener on the other side. That was my first foray into canine land! She did not deserve to be treated the way I treated her. At the time I was young, immature and foolish. Those characteristics, however, did not justify my ending the relationship just as it seemed to be going so well. I told her that I wanted to be free to play the field. But, my immaturity, selfishness, and overall doggishness never allowed me to consider the hurt that that decision caused Ira Nell. At that time I was 18 years old and had no clue as to what I was doing. Today, as a father of a son and a daughter, I can only hope that Michael never treats a woman the way I treated Ira Nell, and that Ashley is never hurt by an immature, selfish jerk. I heard somewhere that the sins of the father are visited on his children. I pray that they are sparred such an experience.

My senior year at Rowan High was bittersweet also because my mom and dad divorced after 20 years of marriage. Their relationship hit rock bottom after years of not getting along very well. I was old enough to understand that two good people whom I loved dearly had sadly sunk into a really bad relationship. Although their three sons and undoubtedly they as well, hoped that the relationship could be salvaged, ultimately it was not to be. From the time I was 13 years old, my mom and dad engaged in sporadic fights, verbally and physically, mainly over his late nights out and early morning arrivals back home. My mom did not take kindly at all to his habitual late arrivals back home, and she never hesitated in letting him know how ticked off that made her. My mom did not back down from bully racist cops and she did not back down from my dad. Unfortunately, I was often caught in the middle of their fights, and by default and by choice, I invariably found myself alternately playing the role of referee and rescuer. For years, whenever I knew my dad was not home by the time I went to bed around 10:00 p.m., I knew that sleep would escape me for hours until he arrived home. I lay awake, drowning in a reservoir of nerves, worry, and fear, listening for the sound of his car pulling into the driveway, dreading and welcoming that moment at the same time. I welcomed it because I knew he was finally home and safe. I dreaded it because I knew that a fight was likely to start and that I was going to have to be referee and rescuer one more time. When he went into their bedroom, I would listen intently for sounds coming from their bedroom. If I heard him snore, I knew I could go to sleep. If I heard talking, I knew I had better stay awake and alert in case the talking escalated into shouts. Whenever shouts ensued, which was rather frequently, I would get up from my bed, make that lonely and scary walk to their bedroom, turn on the light, and plead with them to stop fussing. Depending on how mad they were, they would either heed my plea or get louder and angrier. One of those episodes was particularly frightening one night during my senior year in high school. My dad had come home late one night, and my mom refused to allow him to get into their bed. Every time he came close to the bed, she would throw something at him like a medicine bottle, ink pen, or a notepad, nothing that would actually hurt him. Their verbal exchanges became so loud this time that even my brothers woke up and joined me in a collective plea for calm. As my dad sat in a chair between the closet door and the bedroom door, he suddenly leaped from the chair and yelled, " I know how to put an end to this shit!" He angrily yanked open the closet door and bent down inside the closet. I instinctively grabbed my mother because I knew what he was up to. I placed her in front of me and pushed her down the hallway and out the den door. I went around the side of the house and picked up a wooden baseball bat. I slowly looked around the corner of the house to see if my dad were following us. He was not. I knew what he had done when he went inside the closet. He had grabbed his .38 caliber pistol. I want to think that he was not going to use it and was only trying to frighten my mom into letting him get in the bed. But I was not going to take any chances. Nevertheless, my brothers managed to talk him into putting the gun down. He soon calmed himself, but I was sweating, panting, and confused about what to do next. None of my previous episodes of being a referee had prepared me for this level of hostility and danger. The immediate concern was making sure that my mom would be safe. So, my brothers and I convinced her that she should spend the night at my Aunt Emma's house that night. At the time it occurred and even today, I regard that incident as an extremely frightening experience for all of us, including my dad. In fact, he was so frightened by what could have happened, the next day he took the gun from the closet, drove out to the Leaf River Bridge and threw the gun and the bullets into the river. I was with him when he did that, and felt so relieved that an ominous source of danger had been removed from our lives. That frightening experience is why I am so adamantly and unequivocally opposed to guns. In far too many instances, guns in the home are used to kill a love one, not an intruder. That night, the Harris family came close to making that statement even truer.

Although the gun was out of the house, tension between my mom and dad remained; and I was still tired of my intimate relationship with sleepless nights, tired of trying to keep our family secret from my friends, and tired of being scared that someone was going to get hurt or worse. Finally, one day I told my mom that I thought that she and my dad should get a divorce. Despite their marital difficulties, divorce was unfathomable for both of them. No matter how bad things got, they believed that you stay and work things out and keep the family together. So, neither really wanted a divorce, but in their hearts they knew it was the right thing to do. As a rule, divorce is hard on everybody, especially the children. And for my brothers and me, that rule prevailed quite unpleasantly. After my mom officially filed for the divorce, the judge ordered my dad to immediately move out of our house. He then moved in with my Uncle Sonny Boy and Aunt Dora, who lived a few blocks away.

When the final divorce decree was about to be issued, my brothers and I had to make a very difficult choice that would profoundly affect our relationship with both our parents. One morning the judge summoned my brothers and me to his office for a meeting with him. My mom told us that she was taking us to the meeting, but she would not be allowed to stay. Neither my mother nor we had any idea what the judge wanted with us, and that made us very nervous. She told us that the judge wanted to meet with just the three boys. Nevertheless, we unhurriedly got dressed up in our church clothes while saying absolutely nothing the entire time until, in unison, we said, Okay! when my mom told us to hurry up before we are late. The deafening silence that started while we were getting dressed continued unabated as we rode toward the Forrest County Courthouse, Harold and I in the back seat and Junior in the front. I had this awful feeling as though we were driving to a funeral. My mom parked on the street next to the Courthouse, got out and began feeding the parking meter several nickels. By the time she finished putting the last nickel into the meter, we were already out of the car, standing behind her, stair step from tallest to shortest, which also mirrored out birth order. With the three of us following closely behind her, we began to walk slowly, with heads down and hands in pockets, up the wide, gray-colored steps that had been the stage for so many speeches during civil rights marches in the 1960s. As we wound our way up the remaining steps, I could not help but take a quick glance at the entrance to the courthouse basement and recall the many times I had walk through that entrance to go to the colored restroom and drink from the colored water fountain. I could recall the horrible stench and lingering odor that stayed with you long after you left the basement. As I stood there on the steps for a moment longer, I remembered that the nasty Jim Crow restroom and water fountain were still there, as ugly reminders of just how slow change really comes. Just a few feet away was the very spot where my brother, my friend Ratio and I were arrested for picketing several years earlier. I was going through a wide range of thoughts and emotions that wound up getting all mixed up into one big ball of crap. I was cogitating about the dogged persistence of Jim Crow, my mom's and dad's failed marriage, and my brothers' and my reaction to our parents' breakup. Why the heck were we going to see the judge? When are these white folk going to realize that we will no longer be their niggers? I did my best to shake it off and prepare myself for this mysterious meeting with the judge.

Finally, we arrived at the judge's office on the 2nd floor of the courthouse. My mom told us goodbye and that she would wait for us. After we walked into the judge's plush office, which was impressively accented with brightly polished bookshelves and a long shiny conference table, we felt that this place was too nice to sit just anywhere. So, we just stood there in the middle of this shiny tiled floor, accompanied only by the same agonizing silence that was with us when we started this dreaded trip to the courthouse. When the judge walked into his office, he tried really hard to force a smile as he greeted us, but I could tell he was just as uneasy and uncomfortable as we were. He invited us to join him at the long shiny conference table. After clearing his throat a couple of times and taking a few sips from his coffee cup, he told us that he was handling my parents' divorce, which to me was not exactly a news flash. He went on to say that he was going to ask us something and that he wanted us to think very carefully before giving him an answer. With nods and an unenthusiastic verbal, unison response of yes, we reassured him that we understood his request. He then asked us something that no child should ever be asked or ever be forced to answer. Trying to muster up some degree of sensitivity and concern for our predicament, the judge asked in a very gentle tone of voice, "Boys, which one of your parents do you want to live with?" He followed quickly with the proviso, "I want to make sure you understand that you do not have to give me an answer right now. If you like, I can give you some time to think about it. I know that this is a big decision, and I want you to make sure you give it some thought before deciding." He paused for a few moments to allow time for this dreadful request to register in our hearts and heads. I guess I had known in my head that it was inevitable, but my heart was just not quite ready to deal with this. He then continued with his monologue, "Now you also need to know that whichever parent you choose to live with, that parent will be given sole possession of the house and the other one will have to permanently move out. Do you understand?" Well, none of us had to wait long at all to tell the judge that we wanted to live with our mother, although the same old butterflies that visited me on those scary nights when I lay awake waiting for my dad to come home after he had been out all night, were back for another unwelcome visit. After the judge told us we could leave, he said that he would notify my dad of our decision. I knew that my dad would not be happy with our decision, and when he came by the house to start moving his things, it was painfully clear to me that, in fact, he was hurt. He asked each of us if that was what we really wanted. After we said yes, he stood up from the bar stool, and with a look of deep pain, walked out of the house feeling rejected, by his own children of all people. Forced to face such a vexing decision, I felt my heart being ripped into two parts. I felt like Solomon who asked the two women if he should cut the baby in half so that each could have some measure of satisfaction.

Because my father initially took our decision to live with our mom as rejection of him, for months there were no communications or contact between my father and his three sons. Our decision to live with our mother, however, was not an act of betrayal toward my father, as he believed. We were closer to our mother, and in one sense the decision was actually a no-brainer. Afterall, she was the primary caregiver, nurturer, and like most mothers, was intensely supportive and protective of her children. Nevertheless, my father was understandably hurt and disappointed. We all cried off and on the entire day following that meeting with the judge, regretting that any of us had to be put in such a painful lose-lose situation. But my brothers and I knew that we had made the right choice. To everyone's delight, my parents eventually healed their emotional wounds, remarried other people, and became fairly good friends. My father also resumed enjoying strong loving relationships with my brothers and me. He really seemed to turn things around when he went back to the church and became an active member of the Usher Board at True Light Baptist Church.

Chapter 12

Times are a-changing

During the late 1960s and early 1970s, noticeable progress had been made in the racial landscape in Hattiesburg. With a few exceptions, most of the "Colored Only" and "White Only" signs had been physically removed from water fountains, restrooms, and restaurants; however, the removal of those signs from people's hearts and minds would take much longer. Black children could visit the public library, and the public schools were no longer racially segregated. Black bus riders were no longer required to sit in the back of the bus. Yes, by the time I graduated from high school in 1971, Hattiesburg had outwardly become a much different place than it was when I desegregated Thames Junior High five years earlier. However, Jim Crow was not willing to depart without a fight and without leaving its mark on the community. A disturbing incident occurred that reminded me that there remained plenty of room for improvement in race relations in Hattiesburg, as well as in other parts of the country. That incident occurred in the summer after my senior year in high school as I was preparing to fly back to Mississippi from a two-week visit with a cousin in Chicago. My older brother, James, was also in Chicago on a weekend pass from his Air Force Base in Rantoul, Illinois. College proved not to be his calling, so he entered the military after a semester at USM. On the day I was to fly back to Mississippi, he and my cousin accompanied me to the airport and proffered a fond farewell to me as I entered the Jetway. I took my seat and was thinking how much I was looking forward to getting back home. I enjoyed visiting with my cousin and her family, but I missed my friends and family. I was homesick and could only think about seeing my girlfriend Ira Nell. I was looking for peace and contentment in preparation for the two-hour flight back home. However, neither peace nor contentment would abide me on this day. Not long after fastening my seat belt, a couple of plain-clothed security officers came to my seat and asked me to get up and come with them. I wondered to myself what I had done to be the object of such a request. I knew that I had not violated any laws or airline rules before or after taking my seat on the plane. My mind momentarily flashed back to the incident in the 10th grade when my chemistry teacher sent me to the Assistant Principal's office with a note that yielded no clue to me why I was being targeted. Confused and scared, just as I was while waiting to see the Assistant Principal. I nervously unbuckled by seat belt. When I stood, I felt the stares and glares of suspicious eyes trying to create another hole in my body. As we walked from my seat, I was sandwiched between the two of them in tight formation, apparently to prevent my escape. The three of us exited the plane through the Jetway as my cousin and brother looked on in confusion and concern. The two officers took me to a room in the airport and asked me if I would consent to a body search. I said, "Yes, but what are you searching for?. One of them said "You fit the profile of a hijacker and we want to search you for weapons." I thought, "This is unbelievable. Here I am, homesick and anxious to get back to Hattiesburg, and these people think I want to go to Cuba!" I asked, "What is it about me that matched the profile of a hijacker?" One of the officers answered incredulously, "It is your looks, you know, your Afro hairstyle and your skin complexion." I was immediately swept by incalculable feelings of anger and humiliation. What they were telling me was that my status as a black male and my choice of hairstyles, not any suspicious behavior on my part, resulted in my being subjected to a full body search, with metal detectors and pat downs over my entire body from head to toe. This was an early example of what is rather commonly known today as racial profiling, or driving while black, or in this case, flying while black – the practice by law enforcement officers of selecting individuals for questioning based on the individual's physical characteristics, i.e. race, rather than on any overt suspicious behavior. After failing to find any weapons, and feeling confident that I was not a hijacker, they allowed me to return to my seat. The plane took off and I remember thinking, "When will this ever end?"

The University of Southern Mississippi

I enrolled at The University of Southern Mississippi in the fall of 1971 and quickly became involved with a student organization, the Afro-American Cultural Society. The Afro Society, as it was called, was the primary social organization for the 300 plus black students on the campus. There were no black Greek organizations or any other black organizations on campus. So, the Afro Society was the only organization that provided the much-desired social outlet for black students and at the same time promoted solidarity and unity among black students. My involvement with the Afro Society resulted in my receiving the coveted the Clyde Kennard Memorial Award in 1974. The award was for my demonstrated commitment and dedication to the preservation and strengthening of the Afro Society. Among other acts of volunteerism, I was commended for helping to organize campus marches and protests, assisting with various fund-raisers, and "spinning" records at every Friday night dance at the student union building. Fund-raising and organizing marches were my ways carving out places of respect for black students within the larger university community. There were several issues that prompted campus marches, but perhaps the one that prompted more marches and united us more than any other was our protest of no black professors or administrators.

When we were not upset by some university practice or tradition that we regarded as racially offensive, we created ways to have fun and enjoy college life. One of those ways was for the Afro Society to sponsor a weekly record hop, free of charge. I had the distinct pleasure of being the DJ for those events, which started around 8:00 and ended at midnight. It seemed that I was the logical person to play DJ since I had a huge collection of vinyl LPs and 45s and a decent stereo system. Black students and a few white students would look forward to the weekly record hops each Friday. Even football players, who typically avoided marches and protests, joined their fellow black students in a night of dancing, which always culminated with a Soul Train line. When Mattie Watson and Willie Heidelberg danced down the line, they reminded everyone that they were indeed the best dancers, hands down.

The activities in which I was involved at the University of Southern Mississippi from fund-raising to marches to spinning records were born out of my upbringing in Hattiesburg. Essentially, I did what Daisy Harris and the civil rights movement had taught me to do years earlier– get involved and work to improve the condition of the community. I consider The Clyde Kennard Memorial Award the most meaningful award I have ever received or ever will receive. My receiving the award, however, was not nearly as significant as the fact that the Mr. Kennard was being honored for making the ultimate sacrifice so that future generations of black students at USM would not have to endure the humiliation and insults he suffered.

Point in fact, however, racially motivated insults directed at black students did not disappear from USM in the early 1970s, and many of us dealt with all sorts of racist attitudes from students and faculty. For example, during my sophomore year at USM in 1972, I decided to change my major from political science to Spanish. I chose political science as my original major because I wanted to go to law school, become a lawyer and eventually return to the community to fight injustice. But I realized that I was not going to get there through political science because I found the political theories and the coursework boring and lacking in relevance to my career goals. So, after a few semesters of political science courses, I was faced with three existential choices – stay with political science as a major, in spite of my abhorrence of it, switch to another major, or leave school and go to work with my dad at Hercules. Option three was not a viable option because quitting was not an option. Whether I would go to college was never a dilemma for me. My only dilemmas were where I would go and what would be my major field of study. Staying in the field of political science was not a good option either because of the negative attitude that I had developed toward the courses. Negative attitudes, invariably, lead to poor grades, which I wanted to avoid at all cost. So, the only real viable option I had was to switch majors. The only reason I decided to switch to Spanish was because I took one Spanish course in high school and made an A. So, majoring in Spanish just seemed like the only logical thing to do. In order to officially make the change, however, I was required to get approval from my academic advisor, Dr. Christos Dumas, who was also a political science professor. I went to his office to tell him about my decision to change majors and to get his signature on the change-of-major request form. Dr. Dumas never looked up the entire time I was standing there talking to him; and when he did speak, he uttered one of the most racist remarks of all time. He said, "Anthony, I advise you to not change your major to Spanish. As you know, there is something wrong with black people's tongue that keeps them from pronouncing Spanish words correctly." Obviously, his racist and totally misguided notion that the tongues of black people are naturally malformed and not designed for pronunciation of Spanish words as well as his ignorance of Black Cubans, Black Venezuelans, and Black Puerto Ricans did not permit him to provide advice that was in my best interest. Whatever doubt existed in my mind about changing my major to Spanish had been irrevocably removed by Dr. Dumas' racist remarks. I changed my major to Spanish, in part, because of my anger over his insulting remarks, but also because I really hate it when someone tells me I am not capable of doing something. My general response is, watch me! I majored in Spanish and learned a variety of foreign languages, including Russian, Italian, Portuguese, and Swahili. I even had an opportunity to spend the summer of 1974 in Bogota, Colombia in a Spanish-language immersion program. By the time I graduated from USM in August of 1974, my Spanish-speaking skills were excellent as were my Italian, Portuguese, Swahili, and Russian skills. So many times I wanted to go up to Dr. Dumas and hold a one-sided conversation with him in Spanish, just to show him how wrong-headed he was about my ability as a black person to learn to speak Spanish.

While still a student in the Political Science Department, I was the target of yet another bizarre remark from another of my Political Science professors, although this one had no effect on my career goals. I was waiting outside the classroom one day leaning against the wall waiting for my U.S. Foreign Policy class to begin. The professor walked over to me and said very matter-of-factly: "Young man, you know you are going to go bald, don't you?" Startled a bit by his directness and his authoritative tone, I replied, "No, sir. I don't think I know what you mean. I hope I don't go bald, but if I do, there isn't a whole lot I can do about it." Then he decided to let me in on this amazing insight he seemed to have about the future of my follicles. "I read in *Reader's Digest* this morning, son, that people with hair like yours will eventually go bald because of that thing you use to comb your hair." He was referring to my huge Afro and that thing he was talking about was my rake, a necessity, of course, for maintaining a well coifed 'Fro. "Oh, I didn't read that, but I wouldn't worry much about that if I were you. I'm not." I knew that his remark was not made out of concern for me or whether I would actually become bald some day. Instead, that was his own way of letting me know that he disliked my hairstyle. Like the remark from Dr. Dumas that helped motivate me to stick with my decision to major in Spanish, I treated that professor's comments as motivation to make sure my 'Fro grew even larger.

My brother James had entered the University two years before, and along with his roommate received several pieces of hate mail each week at their dorm. Notes stating that "The KKK is watching you", and "Coons, go home!" were routinely tacked to their residence hall door at Elam Arms. As bad as those incidents were, the insults were not limited to overt acts of racism. As members of the USM marching band, James and several other black students had to decide how to respond to what they regarded as school-sanctioned racism. The signature song for the band was *Dixie*, which for most black people is abhorrent and insulting because of its glorification of the traditions of the old south, including slavery. To register their protest of the song, my brother and his fellow black band members risked expulsion from the band when they refused to play their instruments during the playing of *Dixie*. Those of us black students seated in the stands at the football games registered our own protest by remaining seated as every white spectator stood in a solemn show of sacred reverence for a song that had so much meaning to them and to us, but for much different reasons.

Reverence for the old south along with the celebratory and nostalgic atmosphere at the football games were made even more so by the official mascot of the football team. The team's mascot was a faux-bearded white student dressed as General Nat (short for General Nathan Bedford Forrest, the first Grand Wizard of the Ku Klux Klan) in full rebel regalia, including the obligatory confederate saber. Whenever the team scored a touchdown or field goal, General Nat, with his trusty white mount underneath him, would race up and down the sidelines, raise his saber as though preparing for an assault on Yankee troops, and belt out a well-defined loud rebel yell. Fortunately for us black students, the football team was not very good at that time and did not score very often. We wanted our team to win, but we were so relieved that we did not have to listen to General Nat very often.

As a student at USM, I was generally pretty serious and maintained a high B average and made the Dean's List several times. As a foreign language major, I learned to speak Spanish, Portuguese, Italian, Russian, and Swahili. Nevertheless, I made a few boneheaded decisions that seemed to indicate otherwise. The most notable boneheaded decision came in the summer of 1972 when I took a British Literature course. My friend Lewis and I took the class together, which turned out to be a huge mistake. Although Lewis and I were as close as two friends could be, being in the same class together was a really bad decision. He and I had been friends since grade school and developed a close friendship that is still strong. But I learned that summer that despite our life-long friendship he and I were not good for each other as students in Dr. Orange's British Lit class. On far too many occasions, before class started, he or I would slyly but predictably suggest to the other that we should leave before the professor, Dr. Orange, arrived. Neither of us had sense enough to resist making such a suggestion and even less to say no. Watching fellow students romping around outside throwing Frisbees, hanging out in the bright sunshine, and just generally having a lot more fun than we seemed to be having made it even easier to skip out before class started. I ended up with an F and Lewis got a D. To my credit, however, I repeated the class and earned a B.

Lewis and I were like the proverbial two peas in a pod. Wherever there was one of us, the other was likely somewhere nearby. With such a strong friendship, we could always count on each other to have the other's back. We made sure that we were not veering too far off our path toward graduation and that excessive partying did not interfere with the goal of earning our degrees. If either of us ever thought about messing up, with the exception of the class in which we received poor grades, or behaving in ways that would suggest that we had lost our minds, one of us would perform an intervention. Whether it was reassuring words or a swift, well-placed kick in the butt to set one of us straight, it was done. Never did the other one take offense or take for granted the special friendship that we had.

Another reason Lewis and I were always together, or knew how to reach the other if needed, was that he could not drive. I was his main source of transportation to and from campus, which I did not mind because we lived just a few blocks apart. And because he never took the time to learn to drive and get a driver's license, he did not own a car. The irony of his predicament was that I did not have a driver's license either; but I could drive; and I had a car. Two out of three wasn't too bad, I thought. My reason for not having a driver's license was that after taking driver's education in the 10th grade, I missed school the day the license exam was administered. Due to extreme procrastination and sheer laziness, I continued to drive my yellow Volkswagen for several years without any attempt to secure a driver's license. I was stopped only once, but because the officer knew my dad, he let me off with a warning. Perhaps the one incident that motivated me to finally get my license occurred one evening while Lewis and I were driving home after a night of pretty intense and serious partying. Naturally, I was driving and Lewis was in the passenger seat. I heard words coming from his mouth, but I had no clue as to what they were or what they meant. I wanted to focus only on my driving. If I were stopped, I surely would be in trouble for being inebriated and not having a driver's license. So, whatever he was saying, I tried to tune it out because I was convinced that I could not talk, listen to him, and drive safely at the same time. Then it happened. I made the left turn on to West Pine Street as I had done hundreds of times. Except this time, something was different. I did not remember making the turn. After I crossed the intersection, I asked Lewis. "Lewis, who just turned the steering wheel on this car?" Of course, he looked at me as though I had lost my mind. There were only two of us in the car, and when I looked at him, he was still sitting in the passenger seat. "It was you, boy. You don't remember? Couldn't be me 'cause I been sitting right here." I said, "Lewis. I got to stop this, man. We could have been killed or something." We both agreed that we dodged a bullet that fateful evening and that the good Lord was watching over us that night. Next day, I took the examinations for my driver's license and swore off driving a car while inebriated.

Not long after I got my first and only failing grade in college, I started to become disillusioned, burned out, and bored with college. I was thoroughly enjoying the social aspect of college life, but not the academics. Despite not enjoying being a college student I was doing fine in my courses, British Lit notwithstanding. I was making solid As and Bs in my foreign language courses and in my electives. However, the routine and monotony of going to class every day, not having clear career goals, and questioning the value of what I was doing, seemed to cause me to become restless and burned out with college. In the meantime, the Selective Service System had begun using a lottery draft system to select young men to prepare for and go to war in Viet Nam. The lottery system randomly matched birth dates that corresponded to a set of numbers; and if one's birthday matched a certain number, then one was called up for military service and in all likelihood shipped off to boot camp and eventually to the War. I think I reached rock bottom in my desperation to find relief for my restlessness, disillusionment, and boredom by hoping that my draft lottery number would come up. I stupidly thought that if my number came up, I would not have to take responsibility for doing something different with my life. I would just allow the government to do it for me, I thought. Fortunately for me, my number did not come up, although it was only a few numbers below the cutoff point. Gradually, I began to believe that there was a reason my number did not come up and that God must have a different plan for me. So, I forced myself to reassess my life and career goals in a more reasonable and rational way, in a way that would lead to a positive outcome and not involve risking my life or someone else's.

As sobering as that episode was in forcing me to get my head on straight, perhaps the event that convinced me more than any other to get myself together and stop feeling sorry for myself occurred in the summer of 1973 when I worked as a laborer at Hercules where my dad worked. The company allowed sons of employees to work and earn money for the summer, and my dad decided that that was a pretty good deal. The work was all mindless, meaningless, manual labor and the weather was typically boiling hot. I was in a detail of fellow summer temps that was assigned to the "bull gang." As neophytes and temps in the "bull gang," we would perform such mundane tasks as digging ditches in the mornings and in the afternoon covering them up. My worst assignment, however, was the order from the supervisor to go inside a rail tank car, wearing hot, heavy rain gear, to shovel black gooey, sticky chemical residue and sludge. The sweltering heat inside the huge black cylinder-shaped tank car conspired with the equally blistering heat generated by the heavy rain gear to literally make me sick. The heat and the odor were so intense that my fellow "bull gang" temps and I had to take turn going inside the tank car in ten-minute intervals. After I slowly and painstakingly emerged from the tank car, I think the supervisor realized that I was not cut out for such a strenuous detail; so he assigned me to the less arduous job of sweeping the floor at the smoke house. That was a much easier gig, and I appreciated being able to smell fresh air and wear clothes that were not drenched in sweat. Sweeping floors day in and day out made me realized that, without a doubt, that this was not God's divine plan for me. I certainly appreciated the generous offer by the management at Hercules to hire me for the summer and allow me to earn a rather significant amount of money. They did not have to do that. After all, I do not think that I contributed very much to the company's bottom line, nor do I think they expected me to do so. So, about mid-summer, I finally concluded that if working at Hercules was the alternative to being in college, I was definitely going to stay in school. And I did so with renewed gusto and commitment to getting my college diploma, the first Harris to ever do so.

There were somewhere around 200-250 black students on the USM campus when I enrolled in 1971 and by graduation in 1974, the number doubled. Weekend record hops were our normal outlet for social activities, although, there were several notable concerts featuring soul and R&B artists such as Sly and The Family Stone, Earth, Wind and Fire, and the Temptations. Several times a month, a spontaneous gathering of black students would take place in the front of the Student Services Building. These gatherings became opportunities for us to fellowship, experience a sense of camaraderie, or to rap (the word in those days referred to talking) about issues affecting black students on campus. We also used those opportunities to listen to recordings of speeches by Dr. King, Malcolm X, and one of my favorites, Dick Gregory. Because my mom worked at the local black radio station, WORV, I was able to get demo copies of all types of recordings, including soul, jazz, and speeches by famous black leaders. The album by Dick Gregory, *Dick Gregory at Kent State*, was especially entertaining because he had a unique way of blending stinging social commentary with side-splitting humor. Whether I was rapping or listening or just hanging out on the yard, my countenance was elevated every time I was able to gather with other black students to share common experiences, joys, and challenges.

During many of those gatherings there were intense discussions about the absence of black professors and administrators on the campus. The Afro American Cultural Society had written letters to the President requesting that he hire black professors and administrators, but predictably he ignored our requests. During the course of the discussion, we decided that the time for talking and writing letters, which had proven fruitless, had passed. More direct action was needed. So, following one of those discussions one evening, a hastily organized campus march took place. This was a first for the USM campus; and what made it especially unique and unforgettable was the fact that several black football players joined the march. Some of the black players, while quietly, but solidly behind our efforts, did not regularly attend most social or political events, except the record hops where they could meet girls. There was some light coverage of the march in the campus newspaper; and at the end of the day, we knew that nothing would ever change until the President retired.

Representatives from the U.S. Department of Justice came to campus one day at the request of the local NAACP chapter to investigate complaints by black students regarding the racial climate and the lack of progress in hiring black faculty and administrators. I attended one of those meetings in the Student Union Building along with several other black student leaders. The two Justice Department investigators, both black, asked us about our complaints regarding the racial climate and lack of progress in hiring black faculty and administrators. I answered that one of our issues was that we were sick and tired of listening to the band play *Dixie* and that most of us regarded the song as insulting and racist. The response I received was not what I expected and left me extremely disappointed. The investigator admonished and lectured us that we should not be upset by that song and that we should just ignore it; after all, he said, it is just a song. Upon hearing that comment, we knew that there was no need to continue the discussion with these people. Yes, they were from Washington D. C. and black; but obviously their view of the world was hopelessly different than ours. So we left. If they cannot understand the effects that *Dixie* has on black folk, I said to one of my friends, then there was no hope that they could ever understand how much we wanted black professors and administrators. I left the meeting with a deep appreciation of and sadness over the fact that even some black people just didn't get it. But then I realized that these two clueless black investigators worked for the Richard Nixon Justice Department and that I should not have been surprised at all.

Later that same day the manager of the Saenger Theater invited me, through my mom, to select a group of black students to come to the Theater to preview the movie *Sounder*, starring Cicely Tyson and Paul Winfield. I found about 10 other students who had to be convinced that I was not playing a joke on them. After convincing them that this was a serious matter, we all arrived at the theater at the appointed time. As I walked up to the glass front door of the theater, I realized that previewing this movie at this theater was going to be dually unprecedented for me. And I knew one precedent would be more challenging than the other. First, this was the first time I had ever been asked to preview a movie. I felt like a movie critic – watching a movie free-of-charge and telling someone who would listen what I thought about it. Second, this was the first time I would be allowed to sit in the downstairs section at the Saenger Theater. As a youngster and teenager, I was required to sit in the balcony because of the policy of segregation at the theater at the time. I made a mental note of this observable change in policy and the fact that it had taken decades for someone to change it. Obviously, the theater was under more enlightened leadership, I thought. But the truth is that movie distributors would no longer distribute movies to segregated movie theaters. So, they had to change the policy. Initially, I felt a little strange sitting in what was once the "white" section of the theater. But as I became more engrossed in the movie, that feeling of strangeness and being out of my "place" eventually dissipated. Following the movie we each reported to the manager that we liked the movie very much. He thanked us and informed us that because of our positive reviews, he was going to run the movie at his theater for the general public. He then gave special emphasis to his remark that we were welcomed to come back and sit anywhere we wanted to sit. I was not sure if that remark came from his heart or from some sense of financial or legal obligation. Then I realized that I was becoming a cynic and a skeptic. I was pleased with myself!

Best College Friends

Lewis Slay, Alvin Cooley, Larry Thomas and I were best friends from the beginning of our college days to the end. We developed a friendship bond that has lasted for decades, although it is not as strong today as it was during college. The bond that Lewis and I share is the exception. We will always be close friends. That bond developed over many nights sitting around Alvin's apartment talking about our dreams for the future while listening to the soulful sounds of Bobby Womack, Curtis Mayfield, Bloodstone, Donny Hathaway, or digging on the hard-hitting poetry of socially-conscious Gil Scott-Heron and the Last Poets (*The Revolution Will Not Be Televised!*).

I have many fond memories of our times together as students at the University of Southern Mississippi, but one that I remember with both fondness and vexation was an event during my senior year. Following the homecoming game that year, the four of us and our girlfriends reserved a table at the Top and Bottom Club for a night of celebration and revelry. We reserved the table in the name of "The Family", which is how we saw ourselves. At some point during the evening, Alvin raised his drink for a toast. We all followed his lead and clicked our bottles and glasses. Someone then boomed out a hearty, *Bottoms up!* As I was about to raise my drink to my lips, my girlfriend, shouted at me, *You'd better not! Don't you dare take that drink!* To say that I was taken aback and caught completely off guard is an understatement. And to make matters worse, someone responded, *Hey, Ant. Don't let her talk to you like that. You are a grown man, and she can't tell you what to do!* Defiance or compliance – those were my choices. And neither was a winning choice. And to prove that point, I responded with heart-felt bravado, *Yeah. That's right. You can't tell me what to do!* From that point on, every statement turned into a verbal free-for-all. The other women took the side of my girlfriend and warned their dates that they too had better not drink anymore. This quartet of macho guys and their strongly opinionated girlfriends were not about to let the other side have the last word. As the verbal judo escalated, any semblance of fun or family had completely evaporated into thin air. I left the Top and Bottom Club without my girlfriend, who had accepted a ride from one of the other women. It was not long after that unfortunate incident that my girlfriend and I departed company for good. It was not only that incident that caused the break up. We had a history of incompatibility and intense disagreements over both trivial and major issues, ranging from who my friends should be to how much time we should spend together.

Among my three close friends and me, there were strong ambitions, even if we were not exactly sure what our careers would be. Larry wanted to be a pharmacist, Alvin an architect and Lewis and I lawyers. Lewis and I later modified out career goals; and Alvin and Larry maintained and actually achieved theirs.

Periodically the four of us would make a pledge to commit ourselves to bachelorhood, at least until we reached age 30. We typically made that pledge when one of us was upset with our girlfriend,
or when we had partaken a wee too much of the Mad Dog 20/20,
Tokay, or Strawberry Hill. Interestingly, we seemed to never have
such thoughts when we were libation-free and when we were really
tight with our girlfriends. So, at various intervals during the decade
of the 1970s, long before our 30th birthdays, each of us emerged willingly and enthusiastically from bachelorhood. Lewis was first, I was
second, Alvin third, and Larry last.

Graduation

In August 1974, I graduated with my B.A. degree in Spanish
after having spent most of the summer in Bogotá, Colombia sharpen-
ing my Spanish-speaking skills. But after graduation, I sort of felt
like the dog that chases a car, finally catches up with it, and then is
not sure what to do next. I had the degree, but I was not sure what
I was to do next. With a bachelor's degree in Spanish, no teacher's
certificate, and no desire to be a teacher, I found myself with very few
options. So, I did the only logical thing left for me to do. I went to
work as a long distance operator with the telephone company. In fact,
I had inadvertently broken new ground by becoming one of only two
male long distance telephone operators in the Hattiesburg office of
Southeastern Bell Telephone Company. For the most part I enjoyed
being a telephone operator, but there were a few late nights at the
switchboard when I asked myself, "Is this what you went to college to
do?" Surely, God did not put me on this planet to sit here with a college education and answer telephone calls all day. Despite the drudg-
ery of being a telephone operator, there were also some light moments,
as when a drunken man dialed "0" and became totally flabbergasted
when he heard a man's voice instead of a woman's. After hearing
my standard greeting, "Operator, may I help you?" he responded in
genuine astonishment and disappointment, "Operator? This ain't no
damn operator. You a dude. What you doing on the phone?" My
response was simply, "Sir, you did dial "0" did you not? Well you

have reached the operator and how may I help you?" Reaching a male operator was also an oddity for some Latin American students enrolled at the University's English Language Institute. Because of my Spanish speaking ability, I frequently handled calls from Spanish-speaking callers. While handling a call on one occasion, I heard the caller saying to someone in the background "Es un maricon en el telefono." Not knowing that I understood and could speak Spanish, I politely informed him, "No soy marico!" He said that I was a homo-sexual, and I told him that I was not. Apparently, in his mind only a woman or a gay person would be a telephone operator. Being the professional that I was, I did not allow his comments to interfere with my job of making sure he was connected with his party.

Perhaps, the most interesting caller was a local woman who called an operator everyday to ask one of us to dial a local number for her. One night I had the unenviable pleasure of handling one of her calls. She told me that she was blind and could not see and that she wanted me to dial the local number for her. My first thought was, I know this woman. I recognized her voice and knew that she was no more blind that I was. My second thought was how redundant to say I'm blind and I can't see! But I placed the call anyway and wished her a pleasant day.

After ten stressful and thoroughly unrewarding months of sitting at that switchboard answering and placing 30-35 long distance calls an hour, I decided that I had had enough. Management promised me that I would be allowed to enroll in the company's management training program; however that turned out to be an empty promise. So, I resigned my position with absolutely no idea of what I was go-ing to do with my life. Again, I seemed to do the only logical thing. I went to Anchorage, Alaska to "find myself." Actually, my brother James was stationed at an Air Force base there, and he invited me to stay with him and his wife Kay so that I could look for a job there. That was a very generous offer, and I spent several weeks looking for a job. Finally, I found one – long distance operator of course; but I turned it down because I was getting homesick. I was missing my girlfriend and I wanted to go back to Mississippi to be with her. I also realized that I was in Alaska during the summertime when the weather is nice and the sun shines all day; but I also knew that would not be the case when the season changed to fall and winter. As a Mississippi boy, I realized that I did not want to live in a place that had so much snow, ice, and brutally cold weather. So, I returned to the familiar places and people of Hattiesburg to try again to figure out what in the world I was supposed to be doing with my life.

USM Student (Part Deux)

After returning from Anchorage, Alaska in August of 1975, I found myself unemployed, with no clear direction for my life. I appreciated my brother and sister-in-law offering to help me find my bearings, but the fact of the matter was that I was not fully committed to spending more time in Alaska than I already had. So, it was back to Mississippi to try again to find myself.

As providence would have it, I was visiting the campus at USM one day and met up with a couple of friends from my undergraduate years. After learning about my employment predicament, Marcia asked me if I knew about the graduate program in Counseling at USM. I had not, I told her. She walked me to the Counseling Department where I picked up an admissions application. I submitted the application to the Admissions Office and was admitted to the Master's degree program in Counseling for the fall 1975 school term. Although I had no idea what counseling was about, other than the unpleasantness visited upon my high school classmates a few years earlier, I knew it had to be better than doing nothing, which was my only other immediate alternative.

While in graduate school, I considered an invitation from a group of black men in Hattiesburg to become a member of their organization. Prior to that time, I had never heard of the organization, although they told me that the organization had chapters throughout the nation and the entire world. They tried to impress me; and succeeded in doing so by informing me that their organization was the oldest of its type anywhere in the United States. They also shared with me that they could boast that such great men as Dr. Martin Luther King, Adam Clayton Powell, Reverend Andrew Young, and

Dick Gregory were also members of their organization. I was also impressed with the fact that the organization advocated and strived for high moral and academic standards and had a long-standing commitment to improving the condition of black communities. As it turned out, they had invited four other young black men in town to join. Then, one night all five of us were invited to a meeting with the members of the organization who told us that they were officially inviting each of us to join them as brothers in the number one black fraternity in the world – Alpha Phi Alpha. We all said yes and after 12 months of pledging the charter line, three of us crossed the burning sands on May 1, 1976 into Mu Gamma Lambda Chapter. One of my line brothers dropped out because his church activities seemed to always conflict with pledge meetings, which did not pleased the big brothers. The big brothers, sort of tongue-in-cheek, finally gave him the choice of going to heaven or being an Alpha man. It appeared that he was not going to be able to do both. The former option is still available to him and to his credit the latter became a reality for him a few years later. I was very proud of my membership in this fine organization. It was my first introduction to a group made up exclusively of black men who advocated for the improvement of the black community, and it added immensely to my already burgeoning commitment to black male leadership.

While I was still in graduate school at USM, a racially-motivated incident took place that convinced me that Jim Crow had not completely gone the way of the dinosaur in Hattiesburg. I was looking for an apartment one day and decided to check the newspaper for a listing of vacancies in Hattiesburg. I read an ad in the *Hattiesburg American* advertising a vacancy in a white section of town. I decided that maybe times had changed enough so that a black person could legally and safely live in a white section of town. I called the real estate agent, whose name and telephone number were listed in the ad, and asked him if the apartment were still available. He answered yes and agreed to meet me at the apartment in half an hour to allow me to take a look at it. I arrived at the appointed time, walked up to the front door of the apartment building, and noticed a white gentleman standing in the doorway. I greeted him with a handshake, gave him my name, and told him I was there to look at the apartment per our telephone conversation. Nervously smiling and avoiding eye contact, he informed me that he could not rent the apartment to me after all because someone had just come by and left a deposit. He offered an apology, but I knew it was not sincere. I had just become another victim of the racist practice of not renting apartments in white neighborhoods to blacks. Nevertheless, I completed my master's degree in Counseling in August of 1976 and was offered a position as counselor in the University Counseling Center at the University of Southern Mississippi, at the whopping salary of $12,500 a year.

Going to the chapel and I'm gonna get married!

As a counselor in the University Counseling Center, I felt that I had found my calling. I suppose I was always a people person and my personality and training helped me to embark on a career that made a discernible difference in someone's life. I learned a tremendous amount about therapy and what it takes to be an effective therapist. I developed an abiding appreciation for the fragility of mental health as well as the amazing resiliency that most people possess when facing seemingly insurmountable challenges in their lives.

As an independent man with an income and an apartment, I thought I had finally made it. No more school. No more exams. No more studying. No more civil rights battles (Yeah, right!) I was done with school; and figured that since I had sewn all of my wild oats and had achieved all the education I would ever need, it was time to settle down and find a bride. I loved children; I wanted to start a family, and then embark on the quest for the American Dream. Nearly two years earlier, I met the woman whom I knew would be my bride and accompany on that grand quest. She was from Port Gibson, Mississippi and a freshman at the University of Southern Mississippi, and I was a graduating senior. After dating for several months, I asked her to marry me. She did not say yes, and she did not say no. She said, get a job, and then ask me again. That was a pretty fair bargain and reflected her level-headedness, despite her youth.

She also said that I would have to meet her parents and grand-mother. I thought that was also a fair bargain. So, I drove her to Port Gibson for her Christmas break, in order to save her father a two plus hour drive, each direction and to finally meet Mr. LaNell Frazier, Mrs. LaVada Frazier, and her grandmother, Mrs. Louise Miller. Meeting Mrs. Frazier was easy. She was very kind and graciously welcomed me to her home. She offered me food, which I gladly accepted. I felt at ease with her; and it was easy to see her daughter in her. Meeting her father and Mrs. Miller, however, would be very different in some very interesting ways.

Mr. Frazier was not home when Smithenia and I arrived, which caused me to experience a bit of relief. But that relief soon dissipated when Mrs. Frazier announced that Mr. Frazier would be home in about thirty minutes. This was the moment I was dreading, although I knew it was inevitable. I had no idea how he would greet me – with warm acceptance or cold-blooded rejection. It is one thing to win the acceptance of the future mother-in-law, but the task of winning over the future father-in-law is a much more daunting task. I was in un-charted waters, in the company of people who knew little about me or my background, other than I wanted to marry their second born child. When he did arrive home, the reception I received from Mr. Frazier was not quite what I expected. Following our brief exchange of formal and obligatory pleasantries, he immediately retreated down the hallway to his bedroom, where he immersed himself in his televi-sion shows, by himself. Judging by this unexpected development, I was convinced that I had my work cut out for me if I were going to win his acceptance and blessing to marry his daughter. The fact that he would not engage me in any conversation or invite me to join him in his television watching convinced me beyond a shadow of a doubt that I was failing miserably in my mission to ingratiate myself with him. There was no doubt that he hated me, my pessimistic mind kept telling me. As the hours moved forward, my optimistic-self contin-ued telling me that at some point he is going to say or do something that will make me feel more at ease. My pessimistic-self countered that he would more likely say or do something that would tip this teetering situation in a much different direction. Then it happened.

Like a stealthy lion, Mr. Frazier ran past me, quickly picking up speed as he got closer to his target. To my shock, his target was a shotgun. He grabbed the gun from the gun rack at the end of the hallway, and my heart sank. All I could think was, no doubt the man hates me and that I had failed at the get-the-father-to-like-me efforts. It was all happening so fast. I felt trapped like a cornered prey. There was no place to run and hide. I was stuck in my tracks, momentarily resigned to the fact that I was about to meet my maker. As he ran past me, I slowly began to compose myself and allow myself to breathe. My composure came only after I realized that he was racing down the hallway, running in my direction with his loaded shotgun to go outside to shoot a deer that was crossing the front lawn. I had never seen a deer stalked nor had I ever seen one killed in my entire life, but I was relieved that it was the deer that was the object of his murderous plans and not me. He realized later that I was bothered by what had transpired with the gun and the deer, and in his own inimitable way, assured me that he was not angry with me or hated me. He finally said, thanks for driving Smithenia home. And he even gave me his permission and blessing to marry his daughter. Since that time, he and I have had a great relationship. I regard him as one of the good guys.

My encounter with Mrs. Miller was not as frightening, but she did manage to make a lasting impression on me. During the 15-minute drive to her home, Smithenia attempted to prepare me for this important and pivotal encounter. She reminded me that, as the matriarch of the Frazier clan, Mrs. Miller wielded well-earned power and influence in many family matters, including whether it was okay for me to marry her granddaughter. She also wielded a great deal of love, even though her bravado and persona might suggest otherwise. As Smithenia continued to try to reassure me that Mrs. Miller's bark was worse than her bite, my nervousness began to rapidly escalate to a *TEN* on the *Ten-Point Harris Nervousness Scale*. My palms were clammy and sweaty. I was chatting incessantly about absolutely nothing. I felt a knot tightening in my stomach. In my mounting mental and emotional torment and reticence, I began to wonder whether this trip to meet her family was a good idea or not. After the incident with Mr. Frazier and the wayward deer, I was not overflowing with confidence. We finally arrived at Mrs. Miller's home. I took a few deep breaths as I exited the car. After Smithenia's three short knocks on the front door, Mrs. Miler emerged from behind a latched screen door, hugged her granddaughter, and ushered the two of us into her living room. After acknowledging me with a friendly hello, she offered the couch to us as she re-claimed what had to be her favorite easy chair, which was an arm chair that matched the three remaining pieces of a modern living room suit. She was a stout woman, with a strong, authoritative voice that reminded me of my teachers at Mary Bethune Elementary School – stern, strong, and serious. At once, that thought gave me both comfort and anxiety. Mrs. Miller wore glasses and wore her white hair short and neat. After only a few minutes in her presence, it was clear to me that her physical signs of senior citizen status belied her energy, vibrancy, and vim. After Smithenia formally introduced us, she looked at me with a disarmingly stern look that I had seen many times from my grade school teachers when I had done something egregious, even if I did not know what I had done. She stared at me for a long minute and said, *Boy, it's nice to make your acquaintance, but don't you ever come back to this town, without getting a haircut. And if you don't, you can forget about marrying my granddaughter. If you think I'm playing, try me.* I didn't know it at the time, but that was actually her way of letting me know that I was okay. But she really did not like my huge Afro. And wanting to remain in her good graces, I heeded her warning to get a haircut before the wedding, although my 'fro was still pretty big.

I guess considering my initial anxiety about meeting Mrs. Miller, Mrs. Frazier, and Mr. Frazier the first visit with Smithenia's parents and grandmother went okay. Everyone gave their blessing for me to join the family and become Smithenia's husband. I was relieved and humbled by the process. With their acceptance and blessing fully secured, it was then time to move on and start planning a wedding. But naturally we had to get a marriage license first, which led to another in a series of encounters with Jim Crow.

That encounter with Jim Crow occurred at the Forrest County Courthouse, the iconoclastic symbol of racial segregation in

Hattiesburg and the site of so many marches and demonstrations during the 1960s. In early 1977, Smithenia and I went to obtain our marriage license at the very same courthouse and at the very same Office of the Circuit Clerk where Mr. Theron Lynd, slightly more than a decade earlier, routinely and illegally denied black people the opportunity to register to vote. In order to be granted the marriage license, we had to register our intent to be married by signing our names in one of two large books lying on the counter. One book was black and the other red. Interestingly, in large gold letters, the black book was labeled "White", and the red book with the same color and type of lettering was labeled, "Colored". My bride-to-be and I looked at each other and then at the clerk. I momentarily pondered the obvious irony of the situation. A black book for whites only. How utterly stupid, I thought. The other point of irony was that a little more than a decade earlier, at that same courthouse, I was arrested by police officers who were attempting to enforce an unjust and illegal city ordinance that denied me the constitutional right to protest. In the present situation of trying to obtain a license to get married, once again the ghost of Jim Crow raised its ugly head in the form of another racist law that was designed to remind me that being black in Hattiesburg was synonymous with second-class citizenship. For a moment I seriously considered not participating in this ridiculous ruse and just getting the heck out of there. I felt the anger growing inside me, just as it did when the police officer threatened to feed me to the police dogs in 1965; when a white classmate at W.I. Thames Junior High School spat on me in 1966; when my college advisor told me in 1972 that I would not be able to pronounce Spanish words correctly because of black people's naturally defective tongue; and when a white real estate agent in 1975 refused to rent an apartment to me because of my race. Once again my palms were sweaty, my breathing shallow, and I felt the familiar rush of adrenaline gushing up through my insides. I could feel a knot in my stomach. My anger then became more focused and centered on the present moment. I said to Smithenia, "Can you believe this? They do not even have the courtesy to at least refer to us as black or Afro-Americans. After all these years of struggling and fighting for our rights and our dignity, we have once again become colored and they want us to submit to this Jim Crow practice and sign the colored book before we can get married. Some people just didn't get it." She nervously replied, "Honey, I know that you are angry and that this is not right. I also know that you and many others fought real hard to try to change things like this. You're right. It is a sad reminder that the struggle continues and probably always will. But I love you; and I want to marry you. So, let's be colored for right now and just sign the damn book." She always had a way of cutting to the chase and getting right to the heart of an issue. Because we very much wanted to be married, Smithenia and I endured this shameful reminder of one of the last vestiges of Jim Crowism in Hattiesburg and signed the big red "Colored" book.

My major priority quickly became preparing for my imminent wedding and making sure that my family was on board with the wedding, especially my brother Harold whom I had asked to be my best man; but I was not sure if he could because he was in the Navy at the time and was stationed in Virginia. I was also pre-occupied with making sure that my dad would be at the wedding. He was busy with his job at Hercules but promised me that he would be there. I always saw my dad as a strong, active, healthy man who was never sick. The only medical problem he ever had was surgery to repair a ruptured disc in his back when he was in his early 30s. Then, on February 25, 1977, the day before the wedding, unbeknownst to me at the time, that all changed. On the day of the wedding, while waiting for the wedding ceremony to begin, I took a quick peek from behind the door of the groom's waiting room and noticed that my dad was not seated where I thought he should be. I just figured that he was running late or had stepped out for a few minutes. However, as my best man Harold, the groomsmen, and I were standing at the altar, I still did not see him as I scanned the sanctuary once again. As soon as the ceremony was over, I went straight to my mom and asked about my dad. With a look on her face that revealed an intense struggle between sadness and happiness, she told me that my dad was not there because he was in the hospital in Hattiesburg. He had a heart attack the night before. She said she did not want to give me such bad news before the ceremony because she did not want to spoil this special day for Smithenia and me. My head told me she was right, but my heart told me something different. So, instead of going on a honeymoon, Smithenia and I drove directly to the Forrest General Hospital in Hattiesburg to check on him. Fortunately, he was doing fine and the prognosis was positive. The doctor told him that the positive prognosis could be enhanced if he opted for open-heart surgery. He flatly refused, saying that he was going to live his life as he chooses, take care of himself as best he could, and when his number is up, so be it. That decision did not surprise me at all. He was a stubborn man and rarely changed his mind once it was made up. He had several minor angina attacks later, but for 25 years remained free of any major heart-related problems. My dad worked at Hercules for nearly 25 years and would have worked longer had he not opted for a medical retirement at age 47.

Chapter 13

Farewell Mississippi - Hello Texas

In 1979, after Smithenia and I had been married for two years, we moved to Commerce, Texas where I enrolled as a doctoral student in counseling at East Texas State University. A year later, my beautiful bride gave birth to one of God's loveliest and most precious angels, Ashley Danielle. From the moment I saw Ashley in the delivery room, I knew that this child would change my life. In fact, it did not take long for that to happen, as she became a convenient and a more than sufficient source of motivation for me to immediately and cold-turkey give up my 3-pack-a-day cigarette smoking habit. I simply was not about to expose her little lungs to the hazards and danger of my filthy habit.

No one but God will ever know how pleased I was when that bundle of joy was brought into our lives through His boundless grace and mercy. While driving home alone from the hospital after her birth, I cried tears of joy and thanked God for this precious gift and for blessing her with all of her toes, fingers, and other fully function-ing body parts intact. Even more pleasing was the fact that I had a little girl, which I very much wanted. I had only brothers and just always thought girls were something special. She quickly grew into a beautiful little girl and even more quickly into the apple of her Daddy's eyes.

After arriving home from day care one afternoon, Ashley shared some rather unsettling news with her mom and me. She announced in an uncharacteristically sheepish voice, "Dad, mom, I don't want to be black anymore!" My first reaction was that she was trying to make me laugh. After I saw the anguished look on her pretty brown face, I knew that this was no laughing matter. She was serious. I also knew that Smithenia and I would now have to use parenting skills we never had to use before. She and I immediately saw this as one of those proverbial teachable moments. However, my dear wife gave me that look that said, "Okay. You are the civil rights guy; so, you'd better handle this one!" I took a deep breath, knelt in front of Ashley and asked, "Honey, why do you not want to be black?" "Daddy, Timmy said he doesn't like black people. I don't want him to quit being my friend; so I wish I didn't have to be black." I searched quickly through my mental address book looking for the name Timmy. I then realized that Timmy was a little white boy at the day care and was one of Ashley's best friends. "You're not mad at me are you dad?" I felt like I had just been punched in the solar plexus, as I took in a quick gasp of air. There was nothing in the manual that prepared me for this, I thought. I was not sure if I was supposed to be angry, sad, or both. But some emotion, which I could not identify nor define, was slowly revealing itself in my breathing and in my face. I guess she identified the emotion as anger as she asked if I were mad at her. But I reassured her that I was not angry with her. I took a deep breath to calm and center myself. I had to realize that this was not about me. It was about her. I imagined seeing the dangerous seeds of self-doubt, self-loathing, and low self-esteem beginning to be planted in her little mind. I knew this had to be nipped in the bud *immediately*, before those seeds grew into a major obstacle to a psychologically and emotionally healthy life for her. "Sweetheart, I want you to know that your mom and dad love you very much. You are a beautiful little girl with a beautiful skin color; and God, your mom and dad love your beautiful brown skin. And I want you to love your beautiful brown skin. I want you to know, sweetie, that although you are a beautiful little girl with beautiful skin color that is different than Timmie's, I don't want you to ever think that you are any less than anyone else or any better than anyone else. I love you very much, and I am so proud that you are my beautiful brown little girl." She stopped twiddling her fingers, looked into my eyes, and said, "Okay dad. I love you". Then she gave me one of her special heart melting smiles and hugs. As she skipped along her merry way to play with her dolls, I began to wonder how many other black parents had to do what I had just done. I wondered how many of those parents handled it the way I did. I wondered how many black Ashley's around the country were receiving messages from friends, playmates, and even adults that their worth and dignity were less because of the color of their skin. Most importantly, I wondered, *why*! I figured that most white parents probably never had to deal with such a pivotal moment in their child's life when the child herself questioned her own racial self-identity. I also knew that my words alone, no matter how heart-felt and truthful, would not be enough to instill in this little 5-year old child, a strong and healthy sense of pride in her race and her skin color. Smithenia and I knew that we would have to do something more concretely. We decided that one of the most important things we could do was to begin to surround Ashley with as many icons and images of black people as we could. She loved playing with her huge collection of dolls, all of which were white. So, we went out at Christmas and bought every black Cabbage Patch Doll we could find and *afford*. Our intent was to convey to Ashley that she could see and appreciate her own image in her black dolls and begin to accept and value the blackness and beauty of both her dolls and herself. We also decided that we would furnish our home exclusively with black art that contained positive and uplifting images of black people. We did that not only for Ashley's and her baby brother's benefit, but for ours' as well, as daily reminders of just who we were, racially, and how proud we were to be so.

Ironically, several years later Ashley and I were watching an in-stallment of the acclaimed PBS documentary, *Eyes on the Prize,* when there was a distressing scene of a black man being brutally beaten by a group of white men in Little Rock, Arkansas following the de-segregation of Central High School. I intentionally looked at her facial expressions as she was intently watching this unfortunate and despicable scene. Out of the blue, she blurted out in uncharacter-istic anger, "Daddy, I hate white people!" Again, here was another teachable moment. How many parents have had to deal with such an announcement from an 8-year old before, I wondered? If not *white people*, fill in the blank. It could be black people, homeless people, overweight people, poor people, rich people, etc. I was forced to check my own emotions regarding the scene of the black man being beat-en to be sure I was not unconsciously suggesting to her that I, too, hate white people. I came up with what I thought was a reasonable response. "Ashley, it is not good to hate. That is why those men are beating that helpless black man. Hatred is what is causing them to do this. We don't want that to happen, right? So, let's not hate, okay, because we don't want this type of thing to happen to anyone else." With a look of both relief and confusion, she responded, "Okay, dad. You're not mad are you?" I laughed and gave her a hug and said, "No, sweetheart, I'm not mad. I just want you to know that God wants us to love each other, not hate each other."

Ashley's brother Michael never reported any racial incidents to us as he was going through grade school. Nevertheless, he experienced his share of unique and heart-stopping moments as a child. A couple of humorous and not so humorous incidents caused us to conclude, half-jokingly, that had Michael Vincent Harris been born first, he probably would have been an only child. When he was about three years old, Michael and I were at a basketball game at East Texas State University. He was standing next to me, fixated on the action taking place on the court while I was engrossed in a conversation with a friend. Suddenly, I heard the referee's whistle blow; and the huge crowd of spectators broke into wild laughter. I stopped talking, looked around for Michael, and looked over at the court. And my heart just sank as I discovered the reason for the loud laughter from the crowd and the frantic toots from the referee's whistle. Yes. My dear son wanted to play with the big boys and had run out onto the court to join them in the action. I quickly ran out onto the court, picked him up, and apologized to the referees and the coaches. At that moment I was torn between scolding him and holding him. I chose the latter, although he did cry. He wanted to know why he could not play and could not figure out what the big deal was about. He said that he just wanted to play with the ball and cried only because I told him that he could not. The crowd continued to laugh a little longer and the game promptly resumed.

Another incident with Michael took place one Sunday when I took him to Sunday school. Our normal routine was for me to pull up to the curb, open his door, and kiss him good-bye. In return, he would say good-bye and walk up the steps and into the church. Well, this particular Sunday, however, he decided that instead of sticking with the normal routine, he would come around to my side of the van to say good-bye to me again. I was horrified when I looked in my side-view mirror and saw a rather large vehicle approaching on the left. As the vehicle got closer to where I was parked I was not able to see Michael, but I knew that he, too, was coming around to the left side of the car. I also knew that Michael was much too small to see the oncoming car and too small for the driver to see him. I knew that he would make a wide arc in his path to the driver's side of my minivan. The unsuspecting driver and my equally unsuspecting son were on a sure fatal collision course. Calling out to Michael was not going to prevent what I knew was about to happen. He would have simply thought I was calling him to come to me. Likewise, blowing my horn hoping that the driver would stop was not going to work because the driver would have had no idea why I was blowing my horn. So, instincts took over, and I did the only thing that could be done to prevent an impending deadly tragedy. I quickly opened my door into the path of the oncoming vehicle, which was a large, four-door sedan that was generally referred to as a gas-guzzler. As expected and desired, the sound of crashing metal on metal reverberated throughout the parking lot, as the driver's car collided with the driver's door of my minivan, causing the door to barely hang from its hinges. But it worked. He stopped just a couple of feet from Michael. Of course, Michael was totally oblivious to the presence of the car, and he just kept running toward me. I jumped from my vehicle and hugged him as tightly as I could and told I love him. He said, "I love you dad. Bye!" He had absolutely no idea how close he came to being killed that morning. The driver, who was understandably baffled about why I opened my car door in his path, bolted from his car and ran to me with a crazed and panic look until he realized what had just happened or did not happen. He was not angry with me. He just could not understand why I would intentionally cause him to ram my car door. As he calmed down, he and both reached the same conclusion: losing the car door was no big deal at all. It was replaceable, but my son was not. That incident further deepened my belief in the existential philosophy that when humans fully and unconditionally realize and accept the notion that we can lose those whom we love and care about the most, we tend to value and cherish them even more. After nearly losing my son, I certainly began to value and cherish everyone I loved even more than ever.

I thoroughly enjoyed living in Commerce, Texas. When we moved there in 1979, we had planned to live there for only a few years to complete my doctorate degree, and then return to the University of Southern Mississippi, where I was on a leave of absence. But the place had grown on me and I was hooked. I was hooked by the people, the pace of life, and the quality of life. I could not imagine living anywhere else than in Commerce, Texas. My wife and children shared the same sentiment.

Commerce enabled me to further develop my leadership skills by providing opportunities to become involved in the civic life of the community. My first foray into civic leadership was my helping to found a local group called the Commerce Professional Men's Club (CPMC). Along with a few other local black men, we established CPMC as an organization dedicated to the improvement of the larger Commerce community and specifically, the local black community. We provided need-based scholarships for students to attend college. We held community clean-up campaigns to help beautify some of the blighted areas of the Norris Community, the predominant black community in Commerce. In addition to philanthropic and other altruistic activities, we also established ourselves as a viable political entity. As a political entity, we routinely received endorsement requests from candidates for city and county elections. As a 501 (C) 3 organizations, of course, we could not endorse candidates for political office. However, the candidates believed it was in there best interest to let it be known that they had spoken to the Commerce Professional Men's Club. Norris Community residents frequently sought the Club's advice regarding which candidate or referendum was in the best interest of the community and the City of Commerce. We provided a much-needed service for the Norris Community and the City of Commerce by being a positive force for change and improvement for both.

My second foray into local leadership came when members of the CPMC urged me to file for a vacant position on the Commerce Independent School District Board of Trustees. Initially, I was reluctant. I had no idea what a school board member did, and since my daughter was not yet school age and my son was just an infant, I could not imagine why anyone would want me to serve as a school board member. But I kept hearing that voice from my civil rights days urging me to once again step up to the plate and make a difference. I heeded those voices, filed for the position and won the election by 75 votes, which in a town the size of Commerce was considered a landslide.

Following the completion of my first three-year term in 1987, I ran again successfully and unopposed for four additional three-year terms, serving a total of 15 years, six as the board's first black president. It was during my tenure as a member of the Commerce School Board that I developed a deeper appreciation for public education and for public school teachers. I saw first-hand the enormous dedication and commitment by a wonderful group of underpaid and underappreciated professional men and women who worked tirelessly and successfully to positively impact the lives of young people. Moreover, I arrived at the unequivocal conviction that as goes public education, so goes our democracy. That conviction has led me to firmly oppose the illogical and counterproductive proposition that taking dollars from public education and giving them to private schools is going to somehow improve the very system from which the money is being taken. This democracy will suffer enormous harm if we allow that to happen.

My service as a school board member also tested my belief in free speech and freedom of the press. One night at a board meeting a large group of concerned parents and citizens showed up to demand that two library books be removed from the high school library because of their objection to the profane language and adult themes contained in both books. Both books had received national literary awards; and a committee, per school district policy, approved the books for inclusion in the high school library's holdings. Neither book was required reading

Supporters and opponents of the request to remove the books exerted tremendous pressure on board members and administrators before and during the board meeting. Representatives of the group handed out photo copies of the most offensive excerpts from the book to everyone present. As I read the excerpts, I remember saying to myself that I am not sure whether or not I wanted my kids reading this material. But I also said to myself that if we banned these two books, where would we draw the line? Next time, someone would find objections to some other book, and we would end up with a never-ending series of requests to ban books. I reasoned that banning books is something that is done rather routinely in totalitarian nations. In a democracy, that should never be allowed to happen. Democracies are sometimes not as neat and tidy, when it comes to free expression, as nations that are governed by dictators. In those governments, the government, not the people get to decide what citizens read; and as a result, dissension and controversy are minimized or non-existent. Democracies are not supposed to be that simple. They require us to make tough choices, especially when it comes to deciding how we transmit our history through the written word. Although I would have preferred that my own children not read either book, I was not willing to make that decision for other parents by imposing my judgment about such matters on them. After much discussion and gnashing of teeth, the board wisely voted to not ban the books. My vote to deny the parents' petition to remove the books was an easy one, despite the presence of my pastor, who gave me a look that suggested that if I voted to keep the books, there would be a sermon the next week on the evils of humanism and the moral corruption of our children by way of trashy library books. Despite the potential divisiveness of the board's decision, it was the morally correct thing to do.

Several years later while still a member of the school board, I found myself in the middle of another controversy in Commerce. I did not go looking for it. It just fell into my lap. The local newspaper printed a picture of two black high school football players posing for the photographer with exaggerated smiles and eating watermelon with their white coach sandwiched between them. The caption below the picture stated that the coach was watching over his two players. I immediately reacted to both the picture and the caption. The picture was nothing more than a caricature that perpetuated the stereotype of the happy darkies enjoying a slice of watermelon down on the old plantation. Adding to that stereotype was the choice of words by the writer/photographer in stating that the coach was watching over his players. In my view that was a Freudian reference to the overseer watching over his happy darkies down on the old plantation. I called the superintendent and complained to her that the coaches were wrong in allowing that picture to be taken. If the picture had been taken of the black players sitting around with other players enjoying the watermelon while taking a break from their normal routine, I would not have objected. But this was a staged photo-op; and at several points along the way, some adult knew or should have known that such a photo would likely trigger outrage from the black community. The superintendent and head football coach/athletic director were sympathetic and supportive of my position on the matter. Both expressed their regrets and disapproval of the picture and the caption. However, I realized that I needed to do more than verbally express my outrage. So, I wrote a letter to the editor of the newspaper that was published a few days later. In the letter, I expressed my disappointment with the photographer, editor, and the other adults present during the picture-taking for failing to have the sensitivity and respect for the students, their families, and black citizens throughout the community to prevent the picture from being taken and having it printed in the newspaper. They all had many opportunities to exercise better judgment by realizing at some point, beginning with the request for the young men to pose; the actual snapshot being taken; the development of the film; the writing of the caption; and making the decision to print the caption and the picture, that something was simply wrong about this. I was not upset with the young men because they were too young to have an awareness and appreciation of the historical significance of the caricature of blacks enjoying watermelons. However, the adults on the other hand should have known better.

I knew that I was stepping out on a limb in writing the letter. I knew that some in the community would not like what I had to say. In fact, several rebuttal letters were printed in which I was accused of stirring up controversy. I was even told that if I had not brought it up, no one would have thought anything at all about the picture. And that was precisely my point - no one cared enough to think about what they were doing and what the picture represented to most black people in town. Despite the nasty remarks from some whites in the community, I knew that I had done the right thing. Perhaps, the strongest expression of support, ironically, came in an e-mail message from a white professor in the University's Photography Department. After reviewing the picture again and reading my letter to the editor several times, he wanted me know that my letter and the picture had prompted him to become more intentional in his instruction to his photography students on the critical importance of being sensitive when using members of various racial groups as subjects in their photographs. That was really my point all along in objecting to the picture – raising people's level of awareness and concern about the impact of racially insensitive behavior, whether intentional or unintentional.

A few years earlier, Jim Crow made an unexpected, but not surprising visit to my wife and me. This incident was in sharp contrast to my landslide victory in my first school board election. In the school board election in 1984, the voters of Commerce expressed their support for me as an individual who held strong beliefs about social justice. In contrast to that overwhelming community support, that earlier incident sent a much different message and left a very bitter taste in my mouth. We had been living in an apartment for nearly two years; and after Ashley and Michael started growing and needing more room, we started searching for a house to rent. As a couple with only one child, Smithenia and I were pleased with the size of the apartment. However, with the addition of another child and all of the space needed for two growing children, larger living quarters were an absolute must. While visiting my wife at her job one day, she, a white friend and co-worker and I were discussing options for living in Commerce other than an apartment. We did not like any of the properties listed in the newspaper and were beginning to feel really discouraged. To our surprise and delight our friend told us that she knew a man who owned rental houses in town and who was also a member of her church. She said that if we wanted us to, she would call him to find out if he had a vacancy at one of his properties. We said of course and thanked her being willing to act on our behalf. So, she dialed the man's number in our presence. When she began to speak to him, Smithenia and I smiled at each other, feeling confident that we were about to find a house at last. I could hear our friend asking the prospective landlord about when the house would be available. She repeated what he said, "Next week. That soon, huh?" With those words, Smithenia and I both had really wide grins on our faces as we grabbed each other's hand and gave a tight squeeze. In the interest of full disclosure, our friend then told the landlord that the couple interested in renting his house was black. We could then hear her say, "Oh really. I'm sorry to hear you say that." Our smiles quickly turned to anguish as she hung up the telephone and told us what we had already knew. "He said that he could not rent to blacks. He said he has never rented to blacks because he thought blacks would tear up his house." The man did not know me from Adam. How could he make his mouth even form those bigoted words and assume that because my wife and I are black we are going to tear up his house? To top it all off, she told us that he said that the couple vacating the house was a Japanese couple that was moving back to Japan. He'll rent to someone from another country but not to blacks. How insulting, ironic, and discriminating, I thought.

Kellogg National Fellowship Program

Another unexpected but welcome event emerged in my life when I was selected in 1988 to participate in the W.K. Kellogg Foundation's National Fellowship Program (KNFP). KNFP was designed to provide leadership training for a cadre of current and emerging domestic and international leaders. The objective of the program was to provide the skills necessary to become a better leader, a better professional, and a better human being. An interesting occurrence in the KNFP selection process taught me a very valuable life lesson, although I don't think that was the intent. Several weeks after I submitted my application, I received an invitation to go to Atlanta, Georgia for an interview, which was the final step in the selection process. At the appointed time, I was asked to enter the interview room. It seemed that my heart was racing so fast that it was going to just pop right out of my chest. Seated at a large oval conference table were ten complete strangers who, although friendly and cordial, intimidated the living daylights out of me. I was asked to take the seat at the head of the table. I was offered a glass of iced water, which seemed to rattle noisily from my trembling hands. I was introduced to everyone by the group's leader, but I was thinking that there was no way I was going to remember all those names. This happens a lot when I meet new people. We exchange names, and it is a given that within 10 minutes, no one can recall the other's name, especially if we are certain that we will never see each other again. As I sat in the hot seat at the head of the table, my mind began to wonder, would I ever see these people again or would this be a run of the mill inquisition where I would thank them for inviting me to the interview, leave, and never ever remember anyone's name?

The first question from the assembled inquisitors came from the group's leader, Dr. Larraine Mutasak. She asked if I could be three people, who would they be and why? Before I could finish uttering the name, Ms. Fannie Lou Hamer, another questioner asked, if I could convene an international conference what would be the theme of that conference and name three people I would invited as keynote speakers? Before I could fully gather my thoughts and formulate an intelligent answer on the need for an international conference on world hunger, someone else chimed in with, if you were riding in a limousine with the President of the United States, name three things you would discuss with him? The pattern persisted for another 15 minutes, until Dr. Mutusak thanked me for coming and informed me that I could leave. As I was leaving, one of the questioners walked over to me, extended her hand, and said with a smile, *good luck with all your future endeavors*. Now there's a subtle way of saying, sorry buddy, you didn't make it. At least that is what my pessimistic self was telling me. My optimistic self was telling me that I hadn't done that poorly. A few weeks later, my optimistic-self took a bow and said, I told you so. A letter from the W.K. Kellogg Foundation arrived with an invitation to participate as a Group 9 Fellow in the Kellogg National Fellowship Program. I had the remarkable fortune and blessing to be one of 43 individuals selected to participate in the Foundation's 3-year leadership development program. The lesson learned was that no matter how poorly I think I am doing, I am probably doing much better than I think.

A major requirement of the fellowship program was the selection, development, and implementation of a learning plan, which had to be unrelated to our field of expertise. For my learning plan, I chose to focus on the causes and solutions of domestic and world hunger. The pursuit of that learning plan led me to such desperately poor countries as Zaire (now Democratic Republic of the Congo), Rwanda, South Africa, Kenya, Venezuela, Cuba, Trinidad-Tobago, Russia, and Mexico, resulting in a direct and deeply intense additive to the continuing process of my awakening to a whole new world beyond the U. S. borders.

In 1989, as part of my fellowship activities, I had the occasion to visit Zaire, perhaps the world's most blatant example of man's inhumanity to man and a modern, tragic example of what happens to poor people when their needs and concerns are met with neglect and indifference from a world that has decided that world poverty is someone else's concern. While visiting the capital city of Kinshasa, I had the opportunity to visit Mama Yemo Hospital, which was one of three hospitals in a city of more than 3 million people; and it was the hospital that provided care for the poorest of the poor in one of the poorest cities on the planet. Immediately after walking onto the compound of Mama Yemo, my senses were incredibly stimulated by the sights, sounds, and smells of sick and dying people. Twisted, lame black bodies of all shapes and sizes writhing and moaning in horrible pain were sprawled out along the sidewalk and on the ground. The cries of babies; the wailing of grieving parents; the stench of death and sickness; swarming mosquitoes and flies attached to the faces, arms, and legs of everyone, living or dead, all melded together in a discord of raw emotion, for both victim and visitor. These individuals were outside Mama Yemo Hospital, the host told me, only because there were not enough beds for them inside this run-down cesspool that passed as a government operated hospital. The host went on to explain that even if there were enough beds there would not have been enough room to place more beds in the tiny, hot, overcrowded hospital. As I cautiously stepped over one body after another, I began to seriously wonder if I would be able to get through this visit without losing my lunch. I also wondered what had gone so wrong with humanity that sick and dying human beings had to lie and sleep on the sidewalk and ground at a hospital.

As I continued this mind-boggling and heart-wrenching trek through Mama Yemo Hospital, I was directed to a small examining room where a young Zairian mother was sitting in a small worn-out wooden chair, fanning her sweaty, drained and distressed face while cradling her equally sweaty, drained and distressed black baby in her arms. The American-trained Zairian Public Health Officer told me that the baby was 24 months old, but from her tiny size, she appeared to me to be no older than 12 months. As I struggled to focus my attention on the sight of this precious little baby and away from the mounting stench and the swarm of flies that shared the cramped examining room with all of us, I became concerned with the condition of the seemingly motionless child, nestled in the bosom of her visibly concerned mother, whose tears and sweat had lost their distinction. The Public Health Officer told me to notice that occasionally the baby would slowly move her little head from side to side and intermittently open and close her tiny eyes. A few minutes later I saw movement from the baby and was momentarily relieved, until the Public Health Officer continued with his disturbing description of her condition. He told me very matter-of-factly that when the baby moved her head from side to side and opened and closed her eyes, she was expressing her pain – the only way she could. She was so utterly exhausted and weak from the assault on her tiny body from her illness that she no longer had the strength to cry. Moreover, she was so completely dehydrated that she was unable to shed any tears, despite such a normal human response to unbearable pain. In an unexpected response on my part to this heart-breaking sight, almost immediately, my own tears began to well up and flow. I felt I was a surrogate crier for one of God's suffering children who had been robbed of her natural ability to cry. The Public Health Officer then told me in his now familiar matter-of-fact manner that the baby was dying from a disease in his country they call the slim disease; and in other countries, they call AIDS. Sadly, but far from being uncommon, not only did this baby have AIDS, but her siblings and mother were also infected with the deadly disease. What made the situation even sadder was that the mother knew that as she breastfed her children, she was also passing along the AIDS virus to them, which would surely doom them to unbearable suffering, pain, and an early death. But she also knew that if she did not breastfeed them, they would experience an equally painful death from malnutrition and the concomitant illnesses that routinely shorten the life expectancy of African children. Because of the rampant poverty in Zaire, instant baby formula was non-existent; so her breast milk was the only source of sustenance for her babies. Also, because of the shortage of sterile syringes, doctors often had to administer medication to different patients with the same syringe, thus ensuring the continued spread of HIV.

After hearing the Public Health Officer's explanation of the condition of mother and baby, I knew that I had just been introduced to a completely different concept of suffering, despair, and poverty in one of the poorest cities in one of the poorest countries in the world. Indeed, I had seen suffering, despair and poverty before, in Mississippi, one of the poorest states in the United States of America; but what I had just witnessed was totally unlike anything I had ever seen or heard of anywhere in the USA. I left Mama Yemo feeling sick and just wanting to hug my own precious little children to let them know how much I loved them. Ironically, the experience at Mama Yemo also reinforced and bolstered my faith. One of my initial responses to the heartbreaking scenes at Mama Yemo was to ask God where he was and why did he allow his children to suffer so. The answers were strong and convicting: A short distance from Mama Yemo was the site of Zairians deeply involved in Sunday worship services. The scene of these faithful believers convinced me that if, in the midst of such unfathomable suffering and despair, they could maintain their faith in God, there should never be any reason for me to have doubts about God. I was also reminded of scripture that reassures us that He is always with us, no matter the conditions: *where two or three come together in my name, there am I with them.*

Despite the sadness of watching the awful pain and suffering of that precious baby and her mother at Mama Yemo, other excursions, in sharp contrast, around the Motherland were extremely heartwarming. Not long after arriving in Nairobi, Kenya, the eight African Americans in my group began to have what I called a "Roots" experience, in which each of us started having a rush of emotions brought on by being in the Motherland. The emotions were totally unexpected and further cemented an already strong bond among us. Something special was happening to each of us individually, and initially, unbeknownst to each other; and when we came together to talk about what we were experiencing, it was unlike anything any of us had ever known or experienced before. We spent all of our free time and travel time together talking, sharing, laughing, and just marveling at how lucky we were to be on the continent of our ancestors. Oddly, though, the bonding and sharing of the "Roots" experience among the eight African Americans triggered a surprisingly bitter reaction from several of the white Kellogg Fellows in the group. Some of them felt that we were leaving them out of our "Roots" experience and discussions and that we should take turns riding on their van so that they could learn about our experience. During a very heated discussion one evening when this issue was broached by one of my white colleagues, I responded that this "Roots" experience among the blacks was not about them. It was about us, period. It was not an anti-white thing, but a rare attempt by the black members of the group to fully experience something that we had never experienced before and may never again. I told them that at any time, anyone who wanted to know what I was experiencing should simply come to me and ask. I would be happy to share. However, I did not feel that it was my place to go to them and ride on their van for their convenience and their entertainment. Away from the rest of the group, a white colleague admitted to me that her frustration came from her feelings of jealousy and envy because the black members of the group at least knew where their ancestors came from, and she had no idea.

I also spent an enormous amount of time in private and group conversations with Kenyan men and women who had as much curiosity about me as I had about them. I have a distinct recollection of our octet being invited to a gathering at the home a local business leader in Nairobi, who had also invited several colleagues and neighbors to fellowship and socialize with us. While talking to one of the Nairobian gentlemen about the various tribes in Kenya, he suddenly stopped in the middle of his conversation, looked at me as though he had just experienced an epiphany, slowly rose to his feet, reached out to me with both arms and invited me to embrace; and as we embraced, he said, "Welcome my brother to your homeland. I now see that you are my African brother who lives in the United States." I did not know what to say. Those words were like sweet music to my ears, like hearing my favorite hymn, Amazing Grace. Somewhere in my life scripts, I had been led to believe that Black Africans do not like Black Americans. However, this poignant and completely spontaneous moment forced me to immediately and permanently erase that error-laden script and to replace it with one that allowed me to more fully appreciate my African-ness, even more so because of my light complexion. From the first day in Africa, I was seriously concerned about how I, as a light skinned black man, would be regarded by Africans. Now I could put that concern aside, along with all of the other myths that I had about Africa and African people. I finally found words that I hoped would be appropriate for the moment, "Thanks so much for saying that, sir. I cannot express to you how good those kind words make me feel. You will never know how much I appreciate your acknowledging me as your African brother."

In subsequent days, as I strolled through the streets of Nairobi, I imagined that my nascent and indescribable feelings of joy and excitement must be at least a little like Alex Haley's, when he began writing *Roots*. My overwhelming sense of being connected culturally, emotionally, and spiritually to this land was fortified when Kenyan men and women on the streets would acknowledge me in special ways – a power sign, a smile, or a nod – that let me know that I was indeed their African brother and that neither the origin of my birth nor the amount of melanin in my skin made any difference at all. I was overjoyed beyond description to see with my own eyes that black Africans came in all shades from albino to very dark skin, which enabled me to confidently and fittingly proclaim my African heritage.

One evening several from our group of eight were eating at the restaurant at the Jacaranda Hotel in Nairobi and struck up a conversation with the restaurant manager. Between water refills and bites of our burger and fries, we shared with him our individual and collective excitement about our newfound connectedness to his country. He told us that when he first saw us around the hotel and the restaurant he knew we were black Americans, but thought we were just typical tourists who cared little about his country's authentic, nontouristy culture. The more we talked, the more he was convinced that we were not typical tourists from the States, and that we were genuinely appreciative and respectful of his culture and country. He left the table and returned after about 15 minutes. He then surprised each of us with a totally unsolicited gift that cost him absolutely nothing but was exceedingly priceless to each of us. He was a member of the Kamba tribe and wanted to give each of us an honorary name and membership in his tribe. When my turn came he put his hand on my shoulder and said, "You are Mutua. It means birth of a boy. When a mother gives birth, she always wants a boy. When a boy is born, she shouts Mutua!"

When I left Africa, for the first time ever, I was able to embrace the term African American. Before, I thought that term was a fad and had little relevance to me. I was proud and pleased to be a Black American. But the acceptance of my African-ness by Africans was enough for me to fully realize that my Blackness went beyond being a Black American, and from that moment forward, I could lay claim to being an embodiment of the Diaspora. I was indescribably elated in the knowledge that I would forever be tied to the Motherland of Africa.

On another trip to Africa two years later in August 1991, I had another experience that helped to greatly influence my view of myself and my view of the world. This experience was different than any other, yet was eerily reminiscent of my experience in racially segregated Mississippi. As I sat in the driver's seat in one of two red compact rental cars parked in the parking lot of the Midway Hotel in the town of Middleburg, the haunting reality of being in the most racist country in the world hit me like a ton of bricks.

Although I thought I was prepared to deal with one of humankind's worst examples of inhumanity, what happened in the ensuing moments put a quick end to that misplaced notion. I was now deep in the heart of the Transvaal, one of the most conservative and racist provinces in the Republic of South Africa. The year was 1991 and I was physically in South Africa. Psychologically and emotionally, however, I was in Mississippi and the year might as well have been 1961. Although I had survived American Jim Crowism in Mississippi, South African apartheid in Middleburg was about to teach me another lesson about the deadly combination of power and prejudice.

We exited the two cars that we rented in Bbane, Swaziland, five Americans – three blacks and two whites – and proceeded to the doorway beneath the sign that read "Midway Hotel Restaurant". How interesting, I thought: Midway across the Transvaal…in Middleburg … at the Midway Hotel … in the middle of apartheid. Tired, hungry, and in desperate need of a restroom, we fortuitously stopped at the Midway Hotel after being cautioned earlier in the day by a white South African in another town not to go to that town's local restaurant because it was for blacks only. How odd, I naively thought. I am black as are two other members of our party. Why could the three of us, at least, not eat at the restaurant? As my naiveté started to rapidly evaporate like steam from a whistling teakettle, I suddenly recalled that in South African apartheid society, I was not regarded as black at all. Instead, I was colored. Since apartheid's gestation and birth in 1948, its white minority birth parents tenaciously and unapologetically maintained a three-tier system of racial classification—white Brits and Afrikanners on the top tier, coloreds or mix-race individuals on the middle tier, and dark skin blacks on the lowest tier. Therefore, three separate restaurants would have been needed in order for the five of us to eat – one for the two whites, another for the two dark-skin blacks and one for the colored guy. We quickly exited that little town with dwindling hopes of finding anything approaching a hospitable reception in the next town. However, we did leave with a greater appreciation for the absurdity of apartheid and the inconveniences it causes.

Before we reached the doorway of the Midway Restaurant, I glanced to my left, about fifty yards away in an adjacent parking lot, and noticed a group of blond, grungy-looking white men in their early 30s, standing in a cluster formation. At first I ignored them and tried to avoid too much eye contact. But as they began to angrily and menacingly point their fingers and shake their fists at the five of us it became impossible to ignore them. Our racially mixed group, which would have been entirely ordinary in the United States, suddenly became the object of the individual and collective ire of these disapproving descendents of Dutchmen who, along with the Brits, devilishly devised the apartheid system, using American Jim Crowism as its model. The South African apartheid system was so evil and absurd that it included, for example, something called the "pencil test". If an individual claimed to be colored or even white and a police officer questioned his/her racial heritage, the officer would settle the dispute with a pencil. Typically, a dispute would arise if the non-white individual were caught outside his/her work or township zone, as indicated on his/her internal passport. The officer would run the pencil through the individual's hair, and if the pencil broke, the person was declared black. If the pencil did not break, he/she was white or colored. On the surface such a practice might appear to be humorous and benign, but in reality and at its core, it was dehumanizing, evil, and malignant.

With rare exceptions, custom and law forbade members of different racial classifications to interact, particularly in social settings. The racial composition of our small entourage, then, was taboo under the South African apartheid system; and that was the undeniable and crystal clear message behind the threatening gestures directed at us by these angry white men. As we continued to make our way toward the restaurant and hopefully away from the bona fide threat that those angry men represented, I began to experience an eerie déjà vu and momentarily stopped in my tracks. Distant memories of latent hatred, manifested in obscene gestures by angry white men standing in a parking lot, rose like a slow crescendo in a familiar piece of music. I had seen those faces before. My mind swirled in a whirlwind of intensely powerful memories – memories born during the turbulent and frightening heyday of the civil rights movement in Hattiesburg, Mississippi; memories born out of my own experiences in the civil rights movement; and memories and images passed on to me by my parents and grandparents from their experiences growing up in seg-regated Hattiesburg. The dress of the whites here was different, and the Afrikaaner accents were foreign to my ears; only the hatred was the same.

As Marsha, one of our two white colleagues, called to me to catch up with the rest of the group, my attention returned once again to the angry white men standing in the adjacent parking lot. As I watched their faces contort with expressions of anger and disgust that were born of centuries of deep-seated racial hatred, several more thoughts entered my consciousness: Regrettably, there were many other white men (and women) everywhere who fostered the same twisted logic about race as the men in the parking lot. Refreshingly, however, the winds of change were beginning to blow across the hills and plains of South Africa as manifested in the increasing spirit of cooperation among all races to create a non-racial society. And as these winds pick up velocity and intensity the forces of good will ultimately prevail, although there will always be angry white men standing in parking lots. My final thought was a sincere wish for the South African black majority, as they continue to fight for their freedom, to avoid making the mistake that black America made in not insisting on both inte-gration and equality.

My attention and presence slowly drifted back to Marsha and the other members of my group as I joined them in the slow walk toward the Midway Hotel and Restaurant. Marsha's feistiness and naiveté led her to do something rather inappropriate and drew a quick response from me. She began pointing her finger, shaking her fist, and mouth-ing back to the men in the parking lot. I said, "Marsha, please do not do that. I know you are from D.C., but this ain't D.C. I'm not sure what these guys would do to you and Brad (the other white member of our group), but I have a pretty good idea what they'd try to do to Harvey, Cynthia and me." Fully appreciating the soundness of my logic, she immediately ceased her finger-pointing and fist-shaking, much to my relief. We went inside the Midway Hotel Restaurant and noticed that the only black people there were waiters and custodians. All of the customers were white. Without a word spoken, all of us pivoted, got back into our cars, and drove to Johannesburg for that long-awaited meal.

Once again, apartheid had made its point, and it did not matter whether the point was made with natives or visitors. For the first time, apartheid was no longer an abstract concept to me. I had unwittingly become one of its many victims. Despite this initial encounter with apartheid (and there would be others before I departed the country), I left Middleburg with a deeper appreciation and admiration for the courage, morality, and probity shown by Nelson Mandela, Bishop Tutu, and Steve Biko in their efforts to end the Apartheid system.

Keep Hope Alive

As my three years as a Kellogg Fellow were coming to an end, I began to prepare a response to a set of constantly-asked questions posed to me by my advisors and members of the Fellowship staff: So what? Okay, Anthony you have traveled around the world to 17 countries. You have seen many wonderful and exciting places and met some very interesting people. So what? What are you going to do now to improve your community, your family and your profession? What are you going to do to demonstrate your commitment to volunteerism and leadership? What are you going to do to become a better Anthony Harris? I searched my heart and mind for appropriate and relevant responses to those questions. One of those answers was to establish a mentoring program for African American boys in the elementary grades in Commerce, Texas. I was quietly but strongly moved to make that particular decision because in observing the behaviors and language of some of the young boys and young men in the community, I was disheartened with what I saw and heard. In my growing up in Hattiesburg, my friends and I did not behave in such ways. Members of the "village" expected better from us, and they willingly accepted the responsibility to do what was necessary to ensure that we met those expectations. Consequently, I was convinced that some direct intervention, on my part, with the young men was desperately needed. I was convinced that the best form for that intervention should be to model and demonstrate to them that they did not have to use foul language, accept mediocrity in their school work, and disrespect self and others in order to be noticed. More importantly, however, I regarded the establishment of this mentoring program as another manifestation of those life-sustaining and life-enhancing values and beliefs that had been imbued in my life during the magnificent days of the civil rights movement.

Any doubt or hesitation about starting this mentoring program was removed the first day that my friend Stan and I visited with the boys at their school. We requested that the principal allow us to meet with a hand full of boys who were considered the most challenging. She agreed and arranged for Stan and me to meet with them in a vacant meeting room. We were both dressed in business suits, which was our custom. With a look of fright on their faces, one of the boys raised his hand and asked, "Are y'all from the police? What y'all here for? We didn't do nothing!" I asked why they thought we were from the police department. "Cause y'all dressed up in them clean suits." Stan and I then looked at each other in disbelief; and I thought that something was seriously wrong if young black boys honestly believed that the only black men who wore suits were with the police department. As we walked them back to their classroom following the meeting, one of the boys asked me if he could walk next to me. As we walked together, he had a wide grin on his face; he raised his head, stuck out his chest, and winked and smiled at his friends to let them know that he was proud to be walking next to me. The meeting with them had illustrated the importance of exposing young black boys to successful black men who wore suits, did not necessarily work for the police department and did not gang bang, or spew filthy language in order to be successful. Further, it had illustrated the fact that these little boys yearned for the involvement of positive black men in their lives.

I gave the program a name – Project Keep Hope Alive, knowing that the phrase Keep Hope Alive was a popular and catchy slogan used by the Reverend Jesse Jackson in his 1988 Presidential campaign. As a name for this very timely mentoring program, Keep

Hope Alive went beyond a catchy political slogan. Rather, it became profoundly reflective of my view that hopelessness among our young black males was the real culprit behind startling statistics that show that while black males make up 6% of the total U.S. population, they represent only 3% of college enrollments, and sadly, over 50% of prisoners. Further, I viewed those statistics as not being a black problem, but instead they are America's problem. If we are ever going to reverse that troubling trend, we are ALL going to have work to instill hope in the lives of young people. Show me a young man who has no hope in the future; who does not believe that he is going to live beyond the age of 22; and who, instead of making decisions about a career or a mate, is making decisions about what kind of coffin and clothes he wants to be laid out in, I'll show you a young man who cares little about himself and even less about the life and possessions of others, regardless of race. So, unless hope is instilled and sustained in the lives of young people by investing in their lives on the front end rather than on the more expensive and less sensible back end, nothing else is going to work.

Project Keep Hope Alive was based on the notion that if efforts to rescue black boys are to be successful they must be made before the boys enter the 4th grade. Research done by Dr. Spencer Holland and Dr. Jawanza Kunjufu point out that black boys who do not meaningfully interact with positive black male role models by the time they reach the fourth grade tend to exhibit negative behaviors that can continue for years. Too often these boys end up in "in-school" suspension, behavior management programs, special education classes, and in serious conflict with their peers, teachers and more often than not, their mothers. And if effective intervention is not introduced early enough, far too many of these young boys will succumb to the type of behaviors that generally result in incarceration or premature death. With the enormous growth in the prison industry in our nation, particularly profit-driven privatized prisons, it becomes increasingly clear that these prisons require high levels of occupancy in order to realize a profit. Moreover, the system that created these prisons has already targeted black and brown youth for occupancy of these very expensive prison beds. And in order for investors to realize an acceptable return on their investments, the beds have to remain occupied. Otherwise, empty beds equal low return on investment. As a result, those of us who are trying to fight to save these young men, unfortunately find ourselves in direct competition with the prison industry for these same young men. Ultimately, that competition will be won by the entity that offers the stronger lure to young black and brown males. Thus far, the prisons appear to be winning, given the proliferation of handguns, drugs, and the influence of music videos and records that glorify violence and drugs. All of that is happening against a backdrop of pervasive racism that shows few signs of subsiding. Despite the decided edge the prison system currently has, hope that we can save and reclaim as many of our young men and boys must always stay alive.

So, it was with an understanding of the myriad challenges and potential that black boys face on a daily basis that Project Keep Hope Alive set out to provide positive black male role models for young black boys in the Commerce Independent School District. Securing a six-figure grant from the W.K. Kellogg Foundation helped to ensure the success of the program in its initial stages. Several people suggested that only "at-risk" students be allowed to participate in the program. However, the State of Texas' standard of being "at-risk", which essentially related to academic and economic deficiencies, was too narrowly defined for what I thought was needed in the community. I believed that every black male in our society, regardless of income or academic ability, to some extent, is in fact at-risk. I included my son in the program although he performed quite well academically and was not at all economically disadvantaged, although he often thought that he was.

Programmatically, Project Keep Hope Alive focused on improving the boys' academic performance and on enhancing their sense of self-respect and respect of others. If the boys could not read, write, and compute with a high degree of proficiency, their life options would always be severely limited. So, focusing on helping them to perform well in their schoolwork became the number one priority of the program. In addition, unless they learned to love and respect themselves they would not be able to love and respect others, thus diminishing the quality of their own lives as well as the lives of others. So, activities designed to build self-confidence, self-discipline, and self-respect, such as photography, oratory, martial arts, art, singing, dancing, and creative writing became integral parts of the program's overall efforts to positively impact the lives of these boys and to foster their innate creativity. Young black male college students and other black men in the community spent time after school with the boys mentoring, guiding, and directing them toward success in school and in other aspects of their lives. In order to participate in Project Keep Hope Alive, each child and adult had to agree to three non-negotiable rules: 1. No use of the "n" word. 2. No fighting. 3. No sagging —belts had to be worn and shirts had to be neatly tucked inside pants. I knew that the boys had internalized the importance of adhering to these rules when one reported to me that he heard one of his friends used the "n" word on the playground that morning.

Project Keep Hope Alive was hugely successful in achieving its goals of improving the academic performance of young black boys, instilling in them much-needed hope for the future, and helping them to love and respect themselves and others. The belief that this program was needed in our community was firmly reinforced one afternoon when Ricardo Finley, the program's manager, and I took the boys on a field trip to the Dallas Museum of African American Art. As the museum staff and docents saw 40 little black boys walk up to the front door, I could see the look of dread plastered across their faces. I could tell that they thought that these kids were going to come in and just tear up the place. Instead, mid-way through the museum tour, a staff member with a surprised but pleased look on her face asked me with utmost sincerity, "Sir, what did you do to get these kids to behave so well? We just put a group of high school kids out of the museum because they were acting up." I responded, "Mam, I am not surprised at all that they are behaving so well. I only did one thing. I raised the level of expectation. I simply expect them to behave well; and I let them know that anything less is unacceptable. Whenever we raise expectations, kids will live up to those expectations. Likewise, when we lower expectations, they will likely live down to those expectations."

I have tremendous confidence that the hundreds of boys who went through my program over a period of eight years will continue to live positive lives, full of hope for the future and full of love and respect for themselves and for others. In working with these young men, not only was I continuing my efforts at coming of age, but I also knew that they too were beginning that same never-ending journey.

Ricardo Finely deserves so much credit for the program's success in helping the young men to keep hope alive. He was deeply committed to the boys and to the aims of the program. He did an excellent job in managing the day-to-day operations of the program as well as providing guidance, mentoring, and leadership for the boys. He possessed boundless energy, limitless patience, and an uncanny ability to understand the vision for the program and help convert it to a sound reality. I could depend on Ricardo, whether it was picking up the boys from school, driving them home, picking up food, planning a field trip, securing instructors for the martial arts, arts, choir, and photography programs, directing the choir, doing payroll, or responding to the principal's call for help with one of the boys who might have needed Project Keep Hope Alive's special intervention. Without his involvement with Project Keep Hope Alive, the success of the program would have been non-existent or severely limited. I am forever grateful for his friendship, devotion to the program, and his always positive attitude. Thanks, Rick.

Mixed in with the joys that I experienced with Project Keep Hope Alive was one notable disappointment. At its inception, Project Keep Hope Alive was granted permission to use the University Christian Center (UCC) for our meetings. The UCC, located across the street from the University, operated under the auspices of the First United Methodist Church of Commerce, where my family and I were members. First United Methodist Church was a predominantly white church, located less than a block from the campus. Smithenia and I had worshiped at all-black St. Paul United Methodist Church in Hattiesburg for several years before moving to Commerce. We came to regard ourselves as United Methodists. So, after moving to Commerce, we both started attending church there and later became members because it was the only United Methodist Church in town. And its short distance from the campus, where we lived when I was working on my doctorate degree, made it a very convenient place to worship. Initially, I was reluctant to attend a mostly white church. I suppose it was because the Jim Crow rule against it was still seared into my brain, even though I was no longer living in Mississippi. As time moved on, I became more comfortable worshiping there as did the rest of my family. With the exception of my family and the Talbots (Dave and Phyllis), the congregation was entirely white. Ironically, there were both black and white people in Commerce who questioned our affiliation with a white church. The whites because some thought we belonged with our "own" people. The blacks because some thought we belonged with our "own" people. How ironic and representative, I thought, of a famous quote from Dr. King, who in 1963 had this to say about segregation and the church: *We must face the fact that in America, the church is still the most segregated major institution in America. At 11:00 on Sunday morning when we stand and sing and Christ has no east or west, we stand at the most segregated hour in this nation. This is tragic. Nobody of honesty can overlook this.*

The University Christian Center was just the right size four our meetings with the boys. There was a kitchen, which allowed us to serve a warm meal each day. There was a sizeable meeting area that provided the flexibility to break into small learning and activity groups. The most important convenience was its very close proximity to the campus of East Texas State University. The close proximity allowed the program to intentionally and consistently expose the young men to the college campus, thereby planting seeds in their heads and hearts that college was figuratively and literally within their grasp. In exchange for using the UCC, I promised the Director that at the end of each meeting, I would make sure that the facility would be left in tip top shape. That promise was never broken in the years we used the UCC.

At some point, the UCC changed directors. The agreement that I had with the first director became the object of scrutiny and concern for the new director. His concern was made glaringly evident to me when he informed me one day that Project Keep Hope Alive would have to vacate the premises. Beginning immediately, we would no longer be allowed to use the University Christian Center for our meetings. Naturally, I asked for an explanation; and without hesitating, he said that Project Keep Hope Alive was not a "Jesus based program"; therefore the program and the kids were no longer welcome. The University Christian Center, he said, would be off limits to any group that was not a purely and discernible religious group that was based on the teachings of Jesus Christ. What an awful thing for someone who is a minister to think, let alone utter. So many thoughts went through my head when I heard that bogus explanation. First, who is he to say that the program is *not* Jesus inspired? Second, I was not sure who he had in mind when he uttered those words, but he surely could not be speaking of the Jesus whose words are recorded in Matthew 25:45: *Truly I tell you, whatever you did not do for one of the least of these, you did not do for me.* Nor could he have been speaking of the Jesus I know in Matthew 19:14: *Let the little children come to me, and do not hinder them, for the kingdom of heaven belongs to such as these.* Nevertheless, the new director insisted that Project Keep Hope Alive vacate the premises ASAP. Not willing to accept his decision and his implausible explanation, I appealed the decision to the Administrative Board of the First United Methodist Church; and to my disappointment, board members upheld his decision. The only support I had during that meeting with the Administrative Board came from Mr. Dick Latson, a white business owner who expressed his strong support for Project Keep Hope Alive and his outrage at the decision of the Administrative Board.

I felt betrayed by First United Methodist Church of Commerce. I felt that the leadership of the church had behaved in an obviously hypocritical and prejudiced manner. I was convinced that while the Administrative Board's official reason for their decision was to show support for the new director, who was also the Assistant Pastor of the church, the fact that Project Keep Hope Alive was a program comprised of black boys from the other side of the tracks also figured into the decision by some, no doubt.

Their decision was final, and I knew that I also had a decision to make. And I made it immediately. I decided to discontinue my presence at that church. I reasoned that a congregation that would deliberately turned its back on a group of kids and one of its members warranted neither my presence nor my participation. Although I quit attending church at First United Methodist Church of Commerce, I didn't quit going to church. I visited other churches in the community. Though I had lost faith in my church family, my faith in God was never stronger. To my way of thinking, there was no need to take out my anger and frustration on God. And I didn't. The only fly in the oatmeal was that my wife wanted to remain at First United Methodist Church. She sang in the choir, sang solos at funerals and weddings, served as director of the Children's Choirs, participated in the bell choir, and served on several church committees. She was very connected to the church and to many of the church members. In contrast, my bonds did not run as deeply as hers. Nevertheless, she was terribly conflicted about the situation. She wanted to support me, but she also wanted to continue attending First United Methodist Church. Whenever someone asked her about me and why I was not at church, she would automatically burst into tears. It was tearing her apart. She was very unhappy with the way the church treated me; and she understood my reasons for boycotting First United Methodist Church. On the other hand, she wanted to continue attending out of her commitment to her many church obligations, which I enormously respected. One day, a friend of ours, who was also a member of the church told me something very interesting as she attempted to convince me to return to First United Methodist Church. She said, *Anthony, I hope you will come back to our church. We need you and your family here. You guys represent our commitment to diversity and inclusiveness. That is very important to our church.* I knew she was being very sincere and was speaking from her heart. Her sentiments about my family were genuine. She believed very deeply in what she was saying to me, but I thought she failed to see the bigger picture. So, in my attempt to help her see the bigger picture, I offered a reply. I said, *My presence or that of my family's at First United Methodist Church of Commerce, Texas should not serve as the church's standard for inclusiveness and diversity. It is much too easy to like my family and welcome us into your church. We live in your neighborhood. I am on the school board. I work in the Office of the President of the University. I serve on the city's Planning and Zoning Commission. I am in in the news for all sorts of achievements. My children are well liked. My wife is very popular. With those bona fides, it is so easy to like us. The real test of the church's commitment to inclusiveness and diversity is not its feelings about my family and me. The real test will come when a single, homeless, uneducated black woman with five homeless black children who have no formal education and who come from a different side of the tracks, walk into church service, and want to be part of your church family. When you can open your doors and your hearts to that family, I will stand and applaud your commitment to diversity and inclusiveness.*

I eventually resumed my attendance at First United Methodist Church. I had made my point; and my message was loud and strong: I refused to go along to get along. Principles matter. And God meant it when he said – "Let the little children come to me, and do not hinder them, for the kingdom of heaven belongs to such as these." I had led a conscience-based, faith-based, and Jesus-based one-person boycott of the church. Did I change any minds and hearts? Only they and God know for sure. What I do know is that if they had been paying attention, they would have also known that my boycott was also my way of saying, once again, ain't gonna let nobody turn me 'round. I was not going to be co-opted or marginalized because of my race. I knew that regardless of the final outcome with my disagreement with the church, I did the right thing. And if necessary, I would do it again. Moreover, I returned to worship at First United Methodist Church of Commerce for my wife's sake. I did not want her to go through any more of the emotional stress she was experiencing because of my boycott. At the end of the ordeal, I was convinced that I had made the right decisions – both to leave the church and to later return. Moreover, I was heartened in the knowledge that out of bad comes good and that when one door closes, another one opens. The shiny example of that was when President Jerry Morris, after hearing about Project Keep Hope Alive's ouster from the University Christian Center, located a permanent home for Project Keep Hope Alive on the campus.

March for Family and Community

Another set of major events emerged in my life in 1995 that continued my journey toward coming of age. After attending the Million Man March in Washington D.C. in October of 1995, I returned home to Commerce, Texas full of excitement and strong validation and affirmation of my decision to establish Project Keep Hope Alive four years earlier. However, I left the Million Man March in Washington more motivated than ever to do more and to take a broader leadership role in encouraging black men to begin taking more responsibility and leadership for the condition of our families and communities. Fortunately, there was a black men's organization, The Doers Club, in the area that also wanted to do more. Because these men knew I had attended the Million Man March and had successfully established Project Keep Hope Alive, they asked me if I would organize a march under their auspices. The primary purpose of the march would mirror that of the Million Man March – a call to black men in Hunt County, Texas to be more responsible for our families and communities. I immediately agreed, and we decided that the theme of the march would be *Hunt County Men's March for Family and Community* and that it would take place in Greenville, 15 miles northeast of Commerce.

Tragically, weeks before the march was scheduled to take place, several black churches in the Greenville area were burned. Those disturbing attacks on local churches appeared to be part of national trend in which individuals intentionally torched black churches in an effort to intimidate the community. The fact that the local church burnings took place in Greenville strongly suggested that we should, in fact, be alarmed. Greenville's reputation for racial intolerance was well documented. For years, City officials proudly displayed a banner across the main entrance to the town on Lee Street that read, *Welcome to Greenville, Texas. We Have the Blackest Dirt and the Whitest People.*

In local stores, racks of post cards with an exact replica of the banner were available for purchase.

Greenville is also the site of the arrest, trial, and conviction of Mr. Lenell Geter, a black engineer who was wrongly convicted of the armed robbery of fried chicken restaurant in 1982 on extremely flimsy evidence. During the CBS News Program *60 Minutes'* expose of Mr. Geter's trial, conviction and incarceration, it was clearly shown that Mr. Geter was miles from the scene of the crime at the time it was committed; and that it was impossible for him to have been involved. Following the showing of the *60 Minutes* program, the local District Attorney promptly dropped all charges and arranged to have Mr. Geter released from prison. A year later a made-for-television movie was aired on CBS based on the true story behind the unjust conviction and incarceration of Mr. Geter.

So, it was against such a worrisome and potentially volatile backdrop that the march was planned and organized. In addition, there was such outrage from the entire community over the church fires that black, white and Hispanic citizens, city officials, clergy, and business owners asked us if they could participate in our march as a means of registering their outrage at the burning of the churches. The original intent of our march, however, was not to protest anything, but to make a positive statement about the need for black men to become more responsible for their families and communities. However, given the high level of frustration in all segments of the Greenville and Commerce communities and the strong desire within those communities to publicly take a stand against bigotry and church burnings, we allowed the march to take on the additional goal of sending a message to those responsible for the burnings that black, Hispanic, and white citizens of our community would not tolerate and condone such madness.

Several days before the march was to begin, the Dallas media reported that two Ku Klux Klan groups were planning counter demonstrations, apparently, in support of the church burnings in Greenville. According to media sources, one group was from Waco and was regarded as a non-violent Klan group. The second Klan group was from Arkansas and was considered more prone to violence.

A couple of days before the march was to begin, a reporter from the Fox News affiliate in Dallas called my home in Commerce and asked if I could come to Greenville for an interview. When I arrived, she and her camera and sound crew quickly emerged from their production truck. After brief introductions, she immediately started asking me about the Klan and our upcoming march. Her first question was, "In light of the planned demonstration by the KKK and the increased tension in this community, are you still going to proceed with your march? " Without hesitation, I responded, "Absolutely, we plan to proceed. You see, I grew up in the civil rights movement in Mississippi, where they had real Klansmen, and we did not let those knuckleheads run us away. I am certainly not going to let these wannabes here even come close to intimidating us. We had a freedom song that we used to sing back then and today it is a message that we want to leave with the Klan – Ain't Gonna Let Nobody Turn Me 'Round." The Arkansas Klan group decided to leave town, while the Waco Klan group stayed; and the day before our march they staged a demonstration in downtown Greenville. There was minimal coverage of the Klan march by the media, and very few spectators bothered to show up.

As everyone was lining up to begin the March for Family and Community, it was clear to me that the turn-out and the composition the crowd had exceeded my expectations. There were hundreds of people of all ages, races, backgrounds, and faiths preparing to be a part of this historic event in our community. Each person was there for his or her own reason – curiosity, black male solidarity, anti-Klan, anti-hate, anti-church burning. Each also was experiencing his or her own private personal range of emotions. Standing there in the parking lot of the St. John Baptist Church, my own emotions ran the gamut, as they had done many times during the civil rights movement in Hattiesburg, from relief to anxiety; from uncertainty to resolve; and from calm to frenetic. Despite the tremendous fluctuation in my emotions, I found it reassuring and relaxing to give in to the urge to pause for a private moment of personal reflection and invoke the memory of Mr. Vernon Dahmer and the many other victims of hatred whose deaths had prompted similar public responses from people who wanted to take a stand for love and unity and against hatred and divisiveness. I also yielded to the mounting urge to silently pray to God to ask Him to be with us on this day as he was on January 15, 1966 during the march in Hattiesburg following the murder of Mr. Vernon Dahmer. Not surprisingly, it worked; and it helped to center me in time to speak with the Chief of Police who asked for a private conference with me to discuss some last-minute security arrangements. He told me that there would be several plain-clothes police officers participating in the march, one of whom would be assigned to protect me. "Why do I need personal protection?" I asked. He replied, "Dr. Harris, your comments on television the other day about the Klan, we believe, might have angered a few of our less enlightened citizens who might not agree with your take on the Klan". I told him that I appreciated his efforts to make sure I was safe. My other reaction was to try to identify plain-clothes officers, but I was unable, which is how it should have been. He also told me that there would officers in helicopters and on the ground who would be on the alert for any unusual or threatening activity.

As if worrying about some hate-filled attack on me personally, I was faced with another tense moment that was totally unforeseen. The New Black Panther Party of Dallas publicly announced that they would be in Greenville to participate in the march. They were not specifically invited by anyone associated with the march. However, there was a general announcement to the public that everyone was invited. The problem with the New Black Panther Party was that they made it clear that they would indeed be armed and would not hesitate in using those arms if, in their view, the need arose. Through contacts we had in the Dallas area, we sent word back to them that they were welcome to participate in the march, only if they left their weapons in Dallas. They were not willing to do so and agreed to stay away. I was relieved. The last thing anyone wanted was for there to be violence, either from the Klan or from the New Black Panther Party. The march was a major success and to my relief, there were no incidents.

And I was pleased beyond words to have my 11 year-old son, Michael, marching alongside me from beginning to end, the significance of which was ever present in my mind from the moment I agreed to organize the march. For several reasons, it was extremely important to me to have Michael by my side for the march. The march and my involvement in it were appropriate and effective ways of modeling for him the courage in standing up for one's beliefs in a demonstrable but peaceful manner. Also, I wanted to model for him the importance of stepping up to the plate and being a leader when one is called on to provide that leadership. Finally, I wanted to reinforce in him a deep and abiding concern for the conditions of our communities and to translate that concern into action. Yes, I was overwhelmingly pleased that father and son were together to represent two generations of Harris's to participate in a civil rights march, just as my mother had done with me more than thirty years before.

The results of the investigations of the church burnings were both reassuring and disappointing. A young black man and not some deranged white supremacist had actually set the churches on fire. There was great relief that the torching of the churches was not racially motivated but highly disappointing and sad that a black man would have such little regard for a black church that he would do something as heinous as burn it to the ground. However, the fact that he was mentally unstable helped to explain his actions and ultimately engendered more sympathy for him than outrage. Nevertheless, I was pleased with the results of the march, and anxiously looked forward to what might come next in my life.

Following the March for Family and Community, I was invited by a journalism instructor at East Texas State University to be a guest presenter in his class. He asked me to come to his class to talk with students about the march in Greenville and about the Million Man March in Washington, D.C. Not long after the class started, I discovered that I had been invited by the instructor for a slightly different reason. His first question was, *Dr. Harris, you attended the Million Man March, right?* I replied, *yes, I did.* His next question was quite revealing and went to the real reason I was there. *Dr, Harris, how do you justify attending an event, The Million Man March, that was sponsored by Louis Farrakhan and the Nation of Islam, a group that hates all white people? He is a divisive man who spreads racial strife and hatred everywhere he goes. Help us understand how you can defend your participation in an event that was sponsored by someone as despicable as Louis Farrakhan.* I was caught a little off guard and little befuddled as to why the instructor seemed to be so determined to not only attack Mr. Farrakhan but also to use me as a proxy for everything Farrakhan. I was also taken aback by the fact that as an *invited* guest, I was being treated with such disrespect and contempt. After figuring out what the instructor's agenda, I was faced with two options. One, I could have excused myself and left the room, letting the instructor know that I would not put up with such unprofessional behavior. Two, I could have remained and attempted to convince at least one person, probably not the instructor, in that room that I was unapologetically and unequivocally proud of my participation in the Million Man March. Not surprisingly, I chose option two. So, I turned to the instructor and in a tone that conveyed my strong disappointment with his attitude I replied. *First, I did not attend the march because of Mr. Farrakhan. I attended the march because I support the purpose of the march, which was to encourage black men to return to their roles as leaders in their families and communities. Furthermore, I am not here to defend or attack Mr. Farrakhan. He does not need me to defend him, and there is no shortage of individuals, including you, apparently, who are more than willing to attack him. But, I tell you what you should do, if you really want Mr. Farrakhan to defend himself. Why don't you invite him here, to your class as you did me, so that you can ask him directly about his views on race, politics, and the Nation of Islam?* I saw straight through his one upsmanship game. He was attempting to draw me into a debate about Mr. Farrakhan and the Nation of Islam rather than a discussion of the more important issues regarding the challenges facing black men in our country and how the media report on those challenges. From the back row of the lecture hall, a black student raised her hand to speak. I thought to myself, finally, some back up here. The instructor was attacking me over the issue of Mr. Farrakhan's involvement with the Million Man March. And from the looks on the faces of the students, most of them seemed to be supportive of his comments. So, when I saw the black student raise her hand to make a contribution to the discussion, it was a sense of déjà vu for me. I immediately felt that I was not alone in this ambush.

Somebody's got my back, and I don't have to fight this battle all by myself. I recalled the incident in high school when the white social studies teacher argued in favor of slavery, claiming that slaves were much better off in this country than they would have been in Africa. I challenged his backwards thinking as best I could. Hoping that my black classmate would back me up, I turned to her for some help. But she remained silent. I was out on that limb all by myself. The black student in the journalism class, I thought, was my back up. Surely, she understands the purposes of the Million Man March, and more importantly the challenges black men face in today's society, even if she were not a fan of Louis Farrakhan. Was I wrong! She lit into me as if I had personally insulted her and her entire family. She unloaded on me: *It is people like you who keep things all stirred up. If people like you didn't bring up these things, we wouldn't have to think about them. I'm tired of talking about race.* I quickly replied, *ma'am, that is precisely why I am bringing them up because so many people are not thinking about them. Somebody needs to remind you that the struggle for freedom is not over. The plight of black men in this country is a disgrace. And I am not assessing blame. I am interesting in finding solutions. I believe that we all must remain vigilant when it comes to social justice because the struggle is not over. As you know or should know the song says that We SHALL overcome. It doesn't say that we are getting ready to overcome or that we have already overcome.* By the time I ended my soliloquy, the bell sounded and the class was over. I tried to find that young lady to get a better understanding of why she was so hostile toward me. Unfortunately, I could not find her, and I regretted that a very special teachable moment has passed.

Will that circle be unbroken?

Not long after the successful Hunt County March for Family and Community and the encounter with the journalism instructor and the irate black student, I had an experience that was as equally as dramatic and impactful. This experience occurred while attending the annual meeting of the National African American Male Collaboration in San Francisco in 1997. I attended the meeting as the Collaboration's Vice President and as Executive Director of Project Keep Hope

Alive, which was a founding member of the Collaboration and as the Collaboration's Vice President. During the meeting we had an opportunity to fellowship with a group of young black male ex-offenders who had become participants in Dr. Joe Marshall's Omega's Boys Club and Street Soldiers. Dr. Marshall's program was designed to assist and support the young men in their efforts to remain free of the temptations that landed them in prison in the first place. The eight young men, all in their early 20s and late teens, wanted to share their stories with us about how they ended up in San Quentin Prison and how they were now working to turn around their lives. They all had similar stories to tell about how they made poor decisions and ended up committing criminal acts that landed them in one of the toughest prisons in the country. The common theme and lesson of their stories were poignant and persuasive and served to remind everyone there that the formula for saving young black males is not terribly complicated: Values drive behavior. Change the belief system and value system and you change the behavior.

After a short time the eight young men, seated in wooden folding chairs in the front of at the sanctuary of a small red-brick church, became more comfortable with the format and setting in which our conversations were taking place. Although we were strangers, we were connected by a bond that transcended familiarity, geography and time. As I studied the faces of these young men, I saw my son in them. I saw the faces of my nephews. I saw the faces of the boys in Project Keep Hope Alive. I could not help but pray on their behalf: *There, but by the grace of God, goes I.* I began to wonder what could have possibly caused these young men to have ended up in prison. Was it environment or was it the individual? That question has been debated for generations, and I knew that I sided more with the environment side than with the individual side of that debate. However, I wanted to know specifically how much the educational system had either helped or hindered them during that period of their lives. So, I asked them if school had been a positive or negative factor in his life. As an unapologetic supporter of public education and a 15-year school board member in Commerce, I was not happy with the terse but honest response one young man gave. He said that teachers, counselors, and administrators were absolutely no help to him at all. In fact, he said that the school system and his community had given up on him a long time ago. He then shared something that sent shivers up my spine and brought tears to my eyes. He said that while he was attending school and living among his friends and family in his neighborhood, he was in a circle – a circle made up of teachers, friends, family, and neighbors. He then paused for a moment as he wiped the tears from his eyes, took a deep breath, and slowly exhaled to try to compose himself. With a noticeable tremble in his naturally soft high pitch voice, he went on to say that one day he left his circle. And to his disappointment and hurt no one in his circle even noticed that he had left the circle. It was at that point, he said, that he began to engage in negative behaviors – selling drugs, gang banging, and stealing cars. Although he was disappointed in not being brought back into the circle or receiving visits from by other members of the circle when he was in prison, he did not blame them for his criminal activity. That short but powerful story forced me to engage in my own very personal introspection and to ask myself, who is in my circle –family members, neighbors, friends, co-workers? Who are they? Do I even know if they are still in my circle? If someone left my circle, would I even notice and would I try to reclaim them? Have I checked lately to find out how they are doing in the circle? In whose circle am I? If I left my circle would anyone care? I also automatically started hearing in my head Pops Staples and the Staples Singers singing, *Will That Circle Be Unbroken?* As I continued thinking about the title of that classic gospel tune and even more deeply about the moving interaction with the young man who had left his circle unnoticed, I became more convinced that this event, this day, all of the thoughts that had gone through my head, and all the emotions I had just experienced would be a major step in my life and faith journey. I knew that I had just been taught a very valuable lesson that would require constant vigilance. In fact, when I arrived back at my hotel, I made phone calls to family members and friends to let them know I was calling to check on them and to let them know that I was thinking about them. I vowed to no longer take for granted that members of my circle are okay without the benefit of a phone call or email to verify such.

Another Transition

Although I was perfectly content to live the remainder of my life in Commerce, Texas, circumstances, unfortunately, would not allow that to happen. Professionally, I had made a commitment to a career in higher education administration after nearly a decade of being a faculty member. I was pleased when I was hired by East Texas State University President, Dr. Jerry Morris in 1993 to serve as Assistant to the President. I was hopeful that this position would place me on the path toward achieving my goal of becoming a college president. Following Dr. Morris' retirement six years later, a new president took over. Despite the change in leadership, I remained committed to my career goal of being a college administrator, with increasing determination to eventually becoming a college president. In fact, I was an applicant for the vacant presidency at East Texas State University, which was an intensely bittersweet decision and period in my life. The motivation to apply for the position actually came from my then14-year old son, Michael, of all people. Since the time he was a participant in Project Keep Hope Alive, I had constantly encouraged him to become involved in student leadership at his school as a class officer or as a representative on the Student Council. He had always been lukewarm to the idea, preferring instead to concentrate on his studies and sports. However, as I was driving him to school one day, I plunged into one of my usual discourses on leadership and the importance of stepping up to the plate and accepting the challenge of leadership. After I finished with one of my typical conclusions: "I would really like for you to think about running for president of the student council", he followed with something that just floored me and left me absolutely no wriggle room at all. "Dad, if you want me to step up to the plate and run for president of the student council, why don't you step up to the plate and run for president of ET (East Texas State University)?" He had me! The only sensible thing I could say was, "Well, son you have a point. And I will." I knew that if I were to maintain credibility with my son and not just talk the talk, I would absolutely have to apply for the presidency. I did apply and was especially pleased that again I was modeling for my son the importance of taking risks and becoming a leader.

However, my pleasure and excitement about applying for the presidency soon turned to bitter disappointment and a sense of betrayal. At my request, I met with several representatives from the leadership of the African American faculty and staff organization to discuss my decision to become an applicant for the presidency and to ask for their support. After telling them about my intentions to apply for the position, the representatives said that they were reluctant to support me because they were concerned about the odds of my being successful in the search. They said that they thought that the odds of a black person being selected president were too great for them to throw their support behind me. Instead, they preferred to support a white applicant whom they believed had a much better chance of being selected than I had. I could hardly believe what I was hearing. In a trembling but determined voice I replied, "Since when did we as black people ever have to stop and consider the odds before taking risks? If Martin Luther King, Jr. had considered the odds, do you think he would have led the civil rights movement? If Rosa Parks had considered the odds, would she have refused to move to the back of the bus? If Freedom Riders had considered the odds, would they have rode on buses and trains and gotten their heads bashed in? So, don't give me that bull about odds!" I left the meeting feeling betrayed and dismayed that certain black people on my campus, people with whom I had worked for nearly twenty years and had developed personal and professional relationships, people who knew of my qualifications for the position, and who knew the historical significance of a black person being in the applicant pool for the presidency of that university had turned their backs on me. I was hurt, angry, and disappointed but realized, not for the first time, that sometimes we as black people, not bigoted white people, are obstacles to our own progress.

After the new president was hired, it was clear that he was not interested in retaining me. The new president told me that I could remain in my position as Assistant to the President for one additional year before I would have to go back to my tenured faculty position in the Counseling Department. However, I was not prepared to give up on my career in administration and on my dream of one day becoming a college president, even though the new president had clearly shown that he would not support me in achieving that dream. So, for a period of about two months I was despondent and confused about whether I would really have a future in higher education administration. I loved teaching and for a while reasoned that returning to teaching would not be a bad thing at all if it came to that.

But the wisdom and goodness of the Lord manifested themselves and created a new ray of hope for me. One day while my wife and I were cleaning out my closet and some dresser drawers, two folded up slips of paper fell into my lap as I sat on the side of my bed. I opened them up, and as I started reading them, tears came to my eyes. I handed them to my wife, and without saying a word, we looked at each other and both felt the power of the words written on those two slips of paper. Moreover, we both realized that it was not by chance or coincidence that slips of paper had landed in my lap at that particular time. Written on the slips of paper were two scriptures that I had read the year before at my wife's aunt's funeral. And as I continued to read the scripture, a tremendous burden was miraculously lifted from my shoulders and suddenly optimism for the future was restored. After reading the scriptures, I still had no clue as to where my future plans would lead me. But I was no longer worried, concerned, or bitter. I had been given newfound confidence and hope that a plan was in store for me. In fact, a couple of months later, I was visiting my mother in Hattiesburg, and accompanied her to a civil rights symposium at The University of Southern Mississippi. While attending the symposium luncheon, a gentleman walked over to our table and introduced himself to me as the President of The University of Southern Mississippi. He wanted to know more about me. After I told him where I worked, that I was a native of Hattiesburg, and that I was an alumnus of Southern Miss, he asked me if I had ever considered coming back home to work. I said I would if I were ever asked. So, the next week, I received an e-mail request from the President Horace Fleming asking me to send him my vita. I obliged and soon afterwards, he invited me to come to Hattiesburg for a series of interviews. Apparently, I did well enough in my interviews that he offered me the position of

Executive Assistant to the President. After receiving the offer and accepting it, my mind returned to those two slips of paper that contained the two scriptures. Their meaning had become even more profound and prophetic in my life after I had accepted the offer to return to Hattiesburg and to my alma mater. Both scriptures came from the Old Testament. From Jeremiah 29:11 – *For I know the plans I have for you, declares the Lord God, plans to prosper you and not to harm you, plans to give you hope and a future.* From Proverb 3: 5, 6 – *Trust in the Lord with all your heart and lean not on your own understanding. Acknowledge Him in all your ways, and He will direct your path.* These scriptures not only had brought comfort and hope to my wife's family in their time of bereavement, but they had also brought me enormous comfort and hope at a time when I needed answers about my future. For years, I kept both slips of paper in my wallet and read them whenever I start having doubts about my future.

Chapter 14

Farewell Texas - Hello Mississippi

Returning to Hattiesburg after being away for twenty years was a wonderful experience for me in so many ways. The changes that I noticed were remarkable. One of the earliest changes that I noticed was that once again blacks and whites unmistakably identified me as a black person. While in Texas, I often had to be rather explicit in explaining to some that I was African American and not Hispanic.

More importantly, I was able to observe tremendous changes that had taken place in the City since I left in 1979, some of which were subtle but most were delightfully obvious. There were black members serving on the City Council, the School Board, and the County Board of Supervisors. The Superintendent and Assistant Superintendent of the Hattiesburg Public School System were both black. There were large numbers of black police officers and county deputies. The University had a long string of black student body presidents and homecoming queens. Ms. Oseola McCarty, a black woman from Hattiesburg, brought the national spotlight to the University when she donated her life savings to the University for scholarships for de-serving black students.

There were other encouraging signs that the winds of change had blown across my beloved state. For example, when I walked around campus and in the shopping malls, I sensed that race relations were greatly improved and that those improvements were not superficial. I observed interracial couples going about their business with no ap-parent retributions from anyone. Black and white teenagers appeared to interact with each other in very genuinely friendly ways. The University's student body, with a black enrollment of approximately 28%, had elected four consecutive black student body presidents.

On the other hand, however, several other disturbing trends and incidents occurred that convinced me that there was still plenty of room for improvement in race relations in Hattiesburg. The first was the incredibly disappointing news I learned from an Asian-American colleague on campus who informed me that the two White and Colored marriage license sign-in books that were present when my wife and I applied for our marriage license in 1977 were still being used at the Forrest County Courthouse as recently as 1987.

The other incident occurred one night at a college baseball game when I observed several white baseball fans, who were considered upstanding citizens in the community, making fun of a black man at the game who wore dreadlocks. They seemed to have no qualms at all about publicly showing their racial insensitivity toward a young black man whom I am certain none of them knew at all. To them he was some type of freak who was there strictly for their entertainment. I could feel the anger growing inside me. Here we go again, I thought. My anger was bordering on rage. How dare they make fun of this man! He was not some object placed there for their enjoyment. He was a human being, no different than they, except that all important one – his skin color. And with those dreadlocks, heck, he must be one of those foreigners!!! I was tempted to say something to them that would let them know that I thought they were a bunch of necks with about as much sense God promised the Billy goat. Instead, I decided to do something less confrontational but just as effective. So, I intentionally went over to the young man in plain view of the dreadlock haters, introduced myself to him, and sat and talked with him. I made eye contact with the bigots and made sure they saw me. I actually knew two of the men; and from the guilty looks on their faces, they knew what I was doing and why. I told the young man that I was proud to make his acquaintance, and I wished him continued success in his studies. He never knew he was the object of the bigots' laughter. I did not tell him. Instead, my actions, I felt, accomplished their intent – let the bigots know that I objected to their behavior and let the student know that I cared about him. Both were very powerful messages sent in a very subtle but effective manner.

Another deeply disturbing incident occurred during the spring of 2001 that set the image of the State of Mississippi back another generation. The State Legislature and the Governor approved a plan to allow voters to decide if the State would maintain its current State

Flag, which prominently features the rebel flag, or select a new one without the stars and bars as recommended by a multi-racial blue-ribbon panel. Instead of making the decision themselves to change the flag, the governor and the leaders of the state legislature, in a predictable show of gutlessness agreed to a referendum in which the voters would decide the flag issue, not their elected representatives. The governor and the legislative leadership knew or should have known that the rebel flag would easily win. They clearly lacked the courage to change the flag themselves as was done by the Governor and the Legislature in Georgia, thereby sparing the State immeasurable embarrassment and divisiveness, from which it will take years to recover. Not surprisingly, the voters, by a nearly 2-1 margin, voted to maintain the existing flag with the rebel stars and bars conspicuously emblazoned in the upper left hand corner of the flag. Anyone who understands the history of south knows that the rebel flag was not only the battle flag of a group of people who went to war against the government of the United States of America, but was also a battle flag for the Ku Klux Klan and others racists who oppressed black citizens throughout the South for generations. Not by coincidence, the vote margin nearly perfectly mirrored the racial make-up in the State, thus revealing, not creating, a profound racial divide in the State. In the few counties in which black people were in the majority, the proposed new flag won by a 2-1 margin. In predominantly white counties, the existing flag won by the same 2-1 margin.

In the weeks following the vote, there was a strong sense of pride, as gleaned from numerous gloating letters to the editor, among many reactionary rebel flag supporters, who felt that they had won a great victory for the cause of preserving the heritage and traditions of Dixie and the old south. Many rebel flag supporters felt that they needed to send a strong message to the rest of the country that Mississippi is not going to be pushed around and would not be told by anyone to take down their flag. It was also a clear message to the black minority in the State that the will of reactionary white people still prevails and that they (reactionary whites) are still in charge, despite efforts to improve the state's image. That unfortunate action on the part of the majority of voters was unsettlingly reminiscent of the craziness and stupidity of the Jim Crow era. During the Jim Crow era, whites were willing to foolishly and illogically cling to their symbols of oppression and racism (separate drinking fountains, separate school systems, separate accommodations, etc.), despite the fact that Jim Crowism was and continues to be detrimental to the economic health of the state. That disgraceful decision by 65% of the voters on April 17, 2001 was totally consistent with the prevailing views of the Jim Crow era — racist traditions and symbols of the past are far more important than economic and racial progress for the future. Despite the fact that maintaining such an ugly symbol of racism and oppression like the rebel flag would likely adversely affect the economic condition of the State, the voters defiantly stated that their rebel flag is far more important than economic and social progress.

While driving home one day from work, I saw large block shaped words and a rebel flag plastered to the back window of a pick-up truck driven by a rebel flag supporter that perhaps captured the spirit and sentiment of many of the supporters of the rebel flag. The caption above the rebel flag read, "It's a white thang. You wouldn't understand!" Yes I do understand, I whispered to myself. That is the problem. You understand, I understand, the whole state of Mississippi understands! But it is racist thing, not just a white thing, as this rebel flag supporter would have the reader of his sign believe.

Despite the wrong-headedness of the majority of the voters in the state of Mississippi in that ill-fated election and certainly despite or maybe in spite of the backward thinking exemplified by the driver of the pick-up truck, the voters in the City of Hattiesburg made history 3 months later. On July 3, 2001, Hattiesburg elected its first ever African American mayor in a close election against an incumbent who had served 12 years and had a done remarkable job in fostering unparalleled economic growth in the City. However, with superior organization and with a fresh, clear message about the future of Hattiesburg, Johnny DuPree was elected mayor, thus becoming the mayor of the 3rd largest city in Mississippi — a city that less than 40 years prior, refused to allow black people to become registered voters. On one level, Mr. Dupree owes his election to the majority of voters who voted for him, but at a deeper level, he owes the election to the efforts of those many brave civil rights warriors and trailblazers who were murdered, threatened with murder, beaten, and incarcerated during the 1960s so that subsequent generations of black citizens would have the right to vote for the candidate of their choice. Indeed, had it not been for the Herculean efforts of those unsung heroes, warriors, and trailblazers, Mr. Dupree would not have made history by capturing the Democratic nomination for governor of the state of Mississippi in 2012.

The City of Hattiesburg

Hattiesburg is a wonderful city with an interesting history, apart from its civil rights and Jim Crow history. It is located in southern Mississippi (90 miles south of Jackson and 65 miles north of the Gulf Coast), is the county seat of Forrest County, which has the dubious distinction of being named for General Nathan Bedford Forrest, the first and most powerful Grand Wizard of the Ku Klux Klan. During the 1960s, at the height of the civil rights movement, the city's population was nearly 38,000 and the black population was approximately twenty-eight percent.

Hattiesburg is the home of the University of Southern Mississippi and William Carey University. William Carey University is a predominantly white Baptist college located in a neighborhood that was once all-white and today is all-black. Founded in 1906 and operating for decades as Mississippi Woman's College, William Carey University became co-educational in 1954 and was renamed in honor of the eighteenth century English cobbler-linguist whose decades of missionary activity in India earned him international recognition as the "Father of Modern Missions." The University of Southern Mississippi was founded as Mississippi Normal College in 1910 for the purpose of training teachers. In later decades, its name changed to Mississippi Southern College and finally to the University of Southern Mississippi.

The largest employers in Hattiesburg before and during the civil rights movement were the two colleges and Hercules Powder Company, later Hercules Incorporated. Hercules, the largest employer of blacks, including my father and grandfather, was an international chemical company that produced a variety of chemical, paper, and resin products for industry and retail use. During the decades of the 1940s, 1950s, and 1960s, Hercules, regrettably was a major polluter of the ground water in a heavily populated black section of town located near its vast physical plant, thus becoming an early perpetrator of environmental racism. The pollution came via the infamous Hercules ditch, which snaked through miles of open area in the section of town known as the Gravel Line. The pollutants consisted of untold amounts of poisonous chemicals and toxins from run-off at the plant. It did incalculable damage to the health of residents of the area. The ditch was finally drained and covered in 1971 after local leaders from the black community filed complaints with the company's home office in Delaware.

Hattiesburg's other claim to fame is that in November 1959, John Howard Griffin, the white author of Black Like Me, spent several days in Hattiesburg during his trek across the south as a black man.

Hattiesburg was also a regular stop on the so-called chittlin' circuit for R & B singers who frequently performed at the Hi Hat Club in Palmers Crossing. At all times of the year, but especially during the summer, there would be bright and colorful placards and posters with pictures of such entertainers as B.B. King, Bobby "Blue" Bland, and Ike and Tina Turner nailed to telephone poles all over black sections of town promoting an upcoming concert by one of them.

Hattiesburg was also a regular stop for some gospel music artists, who at the time had not achieved national prominence. My mom was a gospel music DJ at the state's first black-owned radio station, WORV, and frequently promoted such gospel singers at Shirley Caesar, Reverend Clarence Fountain, and the Mighty Clouds of Joy, all of whom were popular but had not yet come to the attention of very many people outside the south.

The City's metro population today is nearly 110,000 and the percentage of African Americans is approximately 37%. Housing patterns today reflect visible changes in demographics and in upward social mobility brought on by improving economic conditions and by mandates from the federal government to end housing discrimination.

Areas of town that were all-white as recent as the 1980s are either all black or desegregated today, indicating a high degree of white flight. White flight is also evidenced by two other trends – the mushrooming construction of new and expensive housing in the exclusive western part of the city that is predominantly white and by the declining number and percentage of white students attending the Hattiesburg Public School System. Even so, black people are visible in prominent positions at local banks, retail establishments, city and county government, school districts, and at both universities.

My dad and the role of providence

My dad was a wonderful provider; and he made many sacrifices to ensure that his family was properly cared for. For most of my childhood, my two brothers, my mom, my dad and I lived comfortably in a three-bedroom, one-bath, and wood-frame house on the corner of Fredna Avenue and Charles Street. There was constant activity inside and outside the house. Every neighborhood has that house where all the kids gather to play, inside and outside. In my neighborhood, that was my house. My parents had only one rule about other kids being at the house. No one, except my brothers and I, was allowed to go inside if they were not home. So, all play was done outside, until one of them was home to supervise any inside play, which was essentially, watching television or playing the record player.

My brothers and I never went without the things we needed. We did not always get all we wanted, but our needs were never left wanting. We had clothes, food, and shelter according to my dad's and mom's ability to afford them. My dad's ability to provide for his family was tied to his ability to earn or borrow enough money to make sure we were sufficiently fed, clothed, and had a roof over our heads. One source of income and borrowing was his employer, Hercules Powder Company. For both profit and employee convenience, the company operated a commissary that sold dry goods, food, and clothing at discounted prices. The company extended credit to employees who could not pay cash. Prior to the start of each school year and at those unpredictable periods of growth spurts, my dad would purchase, on credit, shoes and other clothing for my two brothers and me. The repayments were payroll deducted each payday until the bill was paid in full.

My father's other means for making ends meet was to borrow money from loan companies to supplement his salary at Hercules. Many a day, I would accompany him to several downtown loan companies to make payments on his debts, which were paid in cash – no checks. I never saw my dad write a check his entire life. I am sure it pained him to fork over so much of his earnings to those companies, but the option of not doing so was not part of his make-up. Although he often borrowed money to make ends meet, he believed in repaying his debts.

Some of his creditors did not wait for him to come to them. Several of them actually waited outside the gates at Hercules, parked in their cars during shift changes, in plain view of employees who were leaving and going to work. That is when I realized that my dad was not the only one who borrowed money or made purchases on credit. Every payday, representatives from Max Music Jewelry and Pawn Store, L.B. Price Mercantile, and Sackler Furniture Store would sit in their vehicles and wait for in-debted Hercules employees to make their way to them. Without exception, each payday there were hordes of black men with lunch pails under their arms and hands on their wallets, lined up to make payments to one or more of their vehicle-bound creditors. Typically, they would also cash payroll checks for the employees, primarily to make sure that a payment would be made. Seeing this scene played out every week convinced me this was the norm and that the only reason for working was to pay bills. Those were difficult times, and I thank God for the sacrifices my parents, especially my father, made to take care of the family. I honor him and acknowledge the abundant love he had for his family.

A couple of years into my tenure at USM as the President's Executive Assistant, my dad's heart condition played another pivotal role in my life, just as it had the night before my wedding in 1977. Sunday, March 17, 2002, I had just driven back to Hattiesburg from my bi-weekend trip to Texas to visit my wife and son. My wife asked me the night before when did I plan to drive back to Hattiesburg. I typically would drive back Sunday after church at 1:00. But I told her that I would leave early Sunday morning because I wanted to go ahead and get on the road early. Arriving at my mom's home in Hattiesburg after a tiring 7-hour drive, I unloaded my car. My typical routine was to rest, get a bite to eat, and visit with my mom after unloading my car; but on that day, I decided to go to the car wash to wash off the bugs and road tar that had become attached to my car during the drive from Commerce, Texas to Hattiesburg, Mississippi. I managed to remove the bugs at the car wash, but the tar remained. I knew that it had to come off or it would damage the paint. So, I said to myself, "Woofie will know how to get this tar off. He is an expert in washing cars." I drove the 3-minute trip to his house, but he was not there. Invariably, if he were not home, I would not stay. My typical response would be that I would be back later. But on that day, I decided to stay and wait for him. A few minutes later he drove up to his house, got out of his car, and told me to meet him in the carport. No more than a minute later he walked out the back door and sat on the top step with his back against the storm door. After I asked him how to get the tar off my nearly brand new candy-apple red Mustang, he told me to go to the auto supply store and buy a spray product that will take it right off. After I finished wiping the last bead of water off the car, he told me to pull up a chair next to him and have a seat. I obligingly moved the white plastic patio chair to his left, about 2 feet from him and sat, prepared for a quiet, routine visit with him. He then said, "Son, I cooked some chicken wings and potatoes. Want some?" He then began to make a sound that made me think he was sneezing. So, I paused to let him finish "sneezing" before saying how much I wanted some of his famous chicken wings. It soon became clear to me that he was not sneezing. His face had turned purple. He had lost control of his bladder and was gasping for air as foam mixed with blood started trickling down the corners if his mouth. I placed my hand on his shoulder, desperately called his name several times and shook him; but he did not respond to my words or my shaking. I immediately called 911. I told the operator that I thought my dad was having a heart attack.

261

The operator instructed me to feel for a pulse. After checking his wrist and his neck, I told the operator I could not feel a pulse. The operator then asked if he were breathing. By that time my dad was about to fall over, so I braced him against my leg. With his eyes closed and head tilted back, he lightly let out a puff of air. I told the 911 operator that I thought he was breathing because I had just noticed him exhaling. He said that I needed to lay him down flat to start CPR. My dad weighed well over 240 pounds and there was no way I could do that by myself. So, I banged on the door to get some-one inside to help. Pat, my dad's wife, who was a nurse, bounced out the door. She and I began to administer CPR. She performed chest compressions, and I began to blow puffs of air into his mouth. Between puffs of air and pressing on his chest, Pat and I would yell out his name: "Woofie! Woofie! Come on Woofie! Come on!" Sadly, he did not respond to our efforts to revive him. The paramedics ar-rived and took over, but despite their heroic efforts, they were unable to resuscitate him.

After I returned to my mom's house from the hospital where my father was taken by the paramedics, my cousin Beverly greeted me with a warm and much-needed hug. After the hug, she took my hand; led me to my bedroom; and told me to have a seat. Seated next to me, she shared with me her take on what had just trans-pired. She said, *Ant, you need to know that the Lord had his hand in everything that happened today. He brought you to your dad so that you could be with him when he passed away. Don't ever forget that. He had a purpose. He had a hand in everything. You might not understand it all, but you will. Trust me.*

I knew she was 100% correct. I will always consider it a blessing from God that I was able to be with him in his final moments on this earth. The blessing is especially meaningful when I note that under normal circumstances I would not have been with my dad. If I had stuck with my normal routine, I would have not arrived in Hattiesburg until 9 o'clock at night. He died at 4:30 p.m. It was not accidental or co-incidental that I was placed there at his home at that moment in time. God wanted me to be there with my dad as a final and special time between the two of us. I have great comfort, despite my intense sadness, in knowing that it was indeed God's divine work that made that fateful moment occur. Although his passing was sad, I personally considered it an enormous privilege and a special blessing granted to me by the Almighty to have been present with my dad in his final moments.

Chapter 15

Farewell Mississippi - Hello Texas (Part Deux)

Following my dad's death, I remained at the University of Southern Mississippi for a few months, in my role as the President's Executive Assistant. The President, with whom I had previously worked, Dr. Horace Fleming, resigned his presidency and moved to Mercer University in Georgia. The interim president asked me to stay until a permanent replacement was hired. After the new president was hired, he informed me that he did not want someone working in his administration who worked so closely with his predecessor. So, I was dismissed from my position as Executive Assistant to the President and was given a temporary assignment as a faculty member in the Educational Leadership Department. Without allowing me to complete the semester, the new president informed the Director of Human Resources that he would not adjust my contract to allow me to complete the final two weeks of the semester. Nevertheless, I departed Hattiesburg in November 2002 and moved back to Texas. I left Hattiesburg and my alma mater with strong ambivalence. A reporter with the *Hattiesburg American* called me for an interview after learning that the President had terminated me from my position. She asked me how I felt about the President's decision. I told her that I felt as though someone has just ordered me to leave my own home. Southern Miss was my alma mater and Hattiesburg was my hometown, and I was being told that I was no longer welcomed at either place. The other source of my ambivalence was that while I was unhappy with the circumstances surrounding my leaving Southern Miss, I was very happy to be moving back to Texas to be with my family. I missed them very much, and while the bi-monthly visits were necessary, they were not sufficient. There is nothing like physically being with one's loved ones rather than telephonically being with them.

Moreover, I whole-heartedly subscribe to the notion that God puts us where He wants us to be. Our plan is not necessarily God's plan. So, I concluded that God had placed me in Hattiesburg for a purpose. But I was not sure what that purpose was. Maybe His purpose was for me to be with my father in his final moments. Maybe it was for me to be a comfort to my mother. Maybe it was for me to be a role model and mentor for a number of students and colleagues. Maybe it was for the privilege of knowing Horace Fleming. Maybe it was for all of the above. Regardless, I believed that purpose had been fulfilled, and that God wanted me to be someplace else for a different purpose. So, I left Hattiesburg with much anticipation of what God had in store for me next.

What I quickly discovered was that His plans for me were not the plans I would have had. My plans would have involved finding another job very quickly and transitioning seamlessly back into a normal routine in Commerce, Texas. Instead, His plans actually took me by surprise and shepherded me into an unfamiliar world of doubt, uncertainty, and confusion. I had no idea that I was about to experience the sting of nine straight months of unemployment. That was not my plan for my future a tall. I struggled mightily to try to figure out how to handle this very unfamiliar status as an unemployed, former college administrator and professor. I looked for signs from God that would help me understand why I was in this predicament. I recall pleading with God. I said, *God, you know that I have been trying to be a good father, a good husband, a good neighbor, a good citizen, and good faithful Christian. I go to church every Sunday. I pay my tithes. I treat people with respect. God, why me? Why are you putting me through this?* In case God didn't fully understand the depths of my misery, I thought I would add more to my pleadings. *Please. Help me out here, Lord. I need a job. I am willing to do anything. My family depends on me, and I feel like I am letting them down. I am not a proud man. I am a desperate man. You have blessed me with a loving family, wonderful friends, and a great community. And I have heard your call to serve my fellow man. I am trying to be the person you want me to be. What I am doing wrong, Lord? Just tell me, and I will change it.* God's reply was simple, convicting, and truthful. The message I received from Him went something like this: *Anthony, why not you? Who do you think you are to believe that because you are doing all those things that somehow bad things cannot happen in your life? Besides, all those wonderful things you claim to be doing, guess what? You are supposed to do them. Just be patient and know that I indeed have a plan for your life. You might not understand it or even see it now. Look back on your life. Haven't you been blessed beyond what you deserve? Haven't you spent far more time on the mountain top, basking in the bright glow of achievements and successes in the valley surrounded by misery, despair, and pain? Well, I want you to know what it is like to spend time in the valley so that you will have a better appreciation for what it is like to be in the valley. I also want you to have a better appreciation for what it is like to be on the mountain top. Surely, you will someday find yourself again on the mountain top. And you will feel good about your life in the uplifting and refreshing glow of my goodness and mercy. Know that I am the same whether you are on the top of the mountain or in the valley. Appreciate both. And know that I am with you always and that my plan for you is for the good, regardless of whether you are on the mountain top or in the valley.* Those words of assurance were like sweet nectar and gave me renewed hope that despite my circumstances, I was not alone and that I would be okay.

I had another encounter with God during the period of time when I was in the valley still searching for a job and searching for answers. I was in Corpus Christi, Texas visiting my daughter one weekend and was out jogging along on a familiar five-mile route. At some point in the run, I inexplicably decided to take a detour. In doing so, I ran past a small, white, wooden church that was towered over by marquee sign with a message that was spelled out with black block shaped letters. The message was: *God puts us through these things in order to prepare us for something bigger.* I stopped completely in my tracks. Bam! Once again, I thought, God is talking to me. No. It was not a booming James Earl Jones-type voice coming down from the sky. This encounter was far less dramatic than that. Yet, its message and its meaning could not have been any clearer. While standing there reading and re-reading those words, I took a couple of deep breaths and noticed a smile forming on my face. I looked up to the sky, and gave thanks to God. I said, *God, I hear you. I really do get it. You haven't given up on me. You are preparing me for something. I don't know what it is, but I am willing to be patient, as long as it takes, until you reveal it to me.*

Not many weeks after the Corpus Christi encounter with God, I received a telephone call from a colleague and former doctoral school classmate. He called me for a reference for someone who had applied for a faculty position at his university. After learning about my employment status and out of the pure goodness of his heart, he asked if I might be interested in the position. He knew me and was familiar with my background as a teacher and administrator. I respectfully declined to be considered for that position. I told him that I did not feel comfortable pursuing a position that a friend and colleague was pursuing. He understood my position, but asked me to send him my resume anyway, just in case another position became available. I sent it to him, and a few weeks later, the chair of a search committee invited me to come to Sam Houston State University for an interview for a different faculty position. Apparently, my interviews went well enough that I was offered a faculty position. My search for a job had finally come to an end, after nine months of disappointment and frustration. Providence was at the center of all that was happening to me. I had no doubt about that. Even when I was in the valley, providence was always present. And now that God was allowing me to once again visit the mountain top, his divine providence was in the midst of it all. I accepted the job offer and thoroughly enjoyed the five years I spent with great colleagues and students at Sam Houston State University.

God's next plan for me became evident when Provost Horace Fleming and Dean Carl Martray at Mercer University invited me to apply for a faculty position in the Educational Leadership program. Initially, I was reluctant to leave Sam Houston because certain individuals there thought enough of me to hire me after my extended period of unemployment. But I viewed the Provost's and Dean's invitation as, perhaps, another message from God. So, I applied and was offered the position of Professor of Education. Since 2008, I have enjoyed working with wonderful colleagues and very motivated students at a very fine institution. The only regret at Mercer University is that my former boss, Dr. Horace Fleming, passed away not long after I began my tenure. He and I were looking forward to being reunited as colleagues. But God had his own plan for Horace, as he does for all of his children.

While living and working in Atlanta, Georgia, I completed and published my first book, *Gifts of Moments: Being Somebody to Somebody,* which I describe as a spiritually-based inspirational book. The book started out as a five-minute speech at my Toastmasters Club in Conroe, Texas in 2007. Over time, I began to expand on the theme of the speech, which was about the importance of regarding each moment in our lives as precious, fleeting, and irretrievable. I selected the title after deep introspection and personal reflection on my life and the many gifts and blessings that God has granted me. I realized that moments are gifts granted to us by God. And each gift comes with a covenant...a covenant that requires us to use our gifts in the most beneficial manner possible...not exclusively for ourselves, but more importantly, in service to others. The title also comes from a modification of a quote from Mother Theresa, who said that *one of the great diseases in life* is *being nobody to anybody.* There is ample evidence in the world today that Mother Theresa was absolutely correct in her assessment of humankind. As I pondered her quote, however, I began to realize that people, particularly people of faith, have a sacred obligation to embrace the flip side of that quote. We must embrace the notion that *one of the great joys in life is to be somebody to somebody.* The book contains stories about my life in which I have attempted to be somebody to somebody and have attempted to use my gifts of moments as the covenant requires. We all have stories to share. Our stories need to be shared because someone is waiting to hear how we have dealt with a particular issue with which they are struggling. Thus, in the book, I encourage readers to recall their own stories in which they have been somebody to somebody and have used their gifts of moments as the covenant requires. To illustrate that point, I quote Dr. Maya Angelou, who said that *nothing is more agonizing than having an untold story inside of us.* The feedback that I have received from readers has been very positive. I believe that *Gifts of Moments: Being Somebody to Somebody* has been my gift to some who might need to be reminded that being somebody to somebody trumps being nobody to anybody, anytime.

Chapter 16

20/20 Hindsight

Given the luxury of hindsight, I often reflect on the purposes of the civil rights movement, ponder its successes and failures, and wonder what was actually accomplished. Were the gains sufficient to justify the loss of life, beatings, arrests, and the numerous other forms of terror and intimidation?

At the time the movement was in full swing and while experiencing the turmoil, confusion, and uncertainty that accompany a great social movement, the correctness and appropriateness of what we were doing were never in doubt. We knew that the segregationists, their sympathizers, accomplices and supporters were wrong. No doubt, the anti-civil rights forces represented all that was ugly about Hattiesburg and they reminded me of something my mom and the old folks in church would always say, *God don't like ugly!*

We knew we were right in demanding an end to segregation and the creation of a fully integrated society. We knew we were right in demanding the right to vote, although black people have become the only racial group in the country for which the constitutional right to vote has to be granted periodically with the renewal of the Voting Rights Act. As it comes up for debate in 2012 by the United States Supreme Court regarding whether to end, extend, or modify the law, the very idea that the highest court in the land could throw out the Voting Rights Act is unsettling. Given the current climate of anti-immigration and voter suppression, I believe that the counterbalance made possible by the protections afforded by the Voting Rights Act is not only necessary, but it is also indispensable.

In retrospect, I believe that we were right in demanding an end to the separate but equal doctrine. I believe that a clear message needed to be sent that an end to *de facto* and *de jure* segregation, lynchings, and relegation of black citizens to second-class citizenship was no longer a request. Instead, it became a non-negotiable demand.

Freedom, I contend, is not something you ask for. It is something you must fight for and demand because oppressors do not voluntarily give up their power to oppress.

While I will always believe that the demands and the strategies and tactics used to secure those demands were proper, hindsight permits me to second-guess some of the goals. I regret the fact that in the immediate period following civil rights movement in Hattiesburg there was a major discrepancy in the concept of integration between the white power structure of Hattiesburg and the black community. Black people generally viewed integration as not only the end to segregation, but also as the beginning of respect from and equality and parity with whites. On the other hand, many who made up the white power structure viewed integration, merely as *desegregation* and as an opportunity to increase their control over schools, commerce, and government. Thus, in the early period following the civil rights movement, they were able to project the appearance of creating and embracing change while at the same time continuing their efforts to exclude black people from fully participating in the affairs of the city. Their goal was to avoid sharing power with black people in a meaningful way for fear of permanent erosion of their long-standing dominance of the city's institutions. From my perspective, the white power structure in Hattiesburg fittingly embodied a phrase from the television miniseries, *Roots,* that has always stuck with me. In reference to his determination to capture Chicken George who managed to escape his snare, the Burl Ives character, Senator Arthur Johnson, stated in a hauntingly prophetic soliloquy, *"If brer rabbit can't get you one way, he'll get you another."* Analogously, the white power structure was essentially saying that if they cannot maintain power and control through segregation, they'll just find some way to do it through "integration."

The best example of this unfortunate discrepancy in the root meaning of integration occurred the year after my high school graduation. The Hattiesburg Separate Public School System in the Fall of 1971 merged the two high schools – the historically white high school, S.H. Blair, and the historically black high school, L. J. Rowan and created one high school – Hattiesburg High School. Rowan High

School became a tenth grade attendance center. At first glance, such a configuration may have appeared to be sensible – integrating the high schools and ending the practice of having separate schools based on race. However, as one looks closer at other concomitant actions school system administrators took, school "integration" can only be described as manipulative and self-serving. School system administrators, operating on their own self-serving definition of integration, relegated the principal, band director, and head football coach at Rowan to lesser positions in the new configuration. Mr. James Winters, who had a successful tenure as band director at Rowan, became the assistant band director at Hattiesburg High School. Mr. N.R. Burger, a beloved and respected educator with decades of outstanding service to black children of Hattiesburg, was relegated to principal of the Rowan Tenth Grade Center.

Perhaps most callous and despicable of all of the reassignments was the banishment of Mr. Ed Steele to the school system's athletic director's office as Coordinator of Recreations. Coach Steele, or Head Man as he was often called, was one of the winningest high school coaches, black or white, in the state of Mississippi. He had the distinction of winning four Negro Big Eight State Championships in his seven-year tenure as head coach at Rowan. Not only were his football teams excellent, they were entertaining as well. The home side of the stadium was always filled to capacity. It was very common, also, to see the visitors' side of the stadium completely filled with white fans who appreciated good football. Many of his players went on to successful college careers and several played in the National Football League, including Marvin Woodson, Harold Jackson, Willie McGee, Taft Reed, and Willie Towne. Most graduates, however, went on to successful careers as fathers, husbands, and professionals in fields other than athletics. Not only was he a role model and mentor for athletes, but for those of us who were not athletes he was held him in high esteem. What, other than race, could account for the fact that Coach Steele was not given the opportunity to become the head football coach at Hattiesburg High? The decision certainly was not based on ability and record. Had it been, Coach Steele would have easily become the first black head coach at Hattiesburg High School.

Compounding the relegation in position and title of these three outstanding educators was their loss of visibility, authority, and power, which negatively impacted those of us under their guidance and influence. Prior to the reassignments, these extremely prominent and highly respected men were able to uniquely touch our lives and to create in each of us the determination to succeed, not only academically, but also in life. They kept untold numbers of us, especially boys, from engaging in self-destructive behaviors and helped to make sure we attended school, made good grades, and respected our teachers.

Today such influence is conspicuous by its absence. I contend that in many cities across the south, the demise of young black males began with the demise of our visible and authoritative black male leaders, particularly those in education. I further contend that the demise was deviously planned and implemented by school administrators in the name of school integration. I often wonder if we would have the problems today of gangs, drugs, and hopelessness among our black youth, if the Ed Steeles, Jim Winters, and N.R. Burgers of our nation had been allowed to maintain their ability to influence young people.

Moreover, I wonder if black people would have been better off fighting for authentic equality and equity rather than strictly for "integration". Instead of seeking to go to school with whites and fighting for the right to shop in white-owned businesses, perhaps we should have fought for the maintenance and strengthening of our own institutions – churches, retail and professional establishments, and schools. In terms of improving the community's economic well being, desegregation simply did not work very well for the black community in Hattiesburg. The benefits of desegregation to the black community in Hattiesburg were negligible at best and non-existent at worst. In addition to losing the influence and visibility of our educational leaders, most black-owned businesses gradually closed, which had a direct negative effect on the economic viability of the black community. Most regrettably, however, the overall strength of the village was significantly and probably irrevocably reduced, as the negative values of disunity, complacency, and selfishness replaced the positive and life-sustaining values of commitment to an ideal, self-sacrifice, and care and concern for the group's and not just one's own well-being.

The upside of desegregation was clearly that the vestiges of Jim Crow were destroyed, hopefully, forever. The notion that the color of one's skin should determine which public toilet one uses, the public water fountain from which one drinks, the school one attends and whether one has the right to register to vote, needed to be challenged and eliminated. Also, the notion that skin color should determine who can drive a city bus, serve as police officers and firefighters also needed to be destroyed. Indeed, I can look back with pride and note that in Hattiesburg in 1966, Lawrence Floyd, Jr., Bobby Gibson, Willie McGilvery, and Willie Fluker were the first black police officers; and that Robert Miller was the first black deputy sheriff.

As a result of the civil rights movement in Hattiesburg, S.H. Kress and Woolworth's discontinued their practice of refusing service to black customers at their lunch counters. The movement brought an end to the illegal, annoying and degrading practice of requiring black people to go to a separate window to be served at the ice cream parlor on the corner of 7th Street and Bouie Street; denying black people the right to sit in the front of a public bus; denying black school children access to and use of modern lab equipment and new textbooks; denying black children the right to go to the public library or to visit the public zoo; requiring black people to wash their clothes at black-only laundry mats (which were generally white-owned); requiring black people to go outside and into the basement at the Forrest County Courthouse to use the restroom; requiring black people to use the rear entrance and a separate waiting room at the Greyhound Bus Station; requiring black customers to sit in the balcony at the Saenger Theatre; having separate trash pickup days for blacks and whites; having obituaries of blacks listed in the newspaper separately from whites; and having blacks and whites buried in separate city-owned cemeteries.

Ironically, the civil rights movement, potentially, was as liberating for some whites as it was for blacks. Prior to the evolution of desegregation, many whites were victims of their own destructive and stereotypical thinking about blacks. By breaking down artificially and deviously constructed racial barriers, the movement allowed (in some cases, forced) whites to examine their own racial belief system and to seriously confront the many untruths, myths, and misconceptions about themselves and about black people that they had intentionally accepted as fact. For those who were open to the experience, the civil rights movement offered tremendous relief from the debilitating effects of having to hate, pre-judge or misjudge someone because of the color of his/her skin. For example, when desegregation came to the public schools in Hattiesburg, many white students were able to observe and experience for themselves the authentic characteristics, character, and abilities of black students. They were able to discover that black students could excel academically; could converse in Standard English; and that we were not lazy, not all of us were athletic, had rhythm and big feet, or liked watermelon. To their benefit, some whites discovered that the negative and stereotypical views about black people that they learned from their parents, teachers, and the media were simply not wrong. Had it not been for the civil rights movement, I suspect that many whites would have just remained slaves to their own backward and narrow-minded thinking about race.

Chapter 17

Epilogue

The history-making and life-changing events that occurred during the 1960s in Hattiesburg and in other cities, towns, and villages across the south came about because thousands of brave people of all races embodied the spirit of an elderly black woman whose entire fragile and time-worn being was wholly and unconditionally committed to the struggle for civil rights. When asked if she was physically tired from years of marching and picketing, she responded: *My feets is tired, but my soul is rested!*

To properly honor that remarkable woman's spirit as well as those of all of our deceased and living leaders, we must make sure that each of us lives and breathes the type of unselfish commitment, unwavering spirit, and constant vigilance that brave woman possessed. Each of us has to be willing to selflessly give of ourselves so that the life of another human being is positively transformed. Moreover, because we all belong to humanity and humanity belongs to all of us, we must learn to care about what happens to our sisters and brothers, no matter who or where they are. As W.E.B. DuBois said nearly a century ago, *I must become my brother's keeper; for if I do not, he will surely bring me down in his ruin.* Further, we must remember two clear warnings against complacency and selfishness that Dr. King noted: *No person is truly free until we are all free!* and *Justice delayed for anyone is justice denied for everyone.*

If we are to be successful in fully weaving the multi-ethnic, multi-hue, multi-racial tapestry of our society, we must allow every group to tell its story. By doing so, we help ensure that each group's contributions to the creation of that tapestry becomes visible and viable. And when that happens, our social tapestry is strengthened, not weakened. From those stories, we can further develop an appreciation of the sacrifices and contributions that groups have made and continue to make toward the creation and preservation of our democracy. When that day comes, we will be able to legitimately and proudly proclaim that all Americans have now been invited to and have taken their seats at the table of democracy.

This book has been one attempt to tell several stories that are a tiny part of one group's yet-to-be completed story. It has also attempted to illustrate how those stories have impacted one person's coming of age in the south. More importantly, this book has attempted to honor and offer praise and thanks to the many unsung heroes of the civil rights movement in Hattiesburg. Too often, they have been forgotten or taken for granted. With this book, I want to say thanks to each of them for their sacrifices, wisdom, and example.

No story about the struggle for equality and social justice is complete without mention of the election and re-election of the nation's first African American president in 2008 and 2012. As one who went to jail and fought for the rights of black people to vote in Mississippi, I found it especially gratifying to know that one of the tangible results of that struggle was the two-time election of Barack Obama as President of the United States of America. When the television networks made the calls in 2008 and in 2012 that Barack Obama had won decisively, each time I immediately gave thanks to God and invoked the names and memories of martyrs who had given their lives to the cause of ensuring that black people were granted full citizenship rights, including the right to vote. I remembered Reverend George Lee, Mr. Medgar Evers, Mr. James Chaney, Mr. Michael Schwerner, Mr. Andrew Goodman, Mr. Jimmie Lee Jackson, Reverend James Reeb, Mrs. Viola Liuzzo, Mr. Vernon Dahmer, and Dr. Martin Luther King, Jr. Although they did not live long enough to witness the elections of President Obama, their sacrifices helped make it possible. I have to believe that those and many other martyrs were smiling from heaven when the final results of the elections were announced and Barack Obama was sworn in as the 44th and 45th President of the United States of America. To paraphrase Reverend Jesse Jackson, hands that used to pick cotton are now picking presidents.

Epilogue

They taught me and He enlightened me

To this day, I continue to find strength in the sacrifices made by the many unsung heroes of the civil rights movement in Hattiesburg and in other parts of the country. These courageous men and women, black and white, young and old taught me very valuable lessons about life. They taught me about equality, freedom, and justice. They taught me about forgiveness, atonement, and selflessness. They taught me about love, respect, and loyalty. They taught me about reciprocity, responsibility, and restraint.

They also taught me freedom songs and how to use those songs to inspire myself and an entire congregation of fellow freedom fighters. After I learned the words to my favorite freedom song, *Ain't Gonna Let Nobody Turn Me 'Round*, I adopted it as my everlasting signature song and my personal mantra for dealing with all manner of challenges with which I am confronted. Whenever someone intimates that I am not good enough or not capable of doing something for no reason other than my race, I call upon the words and the spirit of *Ain't Gonna Let Nobody Turn Me 'Round* to help meet those challenges.

Ain't gonna let nobody turn me around
Turn me around, turn me around
Ain't gonna let nobody turn me around
I'm gonna keep on a-walkin', keep on a-talkin'
Marchin' up to freedom land.

Ain't gonna let no water hose turn me around
Turn me around, turn me around
Ain't gonna let no water hose turn me around
I'm gonna keep on a-walkin', keep on a-talkin'
Marchin' up to freedom land.

Ain't gonna let no billy clubs turn me around
Turn me around, turn me around
Ain't gonna let no billy clubs turn me around
I'm gonna keep on a-walkin', keep on a-talkin'
Marchin' up to freedom land.

Ain't gonna let Jim Crow turn me around
Turn me around, turn me around
Ain't gonna let Jim Crow turn me around
I'm gonna keep on a-walkin', keep on a-talkin'
Marchin' up to freedom land.

Ain't gonna let no police dogs turn me around
Turn me around, turn me around
Ain't gonna let no police dogs turn me around
I'm gonna keep on a-walkin', keep on a-talkin'
Marchin' up to freedom land.

Ain't gonna let no Uncle Tom turn me around
Turn me around, turn me around
Ain't gonna let no Uncle Tom turn me around
I'm gonna keep on a-walkin', keep on a-talkin'
Marchin' up to freedom land.

Ain't gonna let nobody turn me around
Turn me around, turn me around
Ain't gonna let nobody turn me around
I'm gonna keep on a-walkin', keep on a-talkin'
Marchin' up to freedom land.

In addition to relying on that precious and inspiring song, I have also learned to rely on the Word to get me through the many toils and snares of life. In my faith journey, I have been taught by my mom, mother-in-law, Reverend Jones, Reverend Booth, and Reverend Sanders to depend on scripture to center me, to motivate me and to inspire me. In addition to inspiring me, Scripture has also held me accountable for my actions. It has been my guide post for doing the right thing and using my gifts of moments to be somebody to somebody. It has also helped me to remain vigilant and engaged in the fight for justice and equality. Perhaps you will find these passages from the Bible as comforting as I have over the years.

- *Faith without works is dead.* (James 2:17)

- *Is not this the fast that I have chosen? to loose the bands of wickedness, to undo the heavy burdens, and to let the oppressed go free, and that ye break every yoke? Is it not to deal thy bread to the hungry, and that thou bring the poor that are cast out to thy house? when thou seest the naked, that thou cover him; and that thou hide thyself from thine own flesh? Then shall thy light break forth as the morning, and thine health shall spring forth speedily: and thy righteousness shall go before thee; the glory of the LORD shall be thy reward. Then shalt thou call, and the LORD shall answer; thou shalt cry, and he will say, Here I am. If thou take away from the midst of thee the yoke, the putting forth of the finger, and speaking vanity; And if thou draw out thy soul to the hungry, and satisfy the afflicted soul; then shall thy light rise in obscurity, and thy darkness be as the noon day: And the LORD shall guide thee continually, and satisfy thy soul in drought, and make fat thy bones: and thou shalt be like a watered garden, and like a spring of water, whose waters fail not. And they that shall be of thee shall build the old waste places: thou shall raise up the foundations of many generations; and thou shalt be called, The repairer of the breach and The restorer of the streets to dwell in.* (Isaiah, 58:6-12)

- *Be patient and you will finally win, for a soft tongue can break hard bones.* (Proverbs, 28:13)

- *Do not get tired of doing what is good. Don't get discouraged and give up, for we will reap a harvest of blessing at the appropriate time.* (Galatians, 6:9)

- *An intelligent mind acquires knowledge, and the ear of the wise seeks knowledge.* (Proverbs, 18:15)

- *Have I not commanded you? Be strong and courageous. Do not be terrified; do not be discouraged, for the Lord your God will be with you wherever you go.* (Joshua, 1:9).

- *For I know the plans I have for you, "declares the Lord, "plans to prosper you…plans to give you hope and a future." (Jeremiah, 29:11)*

- *Trust in the Lord with all your heart and lean not on your own understanding; in all your ways submit to him, and he will make your paths straight.* (Proverbs, 3:5-6)

About the Author

Anthony J. Harris lives in Atlanta, Georgia and is Professor of Education at Mercer University. He previously served on the faculty and in administrative positions at Sam Houston State University, Texas A&M University-Commerce, and the University of Southern Mississippi. He is the author of the book, *Gifts of Moments: Being Somebody to Somebody*. He can be contacted at ajharris007@gmail.com.

Made in the USA
Lexington, KY
25 June 2014